NOBILTÀ DI DAME

NOBILTÀ DI DAME

FABRITIO CAROSO

*A treatise on courtly dance, together
with the choreography and
music of 49 dances*

*Translated from the printing of 1600,
edited, and with an introduction
by*
JULIA SUTTON

*The music transcribed and edited
by*
F. MARIAN WALKER

Oxford   New York
OXFORD UNIVERSITY PRESS
1986

Oxford University Press, Walton Street, Oxford OX2 6DP

Oxford New York Toronto
Delhi Bombay Calcutta Madras Karachi
Kuala Lumpur Singapore Hong Kong Tokyo
Nairobi Dar es Salaam Cape Town
Melbourne Auckland

and associated companies in
Beirut Berlin Ibadan Nicosia

OXFORD is a trade mark of Oxford University Press

British Library Cataloguing in Publication Data
Caroso, Fabritio
Nobiltà di dame.
1. Dancing—Italy 2. Italy—Court and
courtiers
I. Title II. Sutton, Julia III. Walker,
F. Marian IV. Nobiltà di dame. English
793.3 GV1655
ISBN 0–19–311917–X

Library of Congress Cataloging in Publication Data
Caroso, Fabritio.
Nobiltà di dame.
Bibliography p. 65
1. Dancing—Early works to 1800. 2. Ballroom dancing
—Early works to 1800. 3. Dance music. 4. Lute
music. I. Sutton, Julia. II. Walker, F. Marian.
III. Title.
GV1590.C2913 1984 793.3 83–17359
ISBN 0–19–311917–X

Printed and bound in
Great Britain by Biddles Ltd,
Guildford and King's Lynn

Contents

CONTENTS

List of Illustrations

Preface

The labour of love which has produced the present volume was inspired by the pressing need to incorporate the sophisticated dance vocabulary of sixteenth-century Italy into productions of Renaissance dance and music. Twenty years ago the rich repertory in the Italian dance manuals was then unavailable either in facsimile or in English translation. Since then facsimile reprints of the three major Italian manuals by Caroso and Negri have appeared, but English translations are still not published. Meanwhile, demand continues to grow for 'authentic' productions, from Shakespeare in England to Monteverdi in Italy, and dance music continues to be published in modern transcription or facsimile whose accurate interpretation depends upon the recovery of the lost tradition of the dances. It is hoped that this publication of *Nobiltà di dame* in translation and transcription will be a step towards making all dance materials of the period available, so that greater accuracy and truth in concert and stage productions may be attained, and dance may once again take its equal place in our view of the arts in Renaissance courtly life.

In an undertaking of this size and nature, in which precision of translation and transcription are crucial to the recreation of a lost art, the expertise of others has been of great assistance, and is a pleasure to acknowledge here. All who participated gave unstintingly of their time, thought, and—not least—moral support to the endeavour.

The original text and a literal English version supplied by Franco Iachello (currently director of the Kernfysich Versneller Institut of the Netherlands) were the basis of a new idiomatic translation by the editor. Valuable suggestions on the text were then made by three expert readers: Anna Yona (Department of Languages at the New England Conservatory) gave freely of her extensive experience as a professional translator, patiently reading all of the translation word for word with the editor; Barbara Sparti (director of the Gruppo di Danza Rinascimentale of Rome) brought to bear on all of the most problematic passages her years of movement training and teaching in Italy and America, giving critical attention also to the introductory chapters; and my father, Samuel L. Sumberg (Professor Emeritus of the City University of New York), applied his linguist's eye and ear felicitously to matters of style in the translation and prefatory chapters.

The preparation of the musical edition by Marian Walker was aided by another group of active participants. Pamela Jones (Department of Music, King's College, London) and Professor Robert Jones (Vanier College, Montreal) worked on the last phases of the musical edition and commentaries; Tillman Merritt (Professor Emeritus of Harvard University) kindly gave careful scrutiny and constructive suggestions to the discussion of the music (ch. 6); and Anne Hallmark (Department of Musicology, the New England Conservatory) brought her expertise in notation and logic to bear on the same section. On problems in the lute tablature thanks are especially due to James Meadors (Harvard University and New England Conservatory faculties) and Robert Paul Sullivan (New England Conservatory faculty); Michael Morrow (director, Musica Reservata) and Brian Jeffery (Tecla Editions, London) were also consulted. Grateful acknowledgment goes to St. Olaf College, Northfield, Minnesota, for making the transcription possible through two faculty grants and a sabbatical; the transcriber is also beholden to Adolph White (past chairman of the Department of Music of St. Olaf College), Ann Wagner (Chairman of the Department of Dance of St. Olaf), and Daphne Knights (of London) for their unfailing support, encouragement, and help.

Generations of graduate students of the New England Conservatory have given generously of their time and energies to different aspects of this publication, not least of which was proofreading of text and music. To William Warriner, Margaret Pash, Ed Pepe, Susan Brodie, Carol Pharo, and David Hahn goes heartfelt appreciation for the work they did and the provocative questions they asked.

A work of this kind is tested when the dances themselves are brought to life. All of the dancers and musicians, both collegiate and professional, who have joyously performed these dances and given living proof of their charm and viability, have contributed immeasurably to this volume. Caroso's step descriptions, rules for etiquette, choreographies, and music have been incorporated into performances of significant types of aristocratic revels. The New York Pro Musica's 'Entertainment for Elizabeth', for example, recreated the dances in an imaginary masque and ball at the English court; Colorado College's production of 'The Descent of Rhythm and Harmony' was a reconstruction of the final Intermedio of the Medici wedding festivities of 1589, one of the grandest spectacles of the century; the Pennsylvania Orchestra Society's 'Renaissance Revisited' gave the dances in a festive concert setting. Frequent recitals over twenty years by amateur and student groups, especially those at the New England Conservatory in Boston, and at St. Olaf College in Minnesota, also provided ongoing laboratories for the work on *Nobiltà di dame*. Without performance the dances would have remained drily theoretical; with them they became a lively embodiment of a social and theatrical art of the Renaissance, and crowned our labours with delight.

J.S.

1

The Status and Character of
Nobiltà di dame

The full importance of the Italian sources of late-Renaissance dance has only recently been realized in the English-speaking world of 'court' dance. The English manuscripts of the Inns of Court dating from the sixteenth and early seventeenth centuries,[1] and one major French source of the sixteenth century, Thoinot Arbeau's *Orchésographie* (1588) (in two English translations),[2] have been the chief bases for twentieth-century revivals; Italian sources have been represented only by a few highly-edited dances in the manuals of Melusine Wood and Mabel Dolmetsch.[3] The choreographies of the Inns of Court manuscripts need radical 'reconstructions' because they are essentially cue sheets with no music. Arbeau's attraction for modern purposes lies in his detailed correlations between dance steps and music, using a clear but unfortunately unique tabulation. Valuable as his manual is, however, he provides the complete choreographies to very few dances;[4] furthermore, it is not certain how valid his instructions are for dance at the princely courts of Europe (there is no evidence that he was associated with them).[5] The major Italian sources, on the other hand, contain approximately 150 complete dances, both social and theatrical, and are without question representative of dance practises at the great courts of Italy.[6]

---

[1] Most of the Inns of Court MSS date from 1570-1650; they do not explain the steps, nor do those between 1570 and 1600 provide music. See James B. Cunningham, *Dancing in the Inns of Court* (London: Jordan and Sons, 1965), for a complete list. A fuller examination is part of a series of studies in Tudor and Stuart dance and dance music in preparation by John Ward.

[2] See ch. 4 for a complete listing. All references in the present volume are to the Sutton edition (Dover Publications, 1967).

[3] Melusine Wood, *Some Historical Dances* (London: The Imperial Society of Teachers of Dancing, 1952); *More Historical Dances* (London: Imperial Society, etc., 1956). Mabel Dolmetsch, *Dances of Spain and Italy* (1954, reprinted New York: Da Capo Press, 1975).

[4] 'Les Bouffons', a theatrical dance for men; 'La Volte', and several branles.

[5] For further biographical information on Arbeau see Julia Sutton, 'Arbeau, Thoinot', *The New Grove Dictionary of Music and Musicians,* ed. Stanley Sadie (London: Macmillan Publishers, 1980), Vol. 1, pp. 544-5.

[6] See ch. 4 for a complete list of major Italian sources of dance.

It has become increasingly clear, as well, that the strong Italianate influence on European poetry, music, and spectacle in the latter half of the sixteenth century was probably equalled in dance: Italian dancing masters, like other artists and musicians, were attached to courts all over Europe, including those of France, Spain, and the Netherlands.[7] Note also that Caroso's and Negri's manuals are to be found in the royal libraries of Britain.[8] A growing recognition that the level of skill, variety of dance types, and sophistication of choreographic and musical structures in the Italian manuals may be valid outside Italy, and an increasing demand for authentic performances of Italian spectacle (all types of which include dance),[9] now make it imperative that Italian sources be available in English.

The choice of *Nobiltà di dame* for translation and transcription is deliberate. Caroso published two volumes: *Il Ballarino* (1581) and *Nobiltà di dame* (1600, 1605). Together they embody many of the Italian practices of the period. *Il Ballarino* is the more famous of the two, and contains many more dances, but, as will be shown in ch. 6, the corrections and emendations of *Nobiltà di dame* (termed by Caroso himself a second edition of *Il Ballarino*) make logical reconstruction of most of its dances more feasible than those in the earlier volume. The greater detail of *Nobiltà di dame*, not just in the explanations of steps and style, but especially in the correlation of text and music, significantly reduces the guesswork involved. Because so many of the dances (20 of the 49) and even more of the music (30 of the 44 dance pieces) essentially repeat those in *Il Ballarino,* we may speculate that *Nobiltà di dame's* more detailed rules for steps and guidelines about the music may be applicable as well to other dances in the earlier book.

Beyond the light shed by *Nobiltà di dame* on *Il Ballarino,* however, is the possible enhancement of our understanding of material by other Italian dancing masters; Cesare Negri apparently knew *Il Ballarino,* but not its sequel, 'borrowing' many of its rules in his manual;[10] smaller printed sources by

---

[7] See, for example, the listing by Negri of his predecessors, colleagues, and disciples, and where they taught (*Le Gratie d'Amore,* pp. 2-6, hereafter cited as 'Negri'). Another such personage was Baldassare de Belgioioso who, as Baltassar de Beaujoyeulx, was the chief impresario for the famous *Balet Comique de la Royne* (1581), sponsored by Catherine de' Medici, Queen of France.

[8] Now in the British Library. Elizabeth I of England stated that she learned in her youth to 'dance high' in the Italian manner (de Maisse, *A Journal of All That Was Accomplished by Monsieur de Maisse Ambassador in England from King Henri IV to Queen Elizabeth* [1597]; trans. G.B. Harrison and P.A. Jones [London: The Nonesuch Press, 1931, p. 95]).

[9] E.g., Monteverdi, *L' Orfeo* (Mantua, 1607), has a bergamasca as a finale, and Emilio de' Cavalieri's oratorio, *La Rappresentazione di anima e di corpo* (Rome, 1600), calls for dancing of various types in the final ballo.

[10] The slightly later date of Negri's book (1602) does not mean that he followed Caroso. In fact, all evidence suggests that Caroso and Negri were exact contemporaries, and that Negri worked at his book over at least as long a period as Caroso (beginning about 1563). See ch. 3 for further discussion of connections between Caroso and Negri.

Prospero Lutij di Sulmona (1587, 1589), and Livio Lupi di Caravaggio (1600, 1607), employ much the same technical vocabularly and may show Caroso's influence;[11] and the largest staged ballo of the time, in the famous group of Intermedii to *La Pellegrina* (Florence, 1589), was composed and choreographed by Emilio de' Cavalieri with a step terminology that essentially agrees with Caroso's.[12]

In sum, because Caroso's step vocabulary appears in the other known sources of the period, and because *Nobiltà di dame* is the most consistent, clear, and thorough of all the manuals of the time, this publication may help to elucidate *all* the known dance material, from Italy and elsewhere, of the late Renaissance and early Baroque periods.

The chief purpose of the present volume is to present a careful and accurate translation and transcription of *Nobiltà di dame*, given the current state of research into sixteenth-century dance and music. A secondary purpose, to survey this state and give some brief information on the reconstruction of the dances, is served by the prefatory chapters.

Nobiltà di dame is a large and elegant book which was printed with obvious care. The ornate title page and the variety of colophons and capitals underscore the luxury of its production, while the preciousness of the title is clearly intended to suggest the flattering import of its contents. The volume consists of initial prefatory material; Book I, rules for steps, style, and etiquette; Book II, choreographies with music; and at the end three tables of contents. This format is the same as *Il Ballarino*'s, and in fact is essentially that of all the major Renaissance dance manuals. The prefatory material includes a fulsome dedication of the entire volume, and several laudatory poems, to Caroso's patrons, the Duke and Duchess of Parma and Piacenza; a portrait page of the Duke and Duchess; an elaborate balletto choreography dedicated to them;[13] a group of poems praising Caroso; a portrait of the author;[14] and a letter to the reader justifying and extolling the virtues of dance. In Book I there are 68 rules for steps and style, and 24 notes on ballroom and general etiquette for the gentleman and lady. Book II contains 48 dances. Preceding each is at least one dedicatory poem to a lady lauding her beauties and virtues,[15] and an

---

[11] In Lupi's second edition, his passo e mezzo seems to be indebted to Caroso's, and he also uses a term employed only by Caroso, 'cascarda'. See ch. 5 for further discussion.

[12] Included in Cristofano Malvezzi, *Intermedii Et Concerti, fatti per la Commedia rappresentata in Firenze Nelle nozze del Serenissimo Don Ferdinando Medici et Madama Christiana di Loreno, Granduchi di Toscana* (Venice: Vincenti, 1591), Vol. II. Transcribed and edited by D.P. Walker, *Les Fêtes de Florence: Musique des intermèdes de 'La Pellegrina'* (Paris: Centre National de la Recherche Scientifique, 1963), pp. LVI-LVIII.

[13] 'Celeste Giglio'.

[14] Retouched from the portrait in *Il Ballarino* by Giacomo Francho (or Franco).

[15] The next-to-last dance, 'Fulgenti Rai', is dedicated to a sister and brother.

illustration of the opening position of the dance (the last thirteen are not so illustated, but refer back to previous figures). Following each choreographic text is the music, in Italian lute tablature and mensural notation (only the first eight dances are provided with the latter). Both notations are set in single impression movable type. The three tables of contents list the names of the steps, the names of the rules of etiquette, and the titles of the dances respectively.

There are seven different page-heading colophons, six of which are repeated throughout the book, and there are nine different figures showing dancers in various opening positions, which also are repeated as needed. A tenth figure of a geometric rose appears once only, but is applied to both the 'Contrapassi'.[16] Six of the figures are made from plates used in *Il Ballarino,* and are signed by Franco, while two more are made from plates originally by Franco, but retouched. Only two seem to be entirely new: the rose for the 'Contrapasso' (p. 241), and a figure of a couple which appears first opposite 'Nuova Regina', unsigned, and is then repeated elsewhere.[17]

In this translation the exigencies of modern economics have dictated a less sumptuous publication than Caroso's. Thus just the figures are reprinted from the original source once only (at the end of the book for quick reference); in the body of the text the figure which originally appeared with a dance is indicated by a Roman numeral.

[16] See ch. 3 for further information.

[17] The copy of *Nobiltà di dame* used by Forni for the modern reprint (Bologna, 1970) does not contain an illustration for 'Nuova Regina', though it does appear elsewhere in the book. Other examplars carry it, however (e.g., that in the Houghton Library at Harvard).

2

Problems of Translation

Caroso wrote *Nobiltà di dame* in a good, though elaborate Tuscan, and he is ever at pains to demonstrate his fine education. By today's standards his style is often florid, repetitious, pedantic, and pretentious—a mirror of the mannerism of courtly life. In true courtly fashion, however, he can also be elegant, charming, amusing, earthy, and pithy, putting flesh on the dry skeletons of a dancing master and his pupils with his vivid descriptions of awkward movements or disasters on the ballroom floor, and demonstrating the practical and psychological wisdom of a teacher who has dealt with the young for many years. In many ways his instructions are quite precise (if one dances through a choreography carefully one almost invariably concludes with the correct foot), and glaring typographical errors in the text are relatively rare. Yet the manual contains frustratingly ambiguous directions at times; the technical terminology for both dance and music presents a host of puzzles; and Caroso's courtly phrases often have no direct modern counterparts. Hence problems of translation for today's purposes are considerable, and must usually be resolved case by case. Nevertheless, it has been possible to adopt certain general principles for this translation, which aid its primary goal: to provide an accurate, idiomatic, and complete English version of the instructions contained in the original volume for the benefit of those who wish to reconstruct the dances and use the music.

All of the prose in the original has been translated. This includes both the dedicatory letter and the letter to the reader, which are perhaps the most elaborate and ornamental in style, because they provide information on Caroso's life and insight into his conception of the dance. The dedicatory poems have been omitted, on the other hand, for they contain little information and their literary value does not seem to merit poetic effort on the part of the translator.[1]

Caroso's flowery style would probably have been served best by a good sixteenth-century English translation.[2] Today, any attempt to match Caroso's

---

[1] For a summary of the information contained in the dedicatory poems, see ch. 3.

[2] For such an example, see John Dowland's translation, in Robert Dowland's *Varietie of Lute Lessons* (London, 1610), of Jean-Baptiste Besard's *De Modo in testudine libellus* in *Thesaurus harmonicus* (Cologne, 1603), a lute collection and manual.

style would inevitably produce false notes. The procedure followed here has been a compromise—to use modern English in a plain style when rendering straightforward dance instructions, and in a more literary and elaborate style for the ornate literary passages of the original. In striving primarily for clear and idiomatic English, sentences have often been shortened, purely ornamental connectives have been omitted or more appropriate ones freely substituted, tenses and pronouns altered without changing the meaning,[3] and redundant wording or passages often abbreviated. In the choreographic directions especially, brevity and clarity have been sought. Thus in some cases a free translation has been adopted to express Caroso's meaning, while in others an antique flavor has resulted simply because the only satisfactory solution has been to use somewhat antiquated words ('doffing' and 'donning' one's hat, for example). What follows is a discussion of various aspects of the translation in greater detail.

The title of the book and all the dance titles have been retained in Italian with original capitalization, with the translations appended; this follows current practice in music and dance. Most of these titles give no hint of the choreographic type to which the dance belongs but rather are fanciful and allegorical (e.g., 'Altezza d'Amore', 'The Grandeur of Love'), or incorporate a play on words involving the lady to whom the dance is dedicated (e.g., 'Laura Suave', 'Gentle Laura', dedicated to Christine de Lorraine, who married Ferdinando de' Medici in 1589).[4] Dance types that do appear in the titles have been retained in their original form (e.g., 'Gagliarda di Spagna'). But major dance types to which references are made in the course of the text, or which appear as subheadings within the dances or music, have been treated differently: those types that were Anglicized in the sixteenth century have been Anglicized here (thus we have 'pavan' for *pavana*', 'canary' for *canario*', and 'galliard' for *gagliarda*'). On the other hand, those types that were not usually Anglicized at the time (e.g., *passo e mezzo*'), or are unique to Caroso (e.g., *cascarda*'), have been retained without change. Standard dance types appear in lower case; unica or special titles are capitalized.

Because Caroso relates musical time values to dance, including them in many of his step titles, step descriptions, and choreographies, his musical termi-

---

[3] E.g., 'he will do', a literal translation, becomes 'you do' or 'do' without changing the meaning. In the section on etiquette for the lady, however, the discussion is between a *male* disciple and his master, and so the directions for the lady remain in the third person.

[4] In this case the music is a version of the famous 'Aria di Fiorenza', the tune to the ballo by Cavalieri mentioned above, performed at the nuptial celebrations of Christine de Lorraine and Ferdinando de Medici. For a detailed study of this music see Warren Kirkendale, *L'aria di Fiorenza, id est Il ballo del Gran Duca* (Florence: Olschki, 1972). The choice of this music for a dance dedicated to Christine cannot have been accidental on Caroso's part. Since the author of the text of this sung ballo was Laura Lucchesini de Guidiccioni, a double play on words may have been intended.

nology has been retained in the translation. The standard English terms of the period apply in most cases: *semiminima*, semiminim; *minima*, minim; semibreve; breve; and *longa*, long. Caroso adds two more to this series: *semigrave* (equals three semibreves), and *grave* (equals six semibreves); these have been kept also. Other terms, such as *battuta*, beat; *battuta tripla*, triple beat; and *battuta perfetta*, perfect beat, have been translated as simply as possible, though their meanings do not seem to be consistent at all times. In these cases any ambiguities or inconsistencies in the original are reproduced as closely as possible.

All step terms have been translated into English and italicized. Where the English step terminology may not seem to be idiomatic, the choice is deliberate. For example, the term *semigrave stopped step* is used for *passo puntato semigrave*, because 'semigrave' designates a time value, and 'stopped', though inelegant, is a brief and vividly descriptive term whose meaning is made clear in the step description.[5] The purpose of the italics is to mark either a specific movement or a group of movements that function as a single unit, in keeping with Caroso's usage; thus 'five *steps*' refers to five regular walking steps (*passi*), each of which is a single unit of movement, while '*five steps*' refers to the basic grouping of kicks and leaps of the galliard (*i cinque passi*) that together comprise a single unit.

The translation reverts to a word's older meaning, different from that of twentieth-century Italian, when this is clearly what Caroso means, and is confirmed in John Florio's *Queen Anna's New World of Words*, second edition (London, 1611, reprinted Scolar Press, 1973), a contemporary Italian-English dictionary. For instance, '*vita*', whose modern meaning is 'waist', clearly means 'body', 'torso', or 'trunk' in Caroso's usage, a meaning confirmed by Florio, who says it is 'used also for the stature or proportion of man or woman'.[6]

In the original choreographic texts, certain important clues to the steps intended, or to the correlation of dance with music, seem to be embedded. A standardized terminology has been adopted in the translation, and some of the original sentence structures have been maintained even if the results are stilted, in order to keep these clues and permit the reader to deduce what is in the original:

> 1. Semicolons, colons, and periods in the original seem to be equivalent to the ends of musical strains or phrases, as shown in the music by double bars or 'repeat signs'. These have been marked in the translation as periods, except in one case (see 3. below). Stock terms following these punctuation marks often appear in a fixed

---

[5] See Rule VIII.
[6] Florio, p. 603.

order in the text, and may therefore indicate when a new strain is intended. These terms, in order, and their translations are:

Poi, dapoi—then	*Per ultimo, ultimamente*—lastly, last
Dopò—after that	*Al fin(e)*—at the end, conclude
Ciò fatto—this done	*ꝏ, ꝗ, ꝸ, ꝸ et*—and, now[7]
Finalmente—finally	

Since a number of the English terms above are synonymous, the reader must bear in mind that each has been matched to a specific term in the Italian, in order to preserve in the translation clues that may be in the original.

2. Each paragraph in the original normally applies to one complete playing of the music designated for it, whether with or without inner repetitions. The same paragraph structure has been retained in the translation, so that the reader may decide independently what is intended.

3. Instructions to repeat a passage or a group of steps usually follow a semicolon in the original. This formula has been continued in the translation. Thus, 'repeat to the other side' usually means one should repeat the preceding group of steps, going back only as far as the previous major punctuation mark (semicolon, colon, or period). But when, in the original, a new sentence *begins* with instructions to repeat a passage (as in 'Passo e mezzo', Lady's First Variation, p. 178), this seems to signify that one is to repeat from the beginning of the entire paragraph. Again, this punctuation has been retained, and its exact meaning left to the reader to determine.

Certain unvarying formulae have been adopted for some terms or cliché phrases which appear frequently in varied or ornate forms throughout the book, without any discernible difference in ultimate meaning. While such variations and ornamentation are hallmarks of Caroso's age in all the arts, and might add some spice to the text if they were attempted in translation, the editor decided to forego the effort here except in cases where real changes of meaning are intended. The following is a list of some of these formulaic phrases with the original page or the rule in which they appear and the originals for which they may stand:

Repeat to the other side
> *di nuovo tornaranno à fare le medesime attioni per contrario* (p. 94)
> *faranno gli medesimi Moti per contrario* (p. 186)
> *faranno il medesimo per contrario* (p. 290)
> *gli medesimi faranno per contrario* (p. 112)
> *gli medesimi Moti torneranno [sic] à fare per contrario* (p. 112)
> *gli medesimi Moti faranno per contrario al lato destro* (p. 252)
> *i medesimi Moti tornaranno à fare per contrario* (p. 328)
> *il medesimo faranno al lato destro* (p. 94)
> *il medesimo faranno al lato destro per contrario* (p. 103)

---

[7] The variety of signs for this conjunction seems to be purely ornamental.

il medesimo faranno per contrario (p. 98)
il medesimo farà ogni cosa per contrario (p. 157)
il medesimo faranno per contrario al lato destro (p. 231)
il medesimo per contrario (p. 186)
il medesimo torneranno à fare per contrario (p.††2ᵛ)

The Sciolta of this Piece[8]
>*Alla Sciolta della Sonata* (p. 268)
>*La Sciolta della Sonata* (p. 258)
>*La Sua Sciolta* (p. 254)

The Sciolta of this Piece as a Galliard, or as a Saltarello
>*Alla Sciolta della Sonata in Gagliarda* (p. 142)
>*Alla Sciolta di detta Sonata in Saltarello* (p. 114)
>*Alla Sciolta in Saltarello* (p. 361)
>*La Sciolta della Sonata farassi in Saltarello* (p. 224)
>*La Sciolta della Sonata in Saltarello* (p. 142)
>*La Sonata si scioglierà in Gagliarda* (p. 360)
>*Questa Sonata si scioglierà in Saltarello* (p. 173)
>*Quì si scioglierà la Sonata in Saltarello* (p. 279)
>*Si farà la Sciolta di detta Sonata in Gagliarda* (p. 180)
>*Si scioglie la Sonata in Saltarello* (p. 298)
>*Tutta la Sonata si scioglierà in Gagliarda* (p. 112)

The derivation of the term
>*Da che habbie pigliate questo nome* (Rule LVI)
>*Donde deriva* (Rule XXXIII)
>*Donde deriva questo nome* (Rule XVII)
>*Donde derivata sia* (Rule IV)
>*Donde è derivato* (Rule LXV)
>*Donde egli habbi hauuto cosi fatto nome* (Rule XXIX)
>*Donde sia derivato* (Rule LXIIII)
>*Donde sia derivato questo nome* (Rule XX)
>*Donde siano derivati* (Rule XXIII)
>*Donde s'habbia hauuto cosi fatto nome* (Rule LII)
>*Dove derivi* (Rule XXV)

The origin of the [term]
>*Da che deriui l'origine sua* (Rule XXXIIII)
>*Della sua origine* (Rule XXII)
>*Donde s'habbi questo nome hauuto origine* (Rule XLVII)
>*Donde s'habbia tratta l'origine sua* (Rule XXXI)

Turning to the left/right[9]
>*Si han da voltare... à man sinistra* (p. 157)
>*Si voltaranno al lato sinistro* (p. 273)[10]

---

[8] See Glossary for a discussion of the meaning of the terms 'Sciolta' and 'Piece'.
[9] Concerning the ambiguous usages of '*voltare*' and '*volto*', see the Glossary.
[10] Concerning the meanings of '*man*', '*lato*', and '*fianco*', see the Glossary.

Si voltaranno à man sinistra (f. ††2^r)
Si voltassero à man sinistra (p. 267)
Voltando la vita al lato destro (p. 106)
Voltando à man sinistra (p. 114)
Voltandosi al lato sinistro (p. 94)
Voltarannosi alla sinistra (p. 180)
Voltarsi à man sinistra (p. 237)
Volterànno con la vita al fianco sinistra (p. 98)
Volti à man sinistra (p. 263)
Volti alla sinistra (f. ††^{v})
Volti intorno ala sinistra

Wider variants of the terms given above have been translated in full. Apart from these formulae, the translation does not abbreviate Caroso's text.

Single words with multiple meanings pose another type of problem for the translator. Take one of the most significant terms: *tempo*. 'Time' is the translation adopted here most often, each 'time' to be understood in its context. But some instances cannot simply be translated as 'time'; for example, '*quando ogn'uno harà fatto il suo tempo*', 'when everyone has had his turn'. Another example is '*un tempo di Gagliarda*', meaning literally 'one time [through] of the standard galliard pattern', usually | ♩ ♩ ♩ ♩ ♩ ♩ | (translated as 'one galliard pattern'), or '*un tempo di canario*', 'one canary pattern', normally | ♩. ♪♩ |. The most problematic usage of '*tempo*' is when the term indicates either a single playing of the complete piece of music for a dance, or a single playing of one movement of a dance.[11] In a dance of simple construction, such as 'Spagnoletta Nuova' (whose music and dance structure are both A A' A", etc.), each paragraph of the dance instructions begins with an indication of which playing of the entire music it receives. '*Nel terzo tempo*' here means 'In the third time through of the music' or 'In the third playing of the music'. Both of these translations, though accurate, seem awkward and inadequate, however, since they do not carry the dance connotations which seem to be intended by the placement of this phrase at the beginning of each paragraph. The word 'repetition', while perhaps logical, also omits a dance connotation and requires a shift in numbers: that is, '*nel secondo tempo*' becomes 'in the first repetition', an awkward locution. The term 'variation' must be eliminated as a possibility, because Caroso often uses '*mutanza*' in the sense of 'variation';[12] he keeps

---

[11] In this usage the word is synonymous with *volta*, a term that appears twelve times, but only in the rubrics to the music and never in the dance instructions (e.g., 'Laura Suave': '*Questa Sonata farassi due volte*', 'Play this piece twice'). Furthermore, '*volta*' is not consistently employed in the musical rubrics, and '*tempo*' is used instead (three times), though in only one score, 'Furioso', suggesting that one source of music had '*tempo*' instead of '*volta*'.

[12] Florio, p. 327: '*Mutanza*, any shift or change as in a dance'.

'*mutanza*' distinct from '*tempo*', even though one '*mutanza*' often requires one '*tempo*' ('playing') of the music. Thus the term 'variation' has been reserved for the '*mutanza*' family of terms. 'Figure' is perhaps the best translation of '*tempo*' in a dance as straightforward as 'Spagnoletta Nuova', for it is a term which may connote both musical repetition and a discrete segment of a dance which has been choreographed to fit that repetition exactly. In such a dance, the second repetition of the music and the second figure of the dance take place at exactly the same time. But the term '*tempo*' is used in choreographies of more complex structure with several changes of mensuration, a number of strains, and unusual patterns of musical repetition, wherein 'figure' and 'playing' are not synonymous, so that a different approach is necessary. A typical example of such a complex structure is 'Furioso alla Spagnuola', in which occur various subheadings, e.g., '*Si torna à fare di nuovo detta Sciolta in Saltarello à quattro Tempi*' (p. 280), 'Play the sciolta to this piece as a saltarello four more times'; under this subheading appears '*Nel primo tempo di questa Sciolta*', 'In the first playing of this sciolta'. Yet this is actually the seventeenth *section* of the dance![13] With some misgivings, then, the final choice of a word for this context was 'playing', with few exceptions, simply because it seemed to be the best term under the circumstances.[14]

Complicating matters still further is the fact that in some dances repetitions of a strain are called for, yet there is no clear verbal instruction for repetition. In 'Furioso all'Italiana', for instance, the entire first paragraph requires ten playings of the first strain of music, as confirmed by the rubrics in the music, '*Farassi in dieci Tempi gravi*'; yet in another choreography to exactly the same music, 'Furioso alla Spagnuola', not only are twelve playings (*tempi*) of the music specified in the text, but each playing is described in a separate paragraph!

One of the most difficult problems in any translation is ambiguity of meaning in the original. When the original is a manual, such ambiguity is especially irritating and frustrating. Caroso's *intent* in *Nobiltà di dame* was not ambiguity; and undoubtedly he expected his meaning to be entirely clear to his readers. Anyone who has tried verbally to describe a movement or a dance figure to someone who is totally ignorant of it can only sympathize with Caroso's difficulties, admire the degree of clarity he did attain, and rue our total loss of the traditions of movement and terminology on which he instinctively

---

[13] In fact, this dance provides an excellent example of highly varied subheadings and references to these headings in the body of the choreography.

[14] One exception, for example, is '*Tempo Terminato*' (as in 'Amorosina Grimana'), by which Caroso means a symmetrical division of the step patterns in a single choreographic section of the dance. The translation is 'Symmetrical Section'. See 'Conto dell'Orco' for another exception; the word 'figure' has been adopted in this case, since the music clearly must be repeated more than once for each paragraph designated 'tempo' in the original.

and unconsciously depended. In the present translation the strong temptation to 'clarify' Caroso's ambiguities was resisted, and an attempt was made to render them in equally ambiguous English, with a consistent translation in every case. For example, see the list of directions for turning given above; whether these refer to turning around, to curving towards one side or another in passing, or to making a quarter turn to the right or left, is occasionally clear in context, but no effort has been made to impose a precise meaning where none is clear in the original. On the other hand, where the meaning is clear but requires the addition of a word or two, square brackets have been employed to mark off these editorial additions for the reader.

Any translation involves many decisions, and the editor is acutely aware of the questions that remain unanswered, and of the choices that were made among seemingly equal candidates. Those who wish to know exactly what Caroso said should, of course, consult the original text, which is available in reprint. Yet to those who have heretofore been prohibited by language from examining such an important source, this translation is offered in all humility.

3

Caroso's Life

Almost all of the information on Caroso's life presented here has been gleaned from his publications, and much further research into other sources, especially the household accounts and memorabilia of his patrons, remains to be done. A brief statement of what is known and surmised is offered here.

Three volumes bear Caroso's name:

> *Il Ballarino* (Venice: Francesco Ziletti, 1581).[1] Contains 54 rules for performing dance steps, one note on etiquette for ladies, and 80 dance choreographies with music in lute tablature (the first 22 include mensural notation). 200 folios. Reprinted New York: Broude Bros., 1967.

> *Nobiltà di dame* (Venice: il Muschio, 1600, 1605). Contains 68 rules for dance steps, 24 notes on ballroom etiquette for ladies and gentlemen, and 49 dances with music in tablature (the first 8 include mensural notation). 400 pages. Reprinted Bologna: Forni Editore, 1970.

> *Raccolta di varij balli* (Rome, 1630. Published by Giovanni Dini, printed by Guglielmo Facciotti). A reissue of *Nobiltà* with altered title page and dedication leaf. The illustrations are rearranged.

Most twentieth-century references, including both reprints of his books, give 'Marco (or Mario) Fabrizio Caroso' as the full name. Yet in his own works and contemporary references Caroso's name is consistently shown as 'Fabritio Caroso da Sermoneta', with or without a preceding 'M'. Cesare Negri refers to Caroso twice, changing spellings slightly: 'Messer Fabritio Carroso da Sermoneta', and 'Fabricio Caroso da Sermoneta'.[2] It must be assumed, then, that Fabrizio is a modernized spelling, and that the 'M'. preceding the name on the title page of *Il Ballarino* stands not for Marco or Mario, but for *Messer* (Sir, or The Honourable) or *Maestro* (Master or Teacher) as in Negri's first

---

[1] Robert Eitner, *Biographisch-bibliographisches Quellen-Lexikon* (Leipzig, 1900-4), i, p. 341, attributes to Oscar Chilesotti a citing of a first printing of *Il Ballarino* in 1577. This supposed printing has not yet come to light in my current research, and there is no other evidence for it.

[2] Negri, pp. 2 and 4.

reference above.[3] This view is supported by the form of the names of *all* the other contributors to *Il Ballarino:* M. Andrea da Gaeta, M. Bastiano, M. Battistino, M. Oratio Martire, M. Paolo Arnandes, and M. Ippolito Ghidotti da Crema. Contributors of poems in *Il Ballarino* are also designated by 'M'. In *Nobiltà di dame*, Caroso's title is 'Sr'. or 'Sig'. (Signore or Master), as are those of the authors of poems to him (no one else is acknowledged in *Nobiltà di dame* as the choreographer of a dance).[4] It is clear that the 'M'. and the 'Sig'. are employed in the same way by Caroso. Further evidence for the meaning of the 'M'. is to be found in Negri, whose other contributor is 'M. Stefano'.[5]

Since birth records of Sermoneta from this period are lost, Caroso's date of birth must be based on the evidence of the portraits in both his books, each of which states his age. The portrait of 1581 says he is 46, which results in a birth date of 1535; that of 1600 (the same portrait, retouched to show a much older man) says he is 74, resulting in a birth date of 1526. There is no way of knowing, however, exactly when these portraits were made in relation to the dates of publication, for both books obviously took considerable preparation time.[6] Thus the ages given on both portraits may actually be correct.

According to oral history handed down in Sermoneta, Caroso was a native son of peasant extraction who was sponsored by the Caetani, the powerful and ancient ducal family of Sermoneta and Rome.[7] Evidence of the truth of at least some of this history appears in both volumes: four ladies of the family in *Il Ballarino*, and three in *Nobiltà di dame*, are recipients of dance dedications in their honour.[8] Of these seven (an unusually large number for the members of a single family to be named by Caroso), four are designated especially as 'Patrona Mia', one is unique among all the dedicatees to be cited *in memoriam*,[9] and one is especially cited as Caroso's benefactress.[10] How and by whom he was educated we do not know, but it is likely that the Caetani were

---

[3] F. J. Fétis, in *Biographie universelle des musiciens* (Brussels, 1837-44), Vol. III, p. 55, appears to have been responsible for interpreting the 'M.' as 'Marco'. H. Riemann, *Musik-Lexikon*, twelfth ed., ed. Wilibald Gurlitt (Mainz, B. Schotts Söhne, 1959), gives 'Mario' (vol. I, p. 279).

[4] See Florio for definitions of all titles.

[5] Negri, pp. 170, 189, 213, 230. He seems to make a distinction, however, between 'M.' and 'Sig.', the latter apparently designating higher rank.

[6] The earlier date in Eitner, *Quellen-Lexikon*, still would not produce a single date of birth.

[7] Sermoneta, a walled medieval town a short distance south of Rome, is dominated by the fortress of the Caetani; the Palazzo Caetani in Rome is still in active use, now converted to elegant apartments. The last of the line, the Principessa Caetani, died in this century without heirs.

[8] Beatrice Caetana Cesi, Agnesina Colonna Caetana, Giovanna Caetana Orsina, and Cornelia Caraffa Caetana in *Il Ballarino;* Felice Maria Orsina Caetana, Camilla Caetana Caetana, and Laura Caetana della Riccia in *Nobiltà di dame.*

[9] Agnesina Colonna Caetana.

[10] Felice Maria Orsina Caetana, Duchess of Sermoneta. Further connections with the Orsini family are discussed below.

responsible for his upbringing. He shows the same crest in both books, but further research must determine when it was awarded.

By Caroso's own account, he began his career as a dancing master at age 27.[11] The exact geographical perimeters of this career are unknown, but the other patrons besides the Caetani who are named in both volumes support a view that Sermoneta and Rome remained Caroso's chief locations throughout his life. The Orsini family of Rome is, in fact, the most highly represented of all the great families: eight members are cited in *Il Ballarino* and ten in *Nobiltà di dame*; in the former volume one of these, Olimpia Orsina Cesi, is clearly identified as a special patron, while in the latter book it is the Duchess of Sermoneta, Felice Maria Orsina Caetana,[12] who is Caroso's special benefactress. The rose design of the 'Contrapasso Nuovo', furthermore, which is dedicated to Cornelia Orsina Cesi, is undoubtedly intended to evoke the rose emblem of the Orsini family. Additional evidence of the importance of Rome in Caroso's biography is easily found: the chief dedication of *Nobiltà di dame* is to members of noble Roman families, the Duke and Duchess of Parma and Piacenza,[13] who were of the Farnese and Aldobrandini families respectively,[14] and Caroso identifies them as his current patrons. Not only are most of Caroso's patrons identified with Rome, then, but the preponderance of aristocratic Roman family names besides the Caetani and Orsini among the dedicatees of the individual dances in both books testifies to the importance of Rome in Caroso's life.[15] That Tasso (d. 1595) dedicated a sonnet to Caroso which was included in *Nobiltà di dame* is a further indication that Rome was the centre of Caroso's activities, for Tasso was in Rome between 1592 and 1594 as a guest of the Aldobrandini. The reissue of *Nobiltà di dame* as *Raccolta di varij balli* by Giovanni Dini in Rome in 1630, presumably a considerable time after Caroso's death, and eight years after the death of Duke Ranuccio, supports our assumption.[16]

The question remains whether Caroso travelled beyond Rome during his lifetime. No firm answer on this score can yet be given. We do not even know if Caroso ever went to Parma with the Duke. The publication of both manuals in Venice may have been due only to that city's dominance of the music-printing

---

[11] *Il Ballarino*, Letter to the Reader, fol. B^r.

[12] See above.

[13] Ranuccio I, 1569-1622.

[14] The Duchess was a 'niece' (i.e., illegitimate daughter) of Pope Clement VIII, who reigned 1597-1605. He was known as a good family man. Another 'niece' receives a dedication of one dance in *Nobiltà di dame*—'Olimpia Aldobrandina, Nepote di nostro Sig. Papa Clemente VIII' (p. 160).

[15] There is, furthermore, a strong concentration of prominent families from the Sermoneta area.

[16] The rearrangement of the illustrations in *Raccolta* so that a number of them do not match the dance they precede, but have been treated as purely decorative, hints that Caroso's influence and tradition were losing ground.

trade in Italy, or, more simply, to Caroso's finding willing publishers there, though it is certainly possible that he sojourned in Venice for fairly extended periods while supervising the printing of his books. The letters of dedication in both books are signed and dated in Venice, and one dance in *Il Ballarino* is in honour of Madonna Felicita Ziletti, presumably a member of the publisher's family.[17]

Other dedications in both books suggest that Caroso moved in princely circles, and may have travelled to various cities of northern Italy. The entire volume of *Il Ballarino* is dedicated to a member of a prominent Venetian family, Bianca Capello, who had become the wife of Francesco de' Medici in 1579 (one may guess that the volume was originally intended as a wedding gift). Dedications in *Nobiltà di dame* of individual dances to many other ladies of royal blood, among whom the Medici figure prominently, include Maria de' Medici, just crowned Queen of France in 1600; Margarita of Austria, Queen of Spain and cousin to Maria; Leonora de' Medici Gonzaga, Duchess of Mantua; and so on in order of protocol.[18] Certainly Caroso's rules of etiquette, with their detailed instructions for the behaviour of and toward princes and princesses, inform us that he dealt with royalty and was especially involved in training young aristocrats for the long festivities associated with important weddings. Since it was not uncommon at the time, however, for dedications to be made to royalty not personally known to an author, and since these were acceptable both as flattery to the recipient and as self-serving to the author (monetary and other favours normally ensued), we cannot assume that Caroso was an itinerant dancing master at all the Italian courts whose heads he names. So many royal ladies appear in the dedications, in fact, some without family names (e.g., 'Signora Vice-Regina di Napoli')[19] that we can only guess at how many he may have known personally. Until more extensive studies of family

---

[17] *Il Ballarino*, f. 173.

[18] I am indebted to Steven Ledbetter for the following communication: 'Rome, Archivio storico capitolino. Archivio Orsini 103, p. 462: Letter from Cardinal de' Medici [Ferdinando, later Grand Duke of Tuscany], Rome, to Virginio Orsini [in Florence], 1 December 1581: "Alla Granduchessa ho scritto il desiderio di Vostra Signoria circa à Maso [Maestro?] Fabritio Ballerino, et so' che l'amore-voleza sua non harà stimolo per dare ogni sodisfattione che portrà à tutte quelle Principesse con lei insieme, la quale ho piacere di veder così invogliata d'honesti essercitij, et di sentire che si conservi sana, et pregandole prosperità nell'una et nell'altra; . . . " The Cardinal was Virginio's uncle; Virginio himself would have been just about to enter his teens at this time'.

[Translation by J.S.: 'I have written to the Grandduchess Your Highness's wish with regard to Maestro Fabritio, the dancing master, and I know that her good will [towards you] is such that she needs no prodding to satisfy insofar as possible [the desires of] all the Princesses and You too, whom it pleases me to see so desirous of honest exercises, and to hear maintaining good health, and to pray that you prosper in both. . . . '] If one presumes that the 'Fabritio Ballerino' here is Caroso, then the date of this letter may well have implications with regard to the date and dedication of *Il Ballarino*. If it is a response to a letter from Virginio, that letter may be preserved in the Archivio di Stato in Florence. Further archival studies indeed are warranted by the evidence in this letter.

[19] *Nobiltà di dame*, p. 149.

records produce evidence to the contrary, then, it seems likely that Caroso's royal contacts were not quite so broad, nor his travels so extensive as might be supposed at first glance. On the other hand, we may conjecture with some confidence that his reputation was high enough to warrant that his dedications to personages he did not serve directly would be well received.

The poems of dedication function chiefly as flattery and ornament to the more straightforward description of the dances, in the same manner that all the arts and elements of life were then adorned for beauty's sake. Their texts invariably reflect the fondness of the age for allegory, as well as the customary neo-Platonic associations of dancing with godliness and the movement of the spheres. Youth, beauty, grace, gentleness, and charm are the chief virtues extolled in the ladies to whom the poems are addressed, while the occasional mention of a river or geographical place name confirms what the ladies' titles have already revealed. The poetry reflects a well-educated writer versed in the literary conceits of his day, but with so few contemporary sources at our disposal for comparison, it is difficult to say how typical of sixteenth-century dancing masters Caroso may have been.[20]

There is a good possibility that Caroso was the dancing master to many of the Roman ladies to whom he dedicated his dances; such a supposition is based on similar but more specific dedications of dances in Negri's manual.[21] Caroso's professional masters, colleagues, or disciples may well be represented by the contributors to *Il Ballarino* listed above, but in fact nothing is said about them by Caroso. One of them, Paolo Arnandes, may be the same as the 'Gio. Paulo Ernandes romano' who appears on Negri's list of dancing masters just preceding his description of Caroso.[22] According to Negri, Ernandes was from Rome, but also taught in Naples and France before returning to Rome; his specialty was 'many beautiful canary variations'.[23] Giovanni Dini, who reissued *Nobiltà di dame* as *Raccolta di varij balli* with a different dedication, may have been a disciple of Caroso's who had access to the remainder sheets and plates of *Nobiltà di dame*. There is no evidence that Negri knew Caroso personally, as some have suggested,[24] for the two specific references to Caroso

---

[20] We do not know if the dances were specially 'composed' or adapted for the ladies to whom they were dedicated to dance on a special occasion.

[21] Negri, pp. 17-30, where his students are listed under the then governors of Milan, with dates of governorship, thereby placing them in time. Since almost all the dedications of dances to ladies in Negri's book correlate with names on these lists, it is possible to determine that the earliest dances in the book date from about 1563, if one assumes that the dances were composed at the time of the dedications.

[22] Ibid., p. 4; *Il Ballarino*, fol. 106.

[23] Negri, p. 41: '& è stato inuentore di molte belle mutanze del... canario'. Ernandes, whose name suggests Spanish origins, is the only one singled out for this specialty, a matter of some interest because of the possibility that the canary was of Spanish origin (see ch. 3).

[24] E.g., Lawrence Moe, *Dance Music in Printed Italian Lute Tablatures in the 16th Century* (unpublished Ph.D. dissertation, Harvard Univ., 1956), p. 11.

in *Le Gratie d'Amore* refer admiringly only to a book (presumably *Il Ballarino*), and do not cite him as either a personal master or a disciple.[25] These scant mentions are misleading, however, for a number of Negri's rules 'duplicate' Caroso's rules in *Il Ballarino* word for word, while others incorporate phrases or sentences used by Caroso. Nevertheless, the connections between the two masters suggested by these and other concordances among their manuals need not have been personal.

Caroso's rules reflect one whose experience with the young is extensive, while they display the humanistic approach typical of a tutor to the courtiers of the time, such as an insistence on perfect symmetry, the justification of current practice by ancient custom, and the use of terms related to classical verse metres and architecture. The theoretical ramifications of the musical notation also reveal an awareness and an embracing of sophisticated notational techniques of the past and present.

A brief comparison here of the contents of *Il Ballarino* and *Nobiltà di dame* may shed further light on Caroso's life.[26] The greater number of rules for steps in the second book, the entirely new section on etiquette, and the 'corrections' of a number of the dances from *Il Ballarino* make it clear that Caroso continued to function until late in his life as a dancing master, teaching dancing and deportment in an aristocratic milieu which valued them highly as evidence of good breeding and good education. That Caroso deliberately refers to *Il Ballarino* on the title page of *Nobiltà di dame*, suggesting that it is a 'second edition',[27] implies that the first book was a success (in fact, *Nobiltà di dame* can only loosely be called a second edition of *Il Ballarino*, even in the modern sense of a revised and enlarged edition). Acknowledgments to other 'authors' of dances in *Il Ballarino*, including the ever-prolific '*Incerto*', 'anonymous', are entirely absent from *Nobiltà di dame*, and some of these dances are now attributed to Caroso himself (in revised form, to be sure), reflecting the common practice of the period of converting such material and appropriating it when suitable.[28] This appropriation may also indicate the rising status of Caroso, who may now have felt no need of other contributors in order to ensure the sale of his new book. Since the choreographies by these authors in *Il Ballarino* appear to be indistinguishable from Caroso's in their step vocabulary and structure, it seems certain that he was in the mainstream of the Italian dance world of the time.

The most complete information on how dancing masters functioned at the

---

[25] Negri, pp. 2 and 4.

[26] A thorough comparison remains to be done.

[27] *Nobiltà di dame*, title page, '*Libro, altra volta, chiamato IL BALLARINO*'.

[28] E.g., a number of standard dance types in Negri are subtitled, 'messo in uso dall' Autore', which may be loosely translated as 'adapted by the author' (for example, 'Pavaniglia alla Romana messo in uso dall' Autore', p. 132). Negri makes a distinction between such adapted dances and those he has created (such as 'Balletto a tre dell'Autore', 'Balletto for three by the author', p. 137).

end of the sixteenth century is provided by Negri, whose prefatory material is rich in names, dates, places, and activities.[29] From him we learn that dancing masters also taught riding and fencing, were noted for specialities, and opened schools in the cities where they worked.[30] Their noble masters often called upon them to display their manly arts to dazzle visiting dignitaries, or to choreograph expensive performances for these visitors, such as processions of allegorical figures accompanied by music and dancing,[31] the balli of intermedii,[32] or exercises of military precision and skill such as sword dances (*mattacinos*) performed by youths under their direction.[33] Dancing masters went along on lengthy military excursions to entertain and teach their noble masters en route,[34] and many went from Italy to teach at courts in Spain, Flanders, Bavaria, France, Savoy, and Austria.[35] In how many of these activities Caroso shared is unknown, for his texts deal strictly and logically with social dancing and with the etiquette appropriate to aristocratic balls and weddings. We may, then, be grateful to Negri for his braggadocio as well as for his desire to inform his readers beyond the confines of the title of his book,[36] while we seek further evidence of Caroso's work in the archives of noble families.

Caroso's date of death is unknown. It is possible that he was still alive in 1605, at the advanced age of 79 (or 70, if the date in *Il Ballarino* is correct), when a second printing of *Nobiltà di dame* appeared. He was certainly not alive in 1630, upon the reissue of *Nobiltà di dame* as *Raccolta di varij balli,* which may have been designed as a memorial to him. A reference by Alessandri da Narni in his *Discorso sopra il ballo* (published 1620), p. 54, suggests that he, Negri, and Lutij were dead by then: '*Penso io adunque, che se Prospero Lutij, Fabritio Caroso, e Cesare Negri fussero vivi a questo tempo, non usariano molti balli, passeggi, e mutanze, che vedemo nelli loro scritti. Però non mi par bene, che noi quelli imitiamo*' ('Now I think that if Prospero Lutij, Fabritio Caroso, and Cesare Negri were still alive today, they would not make use of many of the dances, passages, and variations which appear in their writings. Therefore[37] I do not think it a good idea that we should imitate them'.).

[29] Negri, pp. 1-30.

[30] Ibid., pp. 2-6.

[31] Ibid., pp. 9-11.

[32] Ibid., pp. 285-296.

[33] Ibid., pp. 8, 11, 13, 14.

[34] Ibid., p. 7.

[35] Ibid., pp. 2-6.

[36] Negri's sobriquet, '*il Trombone*', hints that he blew his own horn! On pp. 7, 11-16, he lists all the notables before whom he was summoned to perform. That he was an exact contemporary of Caroso's, as stated above, is clear despite the fact that his book appeared later than both of Caroso's. He states that he began to teach in Milan in 1554 (p. 3), and cites various events and dates at which he performed.

[37] Florio, p. 370: '*Però*, therefore, whereupon, then'.

4

Late-Renaissance Dance

Dance in Renaissance Society

In the late sixteenth century, it was universally assumed that joyous flirtation and the exhibition through dance of delightful feminine charms and lusty male prowess were vital to social intercourse. All occasions of state, great or small, were celebrated in the ballroom; thus personal adornment and elegance were seen as important artistic contributions to the theatrical ambience of a ball, the social and political aggrandizement of the host, and the matchmaking that was so essential to the perpetuation of the social structure. Dancing skills were cultivated in daily practice by the nobility and their emulators among the middle class, with the assistance of ubiquitous dancing masters like Fabritio Caroso da Sermoneta. The seriousness with which skill at dancing was regarded throughout the entire courtly period (from 1400-1800) was supported in the late Renaissance by a neo-Platonism that found vivid expression in the prose and poetry of the time:

> Dancing, bright lady, then began to be
> When the first seeds whereof the world did spring,
> The fire air earth and water, did agree
> By Love's persuasion, nature's mighty king,
> To leave their first disorder'd combating
> And in a dance such measure to observe
> As all the world their motion should preserve. .
>
> (Sir John Davies, *Orchestra, a Poem of Dancing.* London, 1594)

The neo-Platonic conceit that, in dance, the harmonious movements of the parts of the body paralleled the movements of all human bodies in a well-ordered world, and mirrored on earth the dance of all celestial bodies to the music of the spheres, found its fullest and most explicit expression in those sumptuous spectacles produced for grand occasions at enormous cost, the Italian intermedii, French ballets, and English masques. Here mellifluous poetry on allegorical subjects, music of all varieties for all known musical forces, dances especially choreographed for the occasion, brilliant costumes, and colourful scenery assisted by complex 'machines', combined to produce that perfect delectation and 'sweet assault' on all the senses so amply attested to in all our documents.

Theatrical dances in these spectacles, and in smaller entertainments provided by the nobility for their private pleasure, were not designed to give an audience the choreographer's dramatic or philosophic vision, nor to demonstrate a vast division in skill between amateurs and professionals. In fact, aristocratic amateurs and professional dancers performed side by side in these productions, in which the princes of highest degree often personified the greatest gods.[1] Dance in spectacle, therefore, normally enlarged upon or heightened the standard steps and dance types of the time. Thus, the dance manuals of the period, though their emphasis is on social dance, are extremely important as documentation of basic theatrical dance technique and style, as well as of choreographic patterns for staged dances.[2] It must be borne in mind, furthermore, that because of the high status of dance in the courtly world, and because of the time allotted to it in the daily education of the young, the social dance skills represented in these manuals exceed by far our current expectations of amateur dancing abilities.

From about 1550 to 1610, the period spanned by Caroso, court dance is well documented in plays, memoirs, letters, travellers' accounts, iconography, and most importantly, choreographic and musical sources. Though manuscript sources are few and small, the six dance manuals that appeared in print during this time by Caroso, Arbeau, Lutij, Lupi, and Negri, were not to be equalled again in number or scope until the early eighteenth century. Within them are rules for step patterns and style, valuable instructions on etiquette, and several hundred specific choreographies with music. Their chief authors, Caroso, Arbeau, and Negri, were all old men when their books were published, so unqestionably they documented dance practice for the entire second half of the sixteenth century;[3] but the fact that most of the manuals were reprinted, reissued, or translated up to 1630 is evidence that they continued to be valid into the first third of the seventeenth century, at least in Italy and Spain[4]

---

[1] See, e.g., Iain Fenlon, 'Music and Spectacle at the Gonzaga Court, *c.* 1580-1600', *Proceedings of the Royal Musical Association* (1976), pp. 90-105. The practise continued throughout the seventeenth century (see, e.g., the *dramatis personae* for Lully's ballets in H. Prunières, ed., *Oeuvres complètes de J. B. Lully,* Paris: Editions de la Revue Musicale, 1930-9).

[2] Negri provides several specific theatrical choreographies (pp. 271-6, 219-6). Arbeau gives one ('Les Matassins', pp. 182-95).

[3] Negri's earliest datable dance is 1563 (see ch. 3).

[4] Alessandri's volume refers by name to many dances and dance types, and cites Caroso, Negri, and Lutij. Juan de Esquivel Navarro's later *Discursos sobra el arte del Dançado* (Seville, 1642) uses many of the same terms, and carries on the virtuosic vein represented by Negri, but with a change in style toward greater leg turnout.

(publications in England and France in the first third of the seventeenth century hint that there different fashions were developing).[5]

Primary Printed Sources of Late-Sixteenth- and Early-Seventeenth-Century Dance, with Modern Reprints, Editions, and Translations

Alessandri, Felippo de gli [sic]. *Discorso sopra il ballo.* Terni: Tomasso Guerrieri, 1620.

*Arbeau, Thoinot (pseud. for Jehan Tabourot). *Orchésographie.* Langres: Jehan des Preyz, [1588], 1589; reprinted with expanded title, 1596/Facsimile reprint of 1596, Geneva: Minkoff, 1972.

———. Copy, with an introduction by Laure Fonta. Paris: Vieweg, 1888.

———. Translated into English by C. W. Beaumont. London: 1925. Reprinted New York: Dance Horizons, 1968.

———. Translated into English by Mary Stewart Evans. New York: Kamin Dance Publishers, 1948. Reprinted with corrections, a new introduction and notes by Julia Sutton, and representative steps and dances in Labanotation by Mireille Backer. New York: Dover Publications, 1967. This publication includes a list of translations into other languages, p. 8.[6]

*Caroso, Fabritio. *Il Ballarino.* Venice: Ziletti, 1581/Facsimile reprint, New York: Broude Brothers. 1967.

*———. *Nobiltà di dame.* Venice: il Muschio, 1600, 1605/Facsimile reprint, Bologna: Forni, 1970.

*———. *Raccolta di varij balli.* Reissue, with a new title page, of *Nobiltà di dame.* Rome: Facciotti, 1630.

de Lauze, F. *Apologie de la Danse.* [London]: 1623/Facsimile reprint, Geneva: Minkoff, 1977. Translated, with original text, additional commentary, and music, by Joan Wildeblood. London: Frederick Muller, 1951.

Lupi, Livio. *Mutanze di gagliarda, tordiglione, passo e mezzo, canari e passeggi.* Palermo: Carrara, 1600.

———. *Libro di gagliarda, tordiglione....* Second edition of the above, revised and enlarged. Palermo: Maringo, 1607.

Lutij [Lutius?], Prospero. *Opera bellissima nella quale si contengono molte partite, et passeggi di gagliarda.* Perugia: Orlando, 1587, 1589.

*Negri, Cesare. *Le Gratie d'Amore.* Milan: Ponti & Piccaglia, 1602.[7] Reissued as *Nuove Inventione di balli.* Milan: Bordone, 1604/Facsimile reprint of 1602, New York: Broude Bros., 1969; also Bologna: Forni, 1969.

———. MS translation into Spanish by Don Balthasar Carlos for Señor Conde, Duke of St. Lucar, 1630. Now in Madrid: Bibl. Nacional, MS 14085.

*Contain music for the dances.

———

[5] F. de Lauze, *Apologie de la Danse* (London, 1623), and Marin Mersenne, *Harmonie universelle* (Paris, 1636-7), reveal a more gliding style that contains less airwork. Alessandri's suggestion of a change of style gives no specific information (see ch. 3).

[6] All references in this book to Arbeau are to this edition.

[7] All references in this book to Negri are to this volume.

Five of the sixteenth-century manuals came from Italy, and Negri lists numerous Italian dancing masters working in France, Spain, the Netherlands, and German-speaking countries. Thus it is probable that Italy dominated the realm of dance in the sixteenth century, as it seems to have done in the fifteenth century.[8] The lack of written documentation from other geographical areas does not prove conclusively that Italy was in the vanguard of this art, but it is certainly the Italian manuals which contain the most elaborate and sophisticated steps, the most complex variations on the basic dance patterns, and choreographies of staged dances. While our only printed non-Italian source, Arbeau, is not to be taken lightly—he supplies ample evidence of the dance in France, and is the only adequate instructional source for some dances we know were popular elsewhere, such as branles, 'la volte', and 'Les Bouffons' (or 'matassins')[9]—he is best understood when considered with the Italian sources. As for the English, the Spaniards, and the Germans, little instructional material from these countries survives, though all available evidence indicates they were avid dancers.

There is much work yet to do on the connections between the sixteenth-century manuals, their choreographic similarities and differences, and their possible relationships with the sophisticated dance traditions of the fifteenth century. But even a brief look shows that they are indeed closely interrelated, both choreographically and musically.[10] For example, the relationship between two of the largest manuals, Caroso's *Il Ballarino* and Negri's *Le Gratie d'Amore,* is so close in some areas (e.g., the rules for basic step patterns) as to suggest that if one author were not plagiarizing the other, then both were using a single source or group of sources yet unknown.[11] Because of such connections, then, it is possible to make some general remarks here about all Renaissance dance, paying special attention to Italian style and form, before examining *Nobiltà di dame* in greater detail.

As represented in the manuals, the dances performed at court balls all over

---

[8] On fifteenth-century dance, see Ingrid Brainard, *The Art of Courtly Dancing in the Early Renaissance* (West Newton, Mass.: I. G. Brainard, 1981); 'The Role of the Dancing Master in 15th Century Courtly Society', *Fifteenth Century Studies,* vol. 2, ed. G. Mermier and E. Du Bruck (Ann Arbor: University Microfilms International, 1979), pp. 21-44; 'Bassedanse, Bassadanza and Ballo in the 15th Century', *Committee on Research in Dance (CORD),* II (1969), pp. 64-79; and *Die Choreographie der Hoftänze in Burgund, Frankreich und Italien im 15. Jahrhundert* (unpublished Ph.D. diss., Göttingen University, Germany, 1956). See also studies by Otto Kindeldey, Manfred Bukofzer, Daniel Heartz, and others.

[9] Negri, e.g., refers to this dance, pp. 8, 9, 11, 13, 14, without describing it.

[10] See ch. 2.

[11] Besides the rules for steps of the two authors, we may cite strong choreographic similarities e.g., Negri's 'Barriera' and Caroso's four versions—two in each volume—are unquestionably the same dance in slightly-varied guises; textual similarities, e.g., Caroso's introduction to 'Chiaranzana' (*Il Ballarino,* fol. 116[V]) and Negri's introduction to 'La Catena d'Amore' (p. 277) and 'La Caccia d'Amore' (p. 281), are almost identical instructions on how to deal with the general confusion that may result when these dances are announced; and musical concordances, e.g. between Caroso's 'Tordiglione' (both volumes) and Negri's (p. 196).

Western Europe and England include large group dances of the solemn processional type (e.g., pavan), circular dances (e.g., branles), and progressive longways dances 'for as many as will' (e.g., 'Chiaranzana').[12] There are also couple dances conforming to certain recognized popular types, such as the pavaniglia, passo e mezzo, canary, galliard, or courante/corrente; but the Italian sources especially contain many uniquely created and titled social dances whose choreographic relationships to standard types are not always clear, and may involve a variety of participants, such as trios, two couples, or odd numbers (e.g., five dancers, 'Ballo del Fiore').[13] The chief purpose of most of the dances is social pleasure. Miming dances, like the battle between the sexes in Caroso's 'Barriera'[14] (imitating the Barriers section of the still-popular court jousts), or vaulting *voltes* in an embrace position, as described by Arbeau, enhance the flirtatious flavour of the ball. Dances which are essentially kissing games, like Arbeau's gavotte; choreographed chases, like Negri's 'La Caccia d'Amore'; or mixers, like Caroso's 'Il Piantone',[15] make the sport of love more explicit. Young men may dazzle their ladies with glittering galliards which involve truly balletic techniques, including competitive turning jumps while kicking a tassel raised high above the floor, multiple turns on the ground or in the air, or rapid air beats.[16] The ladies charm with skill, but their role is less athletic, their manner more modest, than the gentlemen's. From simple to complex in pattern, and from easy to difficult in technique, there are dances to suit every taste.

Although stylistic differentiation between men and women reflects their societal roles, the basic aspects of the style are the same for both. These aspects are also perfectly integrated with the garb and social graces of the dancers. Most steps are small, and the torso remains erect with the arms quiet, as in most traditional European folk and social dancing. Footwork is vigorous, complex, skilful, and speedy, exploiting kicking strength, endurance, and elevation (even for the lady). Toes are not pointed; instead, the ankle is flexed, the leg is straight, and the degree of plié (when called for) and turnout are slight.[17] Hands are used for taking, clapping, holding the hilt of a sword, a hat, or a flower, but are not usually raised above the head,[18] nor do their actions involve much energy in the upper arm. In fact, when the gentleman wears his long cape while dancing, one arm has to keep it in place. It goes without saying that only the feet

[12] Caroso, *Il Ballarino,* fols. 176^V-178^r.

[13] Caroso, both publications.

[14] Caroso, both publications; and Negri, pp. 122-4.

[15] Caroso, both publications, and Negri, p. 102.

[16] Caroso and Negri explain all these technical feats.

[17] For kicking gestures Arbeau shows a relaxed ankle, knee, and turnout (pp. 85, 87), but the Italian sources demand straight legs and small turnout, if any (see, e.g., *Nobiltà di dame*, Rules and Note XI; Negri, pp. 52, 64, 68, 85).

[18] For exceptions see Negri, 'La Catena d'Amore', and Caroso, 'Chiaranzana' (*Il Ballarino*) which call for raised arms to allow others to pass underneath.

and the lady's dress ever touch the floor. Social etiquette, such as bowing and kissing one's hand to a partner, is as essential in dancing as in all social relationships among ladies and gentlemen.

In keeping with the social purpose of the dances, body positions are always taken in relation to the partner or other dancers, and encourage the dancers to concentrate on and charm one another. In most dances they do not come closer than required by a hand or arm hold, though a few call for an embrace position.[19] Choreographic paths, then, are also planned vis-à-vis the other dancer or dancers; positions taken in relation to an audience nevertheless include the partner, i.e., 'in prospettiva' apparently means facing each other and the bystanders on a diagonal (see Glossary). It is obvious from the texts, however, that observers' good opinions are highly desirable. A typical social dance for one couple, for example, might consist of opening honours, a lead-in figure that traverses the ballroom, the giving of right hands round and left hands round, a reverse S figure in which the partners exchange places, and a leading-out figure with honours.[20] Another scheme consists of alternating variations for each partner,[21] a third possibility has the couple moving simultaneously and side-by-side,[22] and still another has a refrain of steps and/or paths at the end of each figure.[23] Dances for more participants may include the same figures as couple dances, but with the addition of circles and various kinds of hays.[24]

With regard to compositional technique, little abstract theory or dance aesthetic is expounded in any of the sixteenth-century sources. It is taken for granted, instead, that everyone knows the basic principles of dance construction. While the authors are not concerned with defining, establishing, or justifying their work for posterity, they are eager to justify dancing to their own pupils as a worthy activity on the basis of the theories of the ancients (Arbeau, for example, goes so far as to attempt to correlate specific sixteenth-century dances with the dance types of ancient Greece). Caroso is perhaps the most

---

[19] See Arbeau, 'Lavolta', pp. 119-23, and Negri, 'La Nizzarda', pp. 268-9.

[20] That the common figures mentioned here are connected in some way with the typical figures of eighteenth-century social dances (especially the minuet) seems unquestionable, and perhaps will be proven in the future by the discovery of more choreographic sources than are now known to exist between 1630 and 1700. The presence of the reverse S, the most characteristic figure of the minuet, in both Caroso's and Negri's choreographies, suggests strongly that the origins of the minuet do not lie in France, as often proposed, but in the courtly couple dances of Italy. The possible origins of the minuet were reexamined in my paper, 'The Minuet: Durable Phoenix?', read at the joint meeting of the New England and New York chapters of the American Musicological Society (Spring, 1978), and scheduled for publication by *Dance Chronicle*.

[21] E.g., Caroso, both volumes, 'Passo e mezzo'.

[22] E.g., Caroso, both volumes, 'Pavaniglia'; Negri, 'Pavaniglia alla Romana', pp. 132-5, and 'Pavaniglia...all uso di Milano', pp. 157-9.

[23] E.g., see the 'Pavaniglias' cited above.

[24] E.g., Caroso, both volumes, 'Contrapasso'.

detailed in the matter of practical application of humanistic aesthetics to dance construction. His 'vera' or 'perfetta Theorica' (true or perfect theory), expounded at length and repetitively in Nobiltà di dame, is the only one on which he insists at all times; it is a fundamental law of absolute symmetry, with derived corollaries. If a dancer follows Caroso's rule, he works entirely symmetrically, so that he always begins a new pattern with the left foot and repeats it with the right, and his entire pattern either takes one half of the music and is repeated to the other side for the other half, or takes all the music and is repeated to the other side to another playing of the music. Similarly, if a couple takes right hands round, they must then take left hands round; if the partners move alternately, each must have a turn to either side. The other manuals, including Il Ballarino, are less adamant about symmetry, but normally adhere to it in practice.

Two closely-related principles—improvisation and variation—pervade all the dance manuals of the period, including Caroso's, as they do the music manuals. Basic steps and step patterns are given first,[25] and to them may be appended lists of variants for the would-be improviser to learn,[26] so that he may possess a large repertoire of movements suitable to certain types of dances,[27] such as the pavan, galliard, tordiglione, passo e mezzo, or canary. These variants either divide the basic step patterns into smaller components or substitute one gesture for another; they may consist of steps, hops, leaps, kicks, stamps, or turns, either travelling across the floor or remaining on place, and they take the same amount of time as the original basic step or step pattern.[28] Thus they appear to be identical in nature to the improvised diminutions, passaggi and ornaments so popular in sixteenth- and seventeenth-century music.[29]

The intimate relationship between improvisation and composed variation is plain: to improvise, the performer learns all the basic steps or step patterns, and as many variants upon them as he can, and uses them at appropriate moments

---

[25] By 'step' I mean a single gesture, e.g., falling jump; by 'step pattern' I mean a group of gestures forming a recognizable unit, e.g., ordinary sequence.

[26] See, e.g., Caroso's lists of capers, sequences, falling jumps, and flourishes.

[27] References to a male dancer are deliberate. While some mentions of female improvisation (or choice among new variations) do appear (see Negri, p. 100), the manuals are clearly directed at and ackowledge masculine skill and creativity.

[28] The clearest description of this procedure is given by Arbeau, who says: '... you should be told now that some dancers divide up the double that follows the two simples [in the pavan], and instead of the double comprising only four bars with four semi-breves, they introduce eight minims or sixteen crotchets, resulting in a great number of steps, passages, and embellishments, all of which fit into the time and cadence of the music'. Orchesography, p. 66.

[29] See, e.g., Sylvestro Ganassi, Opera Intitulata Fontegara (Venice, 1535). For further listings see Howard Mayer Brown, Embellishing 16th-century Music (London: Oxford University Press, 1976). Note that the terms gratia, mutanze, and passeggio are applied to both arts (see the Glossary for their meanings in Caroso).

when and how he chooses (he may, of course, invent totally new ones 'in the style' and on the spot if his skill is great enough, but this kind of originality is not demanded). To improvise a whole variation ('*mutanza*') the dancer begins with the basic step-patterns of the given dance type, using suitable step variants from among those in his dance vocabulary, and combines them to make one or more phrases to coincide with the music.[30] What distinguishes a composed dance from pure improvisation is, apparently, the forethought required to combine steps from the well-known vocabulary into an entire and predetermined choreography memorized by the dancers. Ornamentation, on the other hand, appears usually to be improvised: the absence from the written choreographies of some gestures described in the manuals may hint that they are seen purely as ornaments.[31]

Besides variations on the fixed structures of basic step-patterns, the dances in the manuals reveal that the fixed structures of figures may also be varied, so that, for example, a dance in which a couple traces figures simultaneously may have a section in which they alternate solo and accompanying passages.[32] The figures, however varied and recombined, remain recognizable nevertheless. The analogy in sixteenth-century dance composition to the process of composing musical sets of variations on a scheme of fixed length scarcely needs underlining: variation and ornamentation, whether improvised or predetermined, occur essentially within, or upon, a given structure. That variations would have been improvised by the musicians while endlessly repeating an eight-bar strain to a dance, for example,[33] seems an inescapable conclusion. Unfortunately, we have only a few direct examples in the dance manuals of such musical variations,[34] and must refer, instead, to the countless sets of instrumental variations from this period,[35] as well as to the musical manuals.

As has been implied, though originality in dance composition is not ruled out and undoubtedly appears in some of the more interesting, or more dramatic dances, it is not the primary purpose of our dancing masters. In this respect the

[30] Arbeau describes galliard and tourdion variations that equal twelve beats (two standard galliard patterns), and tells how to add steps to make up to twenty-four beats; Negri provides many highly virtuosic galliard variations from two to six patterns in length (twelve to thirty-six beats); Lupi gives 150 galliard variations in his second edition, in phrases up to twelve patterns long (144 beats!).

[31] E.g., Negri's '*tremare di piedi*' (p. 33).

[32] E.g., Caroso's 'Laura Suave', the galliard movement (*Nobiltà*); Negri's 'So ben mi chi ha bon tempo', pp. 222-4.

[33] E.g., the first strain of 'Furioso all'Italiana' is to be played ten times (*Nobiltà di dame*, no. 29).

[34] E.g., Arbeau's tabulations for the fife in duple and triple meter (pp. 40-6) are technically speaking for military music, but may be applicable to dance music; Caroso occasionally varies a repeated passage, as in the last four bars of 'Barriera' (*Nobiltà di dame*, no. 8).

[35] For a general discussion and further bibliography see Kurt von Fischer, 'Variations, part 4: Up to 1600', *The New Grove* (London, 1981), vol. 19, pp. 538-40.

sixteenth-century manuals represent a tradition that is far closer to folk dance and some aspects of early ballet than to the highly personalized theatrical art of the modern choreographer.

The degree to which folk and court dance influenced each other during the Renaissance is unknown. We know that throughout Western dance history the cultivated arts of dance and music have relied on folk and 'exotic' elements (whether real or imaginary) for fresh ideas, renewed vigour, and special character, eventually remaking them in the fashionable courtly or theatrical image until a need for fresh inspiration has been felt once more. We are also aware, however, that the imitation by the lower classes of aristocratic fads and tastes has been a strong force in the history of the performing arts. In the sixteenth century the line dividing court and folk dance appears to have been simply a separation marked by greater attention to elegance, style, and technique on the part of those of gentle birth.[36] Certainly many of the dance figures in our manuals, such as hays, circles, turning one's partner, or changing places, belong to both courtly and country worlds, their origins lost in the mists of time. Other seeming connections appear in some traditional folk dance styles of today: there is a strong resemblance between the galliard kick and the modern Italian tarantella step; the basic step pattern and capers of the galliard also resemble the basic movements, capers and 'galley' or 'gallery' step of traditional English Morris dance (note the apparent etymological connection); the visual and kinaesthetic similarities between the footwork described by the Italian manuals and current Balkan and Greek dance steps are too strong and obvious to be ignored; but the most vivid resemblances exist in the virtuosic male techniques of Basque dance. Unfortunately, documentation *proving* historical interaction between courtly sources and folk styles is still lacking, except in a few cases.[37] In these circumstances, one can only postulate a fairly widespread dance culture whose basic style originally crossed class lines, and from which elements have remained to the present in some areas of Europe while dying out elsewhere. Caroso's dances appear to be in the mainstream of that culture.

Perhaps easier to document than the influence of folk dance on court dance, though still unplumbed, is the influence on dance of the styles and techniques of other manly arts. Fencing and horsemanship, long dominant in the education

[36] There are no manuals of folk dance, as such, from the period; all written materials are, of course, intended for literate people (that is, the gentry). The Italian manuals make no overt reference to folk dance, but Arbeau describes several branles which mimic peasant folk (e.g., 'Haut Barrois', 'Washerwomen'). Many dances given in *The English Dancing Master* of John Playford (first edition, 1651), are referred to in late-sixteenth-century literary sources as folk dances.

[37] See, e.g., Robert Stevenson, 'The First Dated Mention of the Sarabande', *Journal of the American Musicological Society* V (Spring, 1952), 29-31. This originally-lascivious dance does not appear in a manual until the eighteenth century, more than one hundred years after its introduction to Spain from Mexico, by which time its obscene flavour has completely disappeared.

of a gentleman (for whom war was his profession by birth), show close enough relationships to dance in terminology, postures, and techniques to merit considerable further study by dance historians.[38] Arbeau, for example, suggests that dancing is the peaceful counterpart to the art of war,[39] providing as much exercise as fencing or tennis while enabling one to attract the ladies at the same time;[40] he also describes aspects of galliard style in terms of fencing.[41] Negri cites several dancing masters who taught fencing and horsemanship;[42] his references to dances of combat performed by his noble pupils include long swords and daggers, or swords and bucklers.[43] While Caroso makes no direct mention of fencing or related martial arts, his four versions of 'Barriera'[44] and his calls for 'jousting' movements assume it.[45] As important aspects of a noble youth's daily life, the physical arts of dancing, swordsmanship, and riding not only required skill and strength in equal measure, but were seemingly accorded equal status. Anyone attempting to revive the dance style of the Renaissance needs to be aware of the place of dance among the manly arts.

---

[38] See, e.g., Salvator Fabri, *Neuw Künnstlich Fechtbuch* (Nuremberg, 1570); Giacomo di Grassi, *Ragione di adoprar sicuramente l'arme* (Venice, 1570); or Girard Thibault, *Académie de l'Espée* (Antwerp, 1628).

[39] Arbeau, pp. 17-50.

[40] Ibid., p. 12.

[41] Ibid., p. 104.

[42] Negri, pp. 4-6. See also Brainard, 'Role of the Dancing Master in 15th Century Courtly Society', pp. 29-31.

[43] Ibid., pp. 8, 13, 15.

[44] Two in each volume: *Il Ballarino*, fols. 77^r-78^v; *Nobiltà di dame*, nos. 8, 15.

[45] E.g., 'Squilina Cascarda', *Il Ballarino*, fols. 43^v-44^r: '*Giostrando, tutti insieme...*'.

5

Dance Types in *Nobiltà di dame*

The previous chapter attempted to place *Nobiltà di dame* in context with other manuals of its time, and to draw upon them all for general observations about European court dance in the late sixteenth century. This chapter will address *Nobiltà di dame* in particular, briefly surveying its contents and discussing its most common dance types. Most of the comments made here apply also to *Il Ballarino*, because Caroso's conceptions of the dance types do not appear to have changed much from one book to the other, and also because he reuses so many dances.

Numbers of dancers

All of the choreographies in *Nobiltà di dame* are intended for social dancing; if there are any theatrical influences there is no verbal hint of them. There are no dances for soloists,[1] or for groups of male dancers or female dancers only,[2] both of which occur elsewhere with more theatrical implications. Indeed, most choreographies are for one couple, the quintessential social unit. Whether this means a *solo* couple is uncertain. The dedications to individual ladies and the importance given to the onlookers' opinion of the dancers' style and bearing tend to support a theory that one couple at a time was expected to dance before the others at a ball,[3] thus incorporating a theatrical element into a ballroom

[1] Cf. Arbeau's *mauresque*, 'moresca', p. 177. It is not clear whether the numerous galliard variations in Negri, Lutij, and Lupi imply solo performance by a male dancer. In the Florentine intermedii of 1589, Apollo dances an extended solo as he attacks the dragon; the poetic metres of his dance are given, but no specific choreography (Bastiano de' Rossi, *Descrizione del magnificentissimo Apparato E de' Maravigliosi Intermedi fatti per la commedia rappresentata nella felicissime Nozze degli Illustrissimi Don Ferdinando Medici, e Madama Cristina di Lorena, Gran Duchi di Toscana* [Florence, 1589], p. 44).

[2] E.g., Negri, pp. 271-3, a presentation dance for six ladies; pp. 274-5, a dance for six gentlemen dressed as Hungarians. Also Arbeau, 'Les Bouffons', pp. 182-95, a sword dance *(matassins)* for four men, in stage armour and bells.

[3] Iconography of the period bears out this theory, though it is not stated explicitly in the manuals. A century later, P. Rameau's *Maître à danser* (1725) describes this procedure and its protocol in detail; it is not certain to what extent his information applies to an earlier era and another country.

situation. Of the dances for more than two participants, small numbers are still the rule: one dance is for three ('Allegrezza d'Amore'), one for five ('Ballo del Fiore'), four for three couples (the two 'Contrapassi' and two of the 'Furiosi'),[4] and one for four couples ('Furioso in ottava'). No dances for any number of couples either in a circle, like Arbeau's branles, or in longways formation 'for as many as will', like 'Chiaranzana' in *Il Ballarino*, are found in *Nobiltà di dame*,[5] nor are there any two-couple dances of the kind Negri presents.[6] All but one of the dance types are abstract: 'Barriera', in two versions, mimes the actions of that form of tournament, and is the only type that mimics gestures other than pure flirtation and courtliness. Appropriate also to the social context is the fact that in almost all of the dances the partners either dance together throughout, or end together as they began; one exception to this principle is a mixer ('Ballo del Fiore'), and another is quite probably a mixer also ('Il Piantone').[7]

Improvisation

Caroso is clearly more interested in giving specific directions for his composed dances than in teaching the art of improvisation (for example, he provides far fewer variants on galliard steps for *ad libitum* choice by a dancer than any of the other authors of contemporary manuals). Yet frequent references in his texts to such performance show that he recognized improvisation as an important and regular aspect of social dance.[8] Indeed, one may speculate that his lengthy sets of variations on dance types like the pavaniglia, passo e mezzo, or tordiglione, were not intended to be performed *in toto,* but were meant to allow the dancers to select from among his variations those they knew or liked for performance, a process that would give them some freedom.[9] While such a theory is feasible, one must keep in mind that highly skilled amateur dancers can remember long series of dance variations, provided they consist of familiar steps and patterns, and Caroso's texts do not suggest that he intended anything other than a full performance of his dances.

---

[4] 'Furioso all'Italiana' and 'Furioso alla Spagnuola'. Caroso implies that 'Furioso all'Italiana' may be done by twelve dancers.

[5] Negri has two such dances (pp. 277-84), and this formation is common in John Playford, *The English Dancing Master* (London, 1651 and many later editions).

[6] E.g., 'Spagnoletto', pp. 116-17.

[7] The mixer aspect in *Nobiltà di dame* is obscure; it is clearer in *Il Ballarino* (fols. 181^V-84^r) and Negri, p. 102 (Regola LIIII).

[8] See, e.g., his instructions for 'Il Piantone'.

[9] Lutij gives such a series of galliard *'passeggi'* and *'mutanze'* (suggested meaning: '[traveling] passages' and 'variations [on place]'), though without music, and it is clear that they were intended for selection. Lupi does the same for the galliard, tordiglione, passo e mezzo, and canary. Negri's 70 pages of galliard variations have the same purpose.

Steps and Step Patterns

With regard to the step vocabulary of the dances in *Nobiltà di dame*, it is plain that very few steps or step patterns belong solely to a single type of dance, though Caroso recognizes dance types such as the galliard or canary, and his step usage indicates that he considers certain kinds of steps appropriate to each type. [10] Even steps that are most closely identified with a specific dance type, however, like the *cadenza in gagliarda (galliard cadence),* Rule LIX, or the *seguito battuto del canario (stamped sequence in the canary),* Rule XXIII, may be borrowed at will and inserted into another type of dance when desired. [11] Furthermore, there are no purely 'low' walking or purely 'high' leaping dances (air work is introduced into walking passages, and vice versa), nor are there step patterns that can only be performed in duple time *or* triple time. Apparently *all steps and step patterns except canary steps can be danced in duple or triple time.* [12] The complexity of treatment that was available to anyone with sophisticated improvisatory skills is revealed without question in Caroso's composed dances.

Terminology

From the modern standpoint, probably the most important question to address is what Caroso meant by the dance types in his titles or subtitles; [13] what specific kinds of choreographic figures, step patterns, formal structures, emotional affects, pantomime, and musical traits did terms such as 'passo e mezzo' and 'gagliarda' imply to him? The question is significant, for either the definitions of dance types in standard modern references are purely musical, or their choreographic components are generalized and insignificant. [14] Because so many of Caroso's dance types also appear in large numbers in collections of instrumental music of the late Renaissance, closer examination of his assumptions may affect and improve both future definitions and future musical

---

[10] It should perhaps be pointed out here that in his choreographies Caroso does not use all the steps he describes in his Rules.

[11] See e.g., 'Allegrezza d'Amore', a cascarda in which canary steps are called for at the beginning of the second part of each figure.

[12] See ch. 6 for further discussion.

[13] I use the term 'dance type' rather than the more common 'dance form' advisedly, reserving 'form' to mean what it does in music—underlying structure. By 'type' is meant *all* or *any* aspects of a dance which serve to define it and to distinguish it from other types; this may or may not include form.

[14] General definitions of sixteenth-century dance types by title may be found in Stanley Sadie, ed., *The New Grove Dictionary of Music and Musicians* (London: Macmillan, 1981); Friedrich Blume, ed., *Die Musik in Geschichte und Gegenwart* (Kassel and Basle: Bärenreiter, 1949-79); Willi Apel, ed., *Harvard Dictionary of Music,* 2nd ed. (Cambridge, Mass: The Belknap Press of Harvard University Press, 1969); Silvio d'Amico and Francesco Savio, eds., *Enciclopedia dello Spettacolo* (Florence and Rome: Sansoni, 1954-68). There are *no* reliable dance histories or dictionaries dealing with this period.

performances. When Caroso's are the *first* or the chief extant choreographies of an important dance type (such as his passo e mezzi),[15] their exact nature may weigh especially heavily in the formulation of any accurate definitions or sound musical conceptions.

Unfortunately, Caroso himself does not provide any complete definitions of dance types; ours must be gleaned from comments in his Rules, some of the specific step patterns, evidence in the choreographies, the music, and other manuals. Until detailed and extensive studies become available, including statistical analyses of the choreographic components of the dances in the sixteenth-century manuals, our definitions must remain superficial. They are offered here as initial impressions rather than as final syntheses.

Balletto

The term that most often appears in *Nobiltà di dame* as a subtitle to a dance is 'balletto' (e.g., 'Celeste Giglio, Balletto').[16] Thirty-seven of the forty-nine dances in *Nobiltà di dame* are so named, or are referred to as balletti in their choreographies, or elsewhere in the volume. 'Balletto' is associated with other dance types named by Caroso: alta, bassa, canario, gagliarda, passo e mezzo, pavaniglia, saltarello, and tordiglione. A large number of dances with purely fanciful titles are also termed 'balletti'. Thus the term appears to be generic for 'dance'. We find, however, that the term 'ballo' also applies to many dances, appearing within the texts of fourteen 'balletti', and in the Rules as another generic term for 'dance'. Yet both terms seem to be employed in more specific ways as well: neither term applies to the discrete dances in *Nobiltà di dame* that Caroso names 'cascarda';[17] both of the dances with 'ballo' in their titles are playful mixers; and with only one exception[18] *all* of the dances consisting of two or more movements (i.e., different mensurations and different dance types) are called 'balletto'.[19] Since this type of balletto, which I shall call 'balletto suite', is preponderant in *Nobiltà di dame*, as well *Il Ballarino* and *Le Gratie d'Amore,* it and its component dance types will be the focus of the ensuing discussion.

Of the balletti in two movements in *Nobiltà di dame*, most consist of an untitled duple movement and a triple 'sciolta' or 'sciolta in saltarello'.[20] Those in three movements are usually in the order of an untitled duple, a triple 'sciolta' or 'sciolta in gagliarda', and a different triple 'sciolta' or 'sciolta in saltarello'.

---

[15] See the discussion below.

[16] 'Balletto' is used the same way in *Il Ballarino* and *Le Gratie d'Amore*. It seems likely that the term first applied to dances, though it is often encountered in musical collections whose direct connection to actual dance is unknown.

[17] In *Il Ballarino* the term 'ballo' appears with cascarde, however.

[18] 'Il Piantone'.

[19] 'Movement' in this sense is used analogously to 'movement' in a suite or sonata.

[20] The term 'rotta' appears to be a synonym for 'sciolta' in some balletto suites (see Glossary).

The four-movement balletto suites normally follow the same order, adding a 'canario', also in triple. As the word 'sciolta' implies ('loosening' or 'untieing'), 'sciolta' movements are triple versions of the same music as the first movement of the group. The absence in all the dance manuals of the paired or grouped dances of many of the Italian musical collections variously titled 'pavana-gagliarda', 'paduana-saltarello', 'passo e mezzo-padovana-saltarello', and the like,[21] in which each movement of the pair or group is based on the same musical materials in different mensurations, is thus only apparent. Caroso's balletto suites are, in fact, variation suites like those in the musical collections, and what are missing are simply subtitles. The balletto suites in the manuals, then, may provide significant choreographic information for a very large body of music, especially since musical sources from other countries contain similar dance groupings.

It seems likely that the longer balletto suites of more than two movements derive in some manner from the complex sectional Italian balli or the bassa danza-saltarello pairs of the fifteenth century. But this theory cannot yet be fully supported because of a gap that separates the latest manuals of the fifteenth century or early sixteenth century from our choreographic sources of the late sixteenth or early seventeenth centuries,[22] a gap which also renders it impossible to give coherent histories of the individual dance types within the balletto suites. Similarly, connections with eighteenth-century social dances, which were often grouped into suites, are likely, but the present dearth of precise choreographic material from 1630 to 1700 does not permit more than speculation.[23] The exact family tree of our balletto suites cannot be drawn at this time, and a more precise delineation must await the discovery of additional materials.

[21] See Moe, *Dance Music.*

[22] The latest sources using fifteenth-century repertoire include Antoine Arena, *Ad suos compagnones* (Avignon, first dated edition 1529), Robert Coplande, *The maner of dauncynge of bace daunces after the vse of fravnce & other places* (London, 1521) and Jacques Moderne, *S'ensuyvent plusieurs basses dances commune que incommunes* (Lyons, ca. 1529). Negri, by his own account, began teaching in 1554 (see ch. 3) but the earliest dance in his collection may date from 1563 (p. 122). A choreography of a caccia in a letter by Christiano Lamberti dated 1559 (cited in Gino Corti, 'Cinque Balli Toscani del cinquecento', *Rivista Italiana di Musicologia* XII [1977], 73-76), uses the same vocabulary as Caroso and Negri, as does the other MS from the second half of the sixteenth century cited in the same article; the manuscript sources do not explain the steps called for. Since many of the sixteenth-century terms for steps and step patterns are identical to terms in fifteenth-century sources, their precise earlier definitions are essential if we are to establish an uninterrupted history. Such precise definitions are not given, however, and the most we can say presently is that there was a difference in style despite the likeness in terminology; how this difference came about is also unknown.

[23] See list of sources in ch. 4; Raoul-Auger Feuillet's *Chorégraphie* (Paris, 1700) is the first detailed source after de Lauze's *Apologie* of 1623 and Caroso's reissue of 1630 (see bibliography in ch. 4). Playford (1651) is a call book.

Caroso lists three dances in *Nobiltà di dame* as 'bassa', and five as 'alta'.[24] Neither type seems to be choreographically distinguishable from the other dances, and most are also termed 'balletti'. Speculation is natural that the 'basse' are connected in some way to the fifteenth-century 'bassadanze' and the 'alte' to the 'alta danza', or leaping dance. Further study is indicated,[25] but these dances will be considered here with their dance types as Caroso specifies (i.e., balletto; cascarda).

The ensuing discussion attempts to define the standard dance types within Caroso's balletto suites, associating related discrete dances with them, and using evidence from all the other late-sixteenth-century manuals to help define them. The validity of including Arbeau's *Orchésographie,* a French source, among the manuals considered is certainly open to question. Arbeau does not claim acquaintanceship with Italy, and we have no direct evidence that he knew authentic Italian dances or dancing masters (the only Italian dancing masters in France that we know of were at the French court, and the extent of their influence in the provinces where Arbeau worked is unknown). Nor do we know that Caroso knew authentic French dances despite his claim on the title page to Book II that he includes them. Yet that there *were* significant differences in style, steps, and repertoire from country to country seems certain because of the references to them in the manuals and elsewhere.[26] Even the use of the same term in two languages (e.g., pavane, pavana) does not prove that the dance was done *the same way* in each country; variations in style are entirely possible. These cautions should not hinder us, however, from recognizing underlying likeness or even identity when it is truly there. As stated in the previous chapter, I believe that there was indeed a mainstream of late-sixteenth-century dance types and steps, maintained and stimulated by princely marriages, visits by ambassadors, and the huge retinues that travelled with them, and that Arbeau's evidence may therefore be adduced justifiably, though cautiously.

[24] There are six 'basse' in *Il Ballarino* and three in Negri. There are seven 'alte' in *Il Ballarino*, and Negri gives four.

[25] Caroso's 'Bassa, et Alta' is a special case. Angene Feves, in 'The Changing Shape of the Dance, 1550-1600, As Seen Through the Works of Fabritio Caroso' (a paper read at the National Dance Historians' Conference, Harvard University, 1982), has found a close concordance between the choreographies of 'Bassa, et Alta' by Caroso and a choreography incorporated in an instructional poem on dancing by Pedro de Gracia Dei, in his *La crianca y virtuosa dotrina* (cf. Frederick Crane, *Materials for the Study of the 15th Century Basse Danse* [New York: Institute of Mediaeval Music, 1968], p. 17, with a suggested date of 1486). Feves's finding supports the likelihood of old connections for the individual bassa or alta.

[26] E.g., the comments of the Venetian ambassador, Orazio Busino, in the *Calendar of Venetian State papers,* on the revels in the masque *Pleasure Reconciled to Virtue,* 1618: 'They performed every sort of Ballet and Dance as customary in any country soever, such as passamezzi, corents, canaries and a hundred other fine gestures devised for pinching the fancy' (quoted by Mary Sullivan, *Court Masques of James I* [New York: Knickerbocker Press, 1913]).

Pavan

The untitled dances that open most of the balletto suites in *Nobiltà di dame* begin their figures with walking step patterns using, for example, *long Reverences, continences, stopped steps, ordinary sequences, half-double sequences, broken sequences, stopped broken sequences,* and *semibreve steps.* These steps bear marked resemblances to Arbeau's pavane steps,[27] and also to his allemande steps,[28] in their basic movements, the rhythm of their changes of weight, and the syntax of their step patterns, though the dancers do not simply progress in Arbeau's processional manner, and though Caroso's step vocabulary is much more extensive. It seems safe to say that such dances are pavans (or at least pavanlike) even though Caroso does not use the term 'pavana' at all in *Nobiltà di dame* (the closest he comes to it is 'pavaniglia', discussed below). Indeed for all that the Italian musical collections contain many pavane, padoane, or padovani, and that scholars have traced the first musical appearance of a pavana to Italy,[29] only one of our manuals names a 'pavana'— 'Pavana Matthei' in *Il Ballarino*[30]—and this dance is really a balletto suite with a *very* short duple section of walking step patterns, followed by a long 'sciolta' with alternating galliard variations. The reason for the Italians' verbal neglect of the pavan from their manuals is obscure, but by 1581, the date of *Il Ballarino*, the pavan was at least 75 years old. Its basic elements might very well have been taken for granted by then, and no need felt to characterize them, since everyone would know what they were and they were ubiquitous. Evidence of the old age of the dance may perhaps be seen in a vital and pervasive element of most of the pavanlike dances, the division of the steps and musical beats by rapid footwork more suited to fast (or 'high') dance types, especially the galliard; thus pavan and galliard types are frequently blurred.[31]

Pavaniglia

The pavaniglia, a discrete dance, is clearly a series of vigorous and ornate variations on the pavan.[32] The dance may be termed 'pavaniglia' rather than

---

[27] Arbeau, pp. 57-66. His *branle* steps, *simples,* and *doubles* resemble Caroso's *continences* or *reprises, stopped steps,* and *ordinary sequences* or *doubles* in Italian style.

[28] Arbeau, pp. 125-7. His *pas du gauche-grève droite* (step left, kick right), *pas du droit-grève gauche,* followed by three *pas* and a *grève,* strongly resemble Caroso's two *semibreve steps* and an *ordinary sequence.* I suggest that the pavan and allemande are members of the same family.

[29] The first appearance in print is in Joan Ambrosio Dalza's *Intabulatura de lauto* (Venice, 1508).

[30] The dance is ascribed to Battistino (fols. 112[r]-113[v]). The 'Matthei' in the title refers to the dedicatee, Guilia Bandina Matthei.

[31] E.g., 'Forza d'Amore', a galliard which opens with *stopped steps,* that is, as a pavan.

[32] Besides the pavaniglia in *Nobiltà di dame,* Caroso has one in *Il Ballarino,* fols. 36[r]-39[v]; Negri has two pavaniglie: 'alla Romana', pp. 132-5, and 'all'uso di Milano'. The latter more frequently makes a distinction between the lady's choreography and the gentleman's.

'pavana' for reasons that are either choreographic or musical, or both.[33] The lengthy set of variations in *Nobiltà di dame* is elaborate, and *all* the variations are performed simultaneously by both dancers (though some simpler step substitutions are permitted the lady). In this respect the pavaniglia is distinguished from the passo e mezzo, in which the partners alternate passages and variations. The possibility that Caroso intended the music of the pavaniglia to be converted to triple time may in fact ally it even more closely with the galliard than with the pavan.[34] There are certainly steps and passages in the pavaniglia that resemble the galliard far more than the pavan (the *cadenza in Gagliarda*, or *galliard cadence*, for example), but this resemblance in footwork to the galliard is shared by the passo e mezzo, which is *not* described in triple time. Again, the constant intermingling of 'high' and 'low' steps hints at the age of the dance, while it also reflects the passions of the time for ornament and improvisation.

Passo e mezzo

With regard to the passo e mezzo, much ink has been spilled in the attempt to decipher the meaning of the title in dance terms, but to no avail. Literally, of course, 'passo e mezzo' means 'step-and-a-half'. None of the extant choreographies (in Caroso and Lupi only)[35] clarify what this means, and, again, they are quite late when contrasted with the earliest musical examples.[36] Unlike the pavan, for which we at least have a simple (though late) version in Arbeau,

---

[33] The pavaniglia was also kown as the Spanish Pavan, and was popular throughout the sixteenth century. Arbeau's Spanish Pavan (pp. 181-2) is musically concordant with Caroso's pavaniglie, and his very brief choreography also has pavan steps with divisions used in galliards.

    See also Diana Poulton, 'Notes on the Spanish Pavan', *Lute Society Journal* (1961, no. 3), 5-16. She speculates that the title 'pavaniglia' most often alluded to the choreography, while the title 'Spanish Pavan' usually referred to the music, but there do not seem to be enough extant choreographies to support such a theory.

    See also Lawrence Moe, *Dance Music in Printed Italian Lute Tablatures,* pp. 166-7. Richard Hudson, 'The *Folia* Dance and the *Folia* Formula in 17th-Century Guitar Music', *Musica Disciplina* 25 (1971), 199-221, identifies the chord scheme of Caroso's pavaniglia as typical (Hudson equates this chord scheme also with the monica and spagnoletta, an equation that does not apply to Caroso, whose monica ['Celeste Giglio'] and spagnolette do not follow this formula). See also Gustave Reese, 'An Early Seventeenth-Century Italian Lute MS in San Francisco', *Essays in Musicology in Honor of Dragan Plamenac,* ed. G. Reese and Robert Snow, Pittsburgh: Pittsburgh Univ. Press, 1969, pp. 253-80, for triple-time pavaniglie.

[34] The reference to 'Alta Regina' (a cascarda in 'battuta tripla') in the text of the pavaniglia, however, suggests that it may be even closer to Caroso's cascarda or saltarello tempo.

[35] Caroso has four choreographies altogether (in *Il Ballarino*: 'Passo e mezo' [*sic*], 'Ardente solo', 'Dolce Amoroso Fuoco'; in *Nobiltà di dame*: 'Passo e mezzo'). Lupi, in his second edition, provides a full choreography closely related to Caroso's versions, but adds 45 more variations! Caroso's 'Ballo del Fiore' is set to the passo e mezzo antico, but with a different treble and in a shorter version; the choreography is not related in any obvious way.

[36] Hans Newsidler, *Ein Newgeordnet künstlich Lautenbuch* (Nuremberg, 1536).

there is no simple choreography, nor is there any apparent vestige of what may once have been a step or step pattern generic to the passo e mezzo and different from other dances. What is certain is that all passo e mezzo choreographies are elaborated variants of the pavan.[37] Caroso's version in *Nobiltà di dame* bears this out, beginning with simple *stopped steps* which are followed immediately by complex variations employing much of the standard step vocabulary of the manual.

The difference between the pavaniglie and the passo e mezzi in Caroso may have been one of choreographic structure, for his pavaniglie consist of variations performed simultaneously, while his passo e mezzi normally alternate duet and solo passages in which the gentleman does an elaborate variation while the lady performs a walking passage, and vice versa. This alternating structure is identical to that of the tordiglione and a number of galliards, further indication of the connections among these dance types. Interestingly enough, Florio defines a 'passo mezzo' as 'a cinque pace',[38] a term he does not explain, but which the manuals use as a synonym for the basic galliard step pattern.

Although a number of different musical types of passo e mezzo existed, by far the most common were the *passo e mezzo antico* and the *passo e mezzo moderno*[39] Each was based on a typical Renaissance chordal scheme consisting of eight chords on a standard bass melody, the chords and their bass notes appearing at equal intervals throughout the music. Other harmonies could be inserted between the chords, or elaborate melodic figurations could appear over them. The popularity of such chordal series and basses was immense, and innumerable folk songs as well as serious vocal and instrumental works were based on them. Caroso's passo e mezzi are of the simple *antico* variety, each basic chord given four bars, with few interpolations. Because the same melodic figuration appears above each version in both of Caroso's volumes, we may theorize that, in his mind at least, the passo e mezzo was defined by both melody and bass. In many musical collections the passo e mezzo is paired with a triple-time afterdance based on the same chordal scheme (e.g., a saltarello or a galliard). Our sources do not follow this pattern.

Galliard

The galliard, the most vigourous and showy dance of the late Renaissance, often followed the pavan as its afterdance, but was also an independent dance

---

[37] Arbeau, pp. 66-7, cites the passo e mezzo as a faster variant of the pavan, saying that the 'great number of steps, passages and embellishments' which divide up the '*double*' and sometimes even the second '*simple*' will be known by Capriol when he has 'learned the various movements of the feet' from the galliard.

[38] Florio, *World of Words*, p. 360.

[39] See, e.g., John Ward, 'Passamezzo', *MGG* 10 (1962), cols. 877-880.

type.[40] Only one of Caroso's named galliards is a discrete dance, however ('Gagliarda di Spagna');[41] all the others are 'sciolta' movements of balletto suites. Caroso's typical galliard figure most often involves the alternation of the gentleman and lady, each doing a variation to show off before the other, who observes quietly or performs a walking passage at the same time.[42]

The generic step pattern of the galliard was termed *'five steps'* all over Europe (Ital., *'cinque passi'*; Fr., *'cinq pas'*; Eng., *'sinkapace'*); Arbeau explains that the *'cinq pas'* takes six beats, and Caroso and Negri agree that the *'cinque passi in gagliarda'* take the time of a *'tempo di gagliarda'*, also six beats. Caroso's *five steps in the galliard* is a corruption, he says, for it has not really five steps but two (Rule XXXV): two *steps in the air;* the other gestures are not steps but a *limping hop,* a *foot under,* and a *cadence*[43] (worth noting, perhaps, is that Lutij's basic galliard is identical [1589]). Despite the agreement between these two sources, Caroso's lengthy verbal gymnastics to 'correct' the misnomer he claims was made of old arouse suspicion that he is either not identifying correctly the original features that marked the pattern—there are, after all, five changes of weight in his pattern—or that his is not the original one.

Determining what is *the* generic step pattern of the galliard is somewhat complicated by the complete absence of detailed information before the publications of the 1580s, and the sudden explosion into print of literally hundreds of galliard variations in the manuals from 1581-1607. Nevertheless, many of the latter share the same traits: five changes of weight in one *'tempo di gagliarda'* of six minim beats, involving vigorous kicks and leaps, and ending with a *cadence.* The generic step pattern Negri and Arbeau give is identical: four leapt kicks with alternate feet, and a high *cadence* landing on both feet

(Arbeau's rhythm is ♩♩♩♩ ▬ ♩).[44] Because this simple pattern has

four repetitive movements, besides the five changes in weight, it may be close to an unknown archetype. If so, then Caroso's version is a variant; indeed, it is concordant with Arbeau's second variation[45] and is similar to one of Negri's.[46]

Separate Rules for the *limping hop, step in the air, foot under,* and *cadence* define the components of Caroso's basic galliard pattern, but they are also used

---

[40] The earliest reference to it dates from Lombardy, in 1490. The earliest description appears in Antoine Arena's *Ad suos compagnones* (ca. 1519), and reflects its lively, leaping and turning traits, but gives no details as to step patterns or rhythm.

[41] Like the other galliards, it incorporates the *stopped steps* of a pavan type.

[42] E.g., 'Laura Suave'.

[43] For the exact order of the movements see Rule XXXV.

[44] Arbeau, pp. 100-1; Negri, p. 47. The two descriptions read rather differently, but I believe they are the same, if one is careful to perform Negri's *cadenza* as he describes it on p. 31.

[45] Pp. 101-2.

[46] P. 55, first variation.

elsewhere without necessarily identifying the dance in which they appear as a galliard; the terms '*tempo di gagliarda*' or '*cinque passi in gagliarda*', on the other hand, implying the pattern as a whole and also defining the music, are quite literally the footprints that reveal the dance type in the text. The obvious question of chronology has not yet been answered: was the generic step pattern a single entity from its inception which was then separated into its component parts, or was it an agglomeration of well-known and pre-existent individual movements now combined into a distinct and recognizable unit?

Whatever the answer, Caroso's heart is obviously not in his generic pattern, for most of his galliards are elaborate variations whose resemblance to anyone's *five steps*, even his own, often seems invisible. Often, as stated above, his galliards incorporate *stopped steps*, and other walking step patterns, becoming essentially triple-time pavans.[47] Certainly they may employ a whole repertoire of Caroso's favourite lively steps: *knots, flourishes, minim steps, reprises with foot under, half Reverences, falling jumps, dexterous steps,* and *Corinthian steps,* which are light, off the ground and vigorous. As other dance types use this step vocabulary also, the lines of distinction between the galliard and other light and lively dances are hazy too. Then the most recognizable feature is the music, which is usually notated in three minims to a bar, often with a dotted rhythm,[48] each bar equivalent to one of the previous duple dance.

In terms of complexity, Caroso's galliard variations stand midway between Arbeau, who refers to virtuosic capers but gives no details, and Negri, Lutij, and Lupi, whose descriptions make a major contribution to our understanding of the heights of virtuosity and variation to which a dancer could attain.[49] Whatever the differences between Caroso and his contemporaries, however, he shares their view of the improvisatory nature of the galliard, for it is most often in galliards that he simply calls for the gentleman to do a variation *ad libitum,* sometimes supplying a simple one as a substitute for someone who has less skill.[50]

Tordiglione

The tordiglione is probably related in origin to the French tourdion, which we know chiefly as the afterdance to the basse danse of the fifteenth century.[51]

---

[47] E.g., 'Coppia Colonna'; the galliard 'sciolte' in Caroso's 'Barrieras' give no hint of the dance type, while the galliard movement of Negri's 'Barriera' does call for galliard steps.

[48] The dotted rhythm is usually, but not always, in the second measure of a two-bar unit, e.g., 'Alta Colonna'. The music is a galliard; the steps are typical of both the pavan and the galliard.

[49] Negri's entire section on the galliard spans pp. 31-102 of *Le Gratie d'Amore*. Lupi gives 200 galliard variations in his second edition! Negri's great value is that he counts the number of gestures ('*botte*') in each variation and the number of six-beat *tempi di gagliarda* each takes (e.g., pp. 94-101).

[50] E.g., 'Forza d'Amore'.

[51] Antoine Arena, for example, provides only a few hints as to its vigourous character.

Again, there are no early tordiglione choreographies, and again, as with the pavan, pavaniglia, passo e mezzo, and galliard, Caroso's versions in *Il Ballarino* are the first in Italian to be specific or complete; worth noting is that Caroso's tordiglione in *Il Ballarino* is also the first music under that title in Italian lute collections.[52] Whatever their origins or initial differences may have been, in the late sixteenth century the tourdion and tordiglione are closely related, and both are treated as a type of galliard. In Caroso the relationship is clearly spelled out in his 'Tordiglione' (end of first var.):

> It is necessary that you do what I have said above, since galliard variations must finish with a *cadence.*

Arbeau confirms Caroso's choreographic approach, but suggests a difference in tempo to allow for greater elevation in the galliard:

> ... there is no difference between them save that the tordion is danced close to the ground to a light, lively beat and the galliard is danced higher off the ground to a slower, stronger beat.[53]

Such a tempo difference is possible in Caroso too, as he sometimes calls for a galliard and tordiglione to be danced consecutively (e.g., 'Nido d'Amore'). Negri's entire choreography is couched in galliard terms, calling for '*cinque passi, cadenze*', and counting the number of '*botte*' and '*tempi*' in each variation:

> 'questa mutanza e de botte 29 & di quattro tempi di suono' ('this variation has 29 strokes in four patterns [six-beat bars] of music').[54]

The discrete tordiglione by Caroso and Negri also follow the same choreographic figures as most of their galliards—elaborate variations and walking passages performed alternately by the partners—and the steps seem indistinguishable from many galliard variations.[55] The three tordiglione versions of the two masters are all musically concordant—in Caroso a strain of twenty-four minims in twelve duple bars that may be regrouped into four *or* eight bars of triple,[56] and in Negri twenty-four semiminims in four bars.[57] Thus one might theorize that it is the specific music that distinguishes the tordiglione from the galliard (which may be made from any tune) for these Italian dancing

---

[52]   See Moe, *Dance Music*, list of concordances. Florio, p. 568, says the tordiglione is 'a kind of dance in Spain'.

[53]   Arbeau, pp. 94, 96.

[54]   Negri, p. 195.

[55]   *Nobiltà di dame*, original pp. 319-24; *Il Ballarino*, fols. 167-69; *Le Gratie d'Amore*, pp. 193-6; Lupi, *Libro di gagliarda*, etc., 2nd. ed. (1607), pp. 140-217 (full choreography, plus 139 variations for the man, 30 for the woman, no music). Careful study of all galliard and tordiglione variations may show more distinctions between the two types than are superficially apparent.

[56]   See Commentary.

[57]   Negri, p. 196.

masters. The most visible distinction between the galliard and tordiglione in Caroso, however, is that only the subtitle 'galliard' is used for 'sciolte' in balletto suites.

Saltarello

Among the known Italian choreographic sources of the sixteenth century, Caroso is the only dancing master to use the term 'saltarello', despite its frequency in musical sources; his usage is confined to the fast triple 'sciolte' of his balletto suites, whereas in musical sources the saltarello may also be an independent dance type.

References to the saltarello go back at least to the fourteenth century;[58] unlike the other dance types discussed so far, however, the term is still in use in parts of Italy, where it is known as a folk dance.[59] Documenting its precise history throughout six centuries is impossible at the moment. There is no fourteenth-century choreography. In the Italian manuals of the fifteenth century it appears as both a musical term for strains of music within balli indicating mensuration and tempo, and a choreographic term for a particular step pattern; references indicate it was also an afterdance to the bassa danza, based on the same tenor (akin to Caroso's usage in his balletto suites), but there is no choreography extant from the fifteenth century for such an afterdance.[60]

The sixteenth-century saltarello has been equated by some scholars with the galliard as well as with the French tourdion, but without choreographic evidence.[61] Certainly this equation is not upheld by Caroso, whose '*sciolta in saltarello*' movements *follow* galliard movements in balletto suites. None of Caroso's saltarello movements in *Nobiltà di dame* ever specifies the typical galliard figuration alternating variations and walking passages between the two dancers, and no saltarelli use the *five steps* or the term '*tempo di gagliarda*'. Like Caroso's passo e mezzi, there is no clearly identifiable step pattern—there is unfortunately no '*tempo di saltarello*' even—but there are certain favourite steps suited to the two-bar units of fast triple which characterize these dances (that is, in modern terms, they are in compound duple meter): *breve Reverences, broken sequences, falling jumps, reprises with foot under, Sapphic steps, paired minim steps* (each to a '*battuta tripla*' [triple beat]) and *knots*. Many saltarello figures also emphasize flanking movements toward and away from the partner; again, these are all frequent enough in the other dance types to blur distinctions, but a preponderance especially of *broken sequences,*

---

[58] British Library Add. 29987 (Lo).

[59] Near Rome, for example, it is a peasant couple dance.

[60] See Brainard, *Art of Courtly Dancing,* and *Choreographie der Hoftänze.*

[61] E.g., Meredith Ellis Little, 'Saltarello', *New Grove* 16, p. 431. Thomas Morley's statement to this effect in *A Plaine and Easie Introduction to Practicall Musicke* (1597) may be responsible for the misconception.

reprises with foot under, and *Sapphic steps* especially, in an untitled 'sciolta'in fast triple, signals a saltarello.

Cascarda

Caroso is the only author to use the term 'cascarda',[62] and he has eleven of them in *Nobiltà di dame*, twenty-one in *Il Ballarino*. It always denotes a discrete dance, but does not appear otherwise to differ choreographically or musically from the 'sciolte in saltarello'. In fact, a number of cascarde are musically concordant with such saltarello movements ('Allegrezza d'Amore', for example, is concordant with the saltarello movement of 'Alta Vittoria'). As befits separate dances, the cascarde tend to have more dance variations, that is, to be longer and require more playings of the music. One may speculate that the cascarda was a new type of dance in Caroso's day, perhaps even that he invented it, but its close similarities to his saltarello movements suggests instead that it was simply Caroso's term for an independent saltarello. The chief mystery is why neither the term 'saltarello' nor 'cascarda' appears in Negri, although he has many separate fast triple dances or segments of his balletti.

Spagnoletta

The two spagnolette in *Nobiltà di dame* seem to be distinguished from the cascarde/saltarelli only by their use of a well-known spagnoletta tune, the same tune Caroso uses for his two spagnoletta choreographies in *Il Ballarino*.[63] Two of Caroso's four versions use canary steps in one figure (see below for the possible Spanish provenance of the canary), but since some cascarde also use canary steps,[64] this in itself would be no proof of a uniquely 'Spanish' style for the spagnoletta. The last two phrases of the melody, however, are closely allied to standard canary tunes, and here indeed is where canary steps occur.

Canary

The origins of the canary, another of the fast triple (or compound duple) dances, are also uncertain, though it appears to have been comparatively new in Caroso's time. The canary first appears with choreography in *Il Ballarino*, but if this in fact represents its first introduction to Italy, then its rise in popularity must have been explosive, if one is to judge by the number of canary

---

[62] Lupi has one lute tablature titled 'cascarda'in his second ed., but it is in duple time, and while it is concordant with the last two strains of two dances by Caroso ('Le Bellezza d'Olympia', *Il Ballarino*, fol. 66ʳ and 'Alta Cardana', *Nobiltà di dame*, no. 49), these do not resemble Caroso's dances termed 'cascarda' at all. Lupi's *unicum*, therefore, proves nothing.

[63] See Moe, *Dance Music*, pp. 276-7. Negri's 'Spagnoletto' is not the same as this tune, and is in duple time.

[64] E.g., 'Allegrezza d'Amore', second strain of each playing.

variations in all the manuals.[65] It exists both as a separate dance consisting of a series of variations (*Il Ballarino*; *Le Gratie d'Amore*), or as the last dance of a balletto suite.[66] It appears only as such a balletto movement in *Nobiltà di dame*, its typical music remaining quite distinct from the other dance types: it consists always of a short and simple ground bass and chordal scheme, with distinctive dotted rhythms in triple above it, and its mensuration and notation are similar to the saltarello/cascarda types.

The unique stamping movements of the canary appear in all sources, and are certainly related to Spanish dance as we now know it. One may theorize, then, that the canary was introduced into Italy from Spain (which owned the Canary Islands) in the latter part of the sixteenth century, when large portions of Italy were under Spanish rule. It might, therefore, have been perceived as a rather exotic dance. The Italian sources and Arbeau's version are related, although Arbeau's is in duple time; the footwork belongs to the same tradition, and his music is concordant with a well-known canary.[67] Canary steps are incorporated by Caroso into other dances at will, but are always identified as belonging to the canary (e.g., *seguito battuto del Canario, stamped sequence in the canary*), and are always in triple.

Ballo

Caroso's two titled ballo choreographies are his 'Ballo del Fiore' and 'Ballo detto Il Piantone'; the first is a discrete dance, the second has two movements, like many balletti. Additional references to these two dances in the Rules and the Notes reveal them to be popular dance games that were frequently programmed at balls.[68] It is possible that Caroso employed the term 'ballo' in his titles because in his view they were pre-existent popular dances he was simply recording, rather than revising or composing, and that he kept their popular titles to entice his readers to purchase his book.[69] If this view is true, then 'ballo', like 'balletto', would have a specific as well as a generic usage.

Other

As has already been indicated, most of the untitled 'sciolte' within the balletto suites can be identified easily as to type by comparing them with parallel movements specifically named by Caroso in other dances. The same procedure

---

[65] Negri and Caroso supply many variations; Lupi gives over 40 variations (pp. 253-300), without music.

[66] E.g., 'Celeste Giglio'.

[67] Negri, pp. 201f; Michael Praetorius, *Terpsichore* (Wolfenbüttel, 1612).

[68] Also see *Nobiltà di dame*, 'Contrapasso To Be Done in a Circle'.

[69] In other sources of this period, 'ballo' seems to have meant a complex theatrical work (Negri and Cavalieri follow this usage; so does Monteverdi, e.g., 'Tirsi e Clori, ballo').

works for some of the discrete dances titled 'balletto' with no further identification: 'Alta Colonna' has recognizable galliard music and typically intermingled pavan and galliard step patterns; 'Rosa Felice' closely resembles the pavaniglia; and 'Nuova Regina' appears to be misnamed a balletto, being indistinguishable from all the cascarde both choreographically and musically. Though none of the dances lacking specific titles are strikingly different in step vocabulary or figures from the types we have just discussed, some may have other features which set them off either choreographically or musically: although the two group dances titled 'Contrapasso' have allemande-like steps and grand-right-and-left figures (hays) related to the 'Barriera' and 'Furioso' balletti, their title may signify a separate dance type marked by figures in which the dancers approach or retreat reciprocally;[70] the choreography of 'Conto dell'Orco' suggests allemande- and saltarello-type steps combined, but its title may refer to a song or an extra-musical idea now lost.

Changes in Nobiltà di dame

A detailed comparison in all respects of *Il Ballarino* and *Nobiltà di dame* cannot be undertaken here, but there is a marked difference between the two in one respect that deserves mention. In the second book, many of Caroso's revisions of dances which first appeared in *Il Ballarino* are obviously designed to render them more symmetrical. His long-winded and rhetorical insistence on perfect symmetry[71] leads us to suppose either that he personally came under strong humanistic influence in the twenty years between the appearance of the two books, or that he reflects a general trend in this direction.[72] Whatever the truth may be, further evidence of such influence lies in his addition of steps to the Rules of *Nobiltà di dame* which follow classical verse metres (e.g., *spondaic step, dactylic step*). The increased symmetry makes the dances less interesting, though it simplifies learning.[73] The 'new' steps may simply be a case of pouring old wine into new bottles (the *Sapphic step, dexterous step,* and *Corinthian*

---

[70] Violet Alford, for example, describes a modern 'Contrapás' of Catalonia as '... an open Round, a single file of dancers stepping a few steps one way, a few the other, hardly moving from the place on which they began' ('What Folk Song Says of Folk Dance', *Journal of the English Folk Dance and Song Society* IV, [1945], pp. 237f.).

[71] See, e.g., the last paragraph of 'Contrapasso To Be Done in a Circle'.

[72] Arbeau shares Caroso's symmetrical approach with few exceptions, but does not discuss it; Negri is not always so consistent, nor are Lutij and Lupi. The effect of such changes is clear in Feves, 'Changing Shape of the Dance', where she compares Caroso's two versions of 'Bassa, et Alta' with a version of 1486; the version in *Nobiltà di dame* obscures most traces of the fifteenth-century choreography.

[73] That some of the 'new' symmetry is a correction of omissions in *Il Ballarino* is possible, e.g., the gentlemen's variation in 'Dolce Amoroso Fuoco', fol. 174[r] works well with the music if repeated in its entirety to the other side; an internal correction from one *foot under* to two in the third line makes for a better correlation with the music and creates symmetry.

step all involve *reprises with foot under*), or may reflect a growing popularity of variations on that basic step pattern which Caroso felt deserved more detailed identification.

The comments above on the history of the dance types in *Nobiltà di dame* and *Il Ballarino* imply that Caroso was not consciously attempting to be inventive or original. Indeed, all the available evidence, including the other manuals, points to his working with traditional materials. Whether or not his 'corrections' in *Nobiltà di dame* to the dances from *Il Ballarino* are always such, or more often represent an attempt to superimpose new trends on old materials, by 'improving' them in the light of more advanced styles, cannot be determined at this point.[74] Also unknown is the exact age or original authorship of the dances in either book, or the sources, perhaps circulating in manuscripts at the time, from which he drew. One can only look forward to new discoveries of archival materials to provide more oases than now exist in our present desert of information between 1500 and 1581. While we deplore our ignorance, we may at the same time revel in the treasures we have, and explore them more fully while we await new additions to our store.

[74] The evidence produced by Feves, 'Changing Shape of the Dance', is most provocative, but so far unique. Note also that in *Il Ballarino* Caroso 'corrects' earlier versions of the dances, e.g., 'Contrapasso', fol. 173[r], second paragraph. The 'Nuovo' in some of his titles, as in 'Contrapasso Nuovo', is a sign that the new is a variation on the old.

6

The Music

Introductory remarks

Without question the music in *Nobiltà di dame* is 'music for use' in the most fundamental sense. We have no clues as to its authorship.[1] The pieces obviously vary in quality, and some show real care and compositional skill.[2] Most, however, appear to be essentially skeletal, musical 'cue sheets'. On them the expert dance players in the employ of the great families named in the book would have elaborated through improvised diminutions (or variations), during the many repetitions required by the dances.[3] In keeping with its purpose, the style of the music is in general simple, homophonic, and formulaic. Each piece is normally made up of one to three strains of four-bar (or multiples of four-bar) phrases in the same key. Many of the pieces, in fact, seem merely to be assembled, through a pasticcio technique, out of reusable units chosen for their durations rather than for any aesthetic qualities;[4] or else they use standard ostinato basses, chord schemes, or melodies with basses like the passo e mezzo, romanesca, pavaniglia, or canary—such as populate in large numbers the instrumental 'dance' collections of the time.[5]

Nor can we date the music precisely.[6] The many concordances with earlier collections show that the collection spans the sixteenth century. It thus derives from a variety of sources, and hence of notational and possibly choreographic techniques and styles. Thirty of the pieces were included in *Il Ballarino* (1581) and some of them, such as 'Bassa, et Alta', may hark back to early in the century.[7] However, the music, like the choreography, may have been 'corrected' and 'revised' to some degree, whatever its origins, according to Caroso's needs and the prevailing fashion.

---

[1] References in the text and commentaries to 'Caroso's music' are not intended to imply that he was the composer.

[2] E.g., 'Alta Gonzaga', which exhibits sophisticated use of sequence and motivic imitation.

[3] For an example of written-out diminutions see 'Passo e mezzo'; for a set of variations, see 'Celeste Giglio'. For further information on sixteenth-century techniques of elaboration, see Brown, *Embellishing 16th-Century Music*.

[4] E.g., all the cascarde.

[5] For a study of concordances of Italian dance music see Moe, *Dance Music*.

[6] But 'Laura Suave', is based on Cavalieri's 'Aria di Fiorenza' of 1589 (see ch. 2).

[7] See the Commentary.

Some of the musical characteristics of the major dance types in *Nobiltà di dame* have been given in the previous chapter. The following discussion concerns the way in which the music may correlate with the text, and the various solutions to problems of transcription.

Text and music

A complete examination of all the complexities involved in reconstructing even the simple dances in *Nobiltà di dame* is not possible here.[8] Nevertheless, general observations about the rhythmic interrelationships between text and music have enabled the editors to solve many problems of musical transcription, to detect many errors, and to identify exceptional cases which may seem to be in error, but are intended. Furthermore, when text and music are read together many of the dances in *Nobiltà di dame* may be reconstructed so that they make sense both choreographically and musically. (Here the textual and musical clarifications and corrections of *Il Ballarino* in *Nobiltà di dame* contribute materially to our understanding of the correlations of text and music in the earlier volume, and in Negri's manual as well.) Even so, the numerous ambiguities and exceptions that remain allow legitimate differences in the rhythmic interpretation of many choreographies. It is hoped that the information presented here will assist the interpreter to make independent and logical decisions.

In *Nobiltà di dame* the most important element linking dance text and music is time (in the sense of relative duration), and many hints as to the correlations between them are to be found in both. The music in the original is normally given for one playing only, yet the text almost always requires repetitions of the music. But rubrics in the *music* specifying the number and nature of the repetitions are rare, so any such information in the text is vital. Just as important are textual comments on the relative durations of the components of a dance—the individual dance movements of a balletto suite, the individual dance figures, the phrases within the figures, and the steps and step patterns within the phrases. Most often, however, we must look for such hints in both the music and the text, for music and text are essentially interdependent.

The large structural divisions of the text and music tend to correlate quite simply. Subheadings in the texts of balletto suites generally correspond to subheadings in the music (when given) or new mensural signs. A paragraph in the text normally coincides with one playing of all the music of one movement or dance (including internal repetitions). In fact, the text normally indicates which playing of the music is intended by beginning the paragraphs, '*Nel*

---

[8] For a performing edition of twelve dances see Julia Sutton, *Renaissance Revisited,* notated by K. Wright Dunkley (New York: Dance Notation Bureau, 1972): 'Allegrezza d'Amore', complete; 'Passo e mezzo', five figures; and three variations of the 'Canary', are from *Nobiltà di dame.* The other dances are from Arbeau and Negri.

secondo tempo', *'Nel terzo tempo'*, etc. ('In the second playing', 'in the third playing', etc.).[9] To correlate one paragraph with its music, the major and minor divisions of sentences and clauses normally can be coordinated with the major and minor divisions of strains and phrases. In the *text*, major divisions are marked by specific punctuation: a period, semicolon, or colon followed by *'poi, dapoi'* or *'dopò ciò fatto'*, usually designates the end of one strain or phrase and the beginning of another. The word after the punctuation sign may actually indicate which new strain is intended.[10] The direction to 'repeat to the other side' after a semicolon or colon, however, usually refers to the entire text from the previous major punctuation mark, and may be assumed to require a repetition of the music to that text, whether or not this repetition is marked by a 'repeat sign' or is actually written out.[11] In the *music*, major segments within a movement (strains) are marked off by 'repeat signs', and normally consist of four-bar phrases, or multiples thereof, while musical units subdividing the phrases are commonly two bars long.

As for lesser divisions in the text, steps and step patterns are often paired, fitting the smaller musical divisions. Certain formulaic groups of steps which constitute a recurring refrain in each figure or variation of some dances probably match the cadential formulae in the music.[12] Correlating step values in the text with note values in the music, however, is not nearly such a simple matter as correlating large structural divisions. To correlate a text passage with its strain, the time values must be applied which Caroso specifies for the steps, either in his Rules or in the choreography itself. Then the steps or step patterns to which he has not given specific time values must be sensibly coordinated with the music through good guesswork. Both stages present complex problems, for even the time values given in the Rules do not seem always to apply in the dances themselves (for example, dances in triple call for steps described in duple, and vice versa).[13] Quite frequently, in fact, the sum of the normal time values (whether given or implied) in the text for a single playing of the music does not appear to equal the sum of the time values in the music.

The key to many of the apparent contradictions between text and music lies in the mensural system of the sixteenth century,[14] for an important theoretical

[9] See ch. 2 for a more detailed discussion and examples.

[10] See ch. 2 for the complete list of such words and their translations here.

[11] E.g., the music to 'Spagnoletta Nuova' consists of three repeated strains, but all repetitions are written out.

[12] E.g., the codettas in the 'Pavaniglia', consisting of a *hop*, a *step in the air*, and a *cadence*, probably coincide with bar 8.

[13] E.g., the *ordinary sequence* is described in duple but also used in triple dances; the *broken sequence* is described in triple but also used in duple dances.

[14] For detailed explanations of the late-Renaissance mensural system, see ch. 7 n.l. The terminology used here will refer to that system. Note, however, that the term 'perfection' as understood in the mensural system (and used here) is *not* synonymous with Caroso's term, *'battuta perfetta'*, which appears to mean a duple semibreve (termed 'imperfect' in the mensural system). Cf.

principle of time values is implied, though never articulated by Caroso and the authors of the other dance manuals of the period: *the time values of the steps and step patterns may be interpreted as if they were note values in the mensural system,* and therefore subject to its concepts of imperfection and perfection, proportion, and 'resolution'.[15] That is, a single note or rest may represent either duple (imperfect) or triple (perfect) subdivisions by the next smaller value, as indicated by mensuration signs;[16] it may be related to other notes in different mathematical ratios (proportions) according to the meanings of specific proportional signs. Under certain circumstances, two consecutive equal time values shown as duple may be intended to be 'resolved' unequally, changing from duple to triple within the same time span, while two consecutive unequal time values shown as triple may be intended to be 'resolved' equally, changing from triple to duple. In the late sixteenth century, however, the mensural system was gradually evolving into the modern one, and the notation in *Nobiltà di dame* reflects the confusion of a transitional period: notational devices may be within or outside the proportional mensural system, even in the same piece.[17] There are equal problems in the texts, not only because here too are contradictions and inconsistencies, but especially because the same notational concepts appear to be applied differently in the text and in the music. Again, it is only possible to call attention here to some of the norms of the step terminology in the book, to explain how they relate to the musical notation, and to concentrate on practical ways of applying them when correlating text and music.

In the music of *Nobiltà di dame* triple note values are normally distinguished from duple by a dot of addition, in the modern way.[18] The terminology of many steps and step patterns, however, does not distinguish between duple and triple values;[19] in these cases (e.g., *semibreve steps*) step values may be interpreted as if they were note values in mensural notation—that is, depending upon circumstances, the same steps may be either duple or triple (imperfect or

Adriano Banchieri, *Conclusioni nel suono dell'organo* (1609), for a definition of '*tempo perfetto*' as duple, cited in Michael B. Collins, *The Performance of Coloration, Sesquialtera, and Hemiolia (1450-1750)* (Ph.D. dissertation, Stanford University, 1963; University Microfilms 64-1598, Ann Arbor, Michigan, 1977), pp. 84-85, n. 54.

[15] See op. cit., ch. 5, for a detailed discussion of resolution.

[16] See below for a discussion of mensuration signs and proportions in *Nobiltà di dame*.

[17] E.g., 'Alta Gonzaga', which contains the only example of coloration to indicate *hemiola*, though the triple semibreves that run throughout this piece are dotted in modern fashion. For a detailed study of notational developments at this time, see Helmut Hell, 'Zu Rhythmus und Notierung des "*Vi Ricorda*" in Claudio Monteverdis "*Orfeo*"', *Analecta Musicologica* 15, Studien X (1975), 87-157.

[18] This statement is true in the mensural staff notation in *Nobiltà di dame*; in the tablature longer note values are often only implied, but where shown they are dotted for triple.

[19] For exceptions, see below.

perfect)[20]—and this potential extends as far down the hierarchy of time values as the minim.[21] The concept of imperfection and perfection is applied loosely to step values, but essentially in triple dances larger step values are normally triple but may be duple in the same dance.[22] On the other hand, there are a number of dances whose music is barred in duple but which are apparently intended to be grouped in triple; until a decision is made as to whether this is so in any given case, it may not be possible to correlate steps and music sensibly. In both cases, the step terminology is the same, but it is the way in which this terminology is used, together with clues in the music, which permits us to understand its intent. Particularly important is the total number of step values in a clause, sentence, or paragraph when compared with the music.

The dances just cited that are barred in duple semibreves but are clearly intended to be grouped in triple, can well exemplify the foregoing discussion.

Here three bars of two minims: C♩ ♩ | ♩♩ | ♩ ♩ | seem designed to be performed as two 'bars' (or groups) of three minims: 3 ♩ ♩ ♩ ┊ ♩ ♩ ♩ | .The most important clue to this kind of grouping is when the total number of *semibreve steps* (or their equivalents) for a strain is four or eight, while the music of that strain comprises six or twelve bars.[23] Only by treating the *semibreve steps* as triple in such cases can text and music be correlated. Additional musical clues to such a grouping occur when there are basic changes of harmony every three minims, and when the fingering dots in the tablature, indicating the first finger of the right hand (normally used on weak beats), appear on notes or chords immediately following barlines (that is, are used on what look like strong beats).

Characteristic of most triple dances is the rhythmic oscillation between two groups of triple beats and three groups of duple beats (*hemiola*), each supported by the duration of the harmonic bass. Both the melody and the steps of the choreography may move in shorter time values that may be regrouped convincingly either to coincide with the bass rhythm or to be in syncopation with it. Here again, the clues to *hemiola* are textual and musical, reversing those just described.[24]

---

[20] The terms 'imperfection' and 'perfection' as used here are not necessarily related to the tactus; the principle is employed in *Nobiltà di dame* regardless of whether the triple value is equal to, smaller than, or larger than the tactus.

[21] Traditionally, mensural notation had forbidden triple division of the minim.

[22] By larger step values is meant those that, if triple, would span a whole bar (e.g., 3|o. | in galliards, 3|♩. | in saltarelli), or multiples of whole bars (e.g., *long Reverence* = 3 o. | o. | o. |).

[23] E.g., 'Contrapasso Nuovo'. See ch. 7, for editorial procedures.

[24] For examples which play with the various possible levels of ternary grouping, see 'Bellezza d'Olimpia' and 'Tordiglione', and their commentaries.

In *Nobiltà di dame* there are two instances which do in fact attempt to distinguish triple values from duple values. The first occurs in fast triple dances, where barring is by the dotted minim (saltarelli, cascarde, and canaries). Here the term '*battuta tripla*' ('triple beat') may be employed. As explained in 'Amorosina Grimana', a '*battuta tripla*' equals a dotted minim ('two triple beats, which equal one semibreve beat').[25] Since the term is not always used in fast triple dances, however, the possibility that a '*minim step*' or its equivalent may be worth three semiminims (that is, may be perfected), always exists.[26] Further confusion may arise when other adjectives are used for the same step values such as 'two quick steps'.[27] The second instance consists of the *grave* and *semigrave* step types, equalling six and three 'ordinary' beats respectively, according to the Rules.[28] The definitions of these steps are more precise in *Nobiltà di dame* than in *Il Ballarino*, where 'grave' means only 'slow'. The terms are used in only a small group of dances, however, and not consistently,[29] and if they represent an attempt on Caroso's part to differentiate between larger duple and triple values in slower dances in the same way as he applies '*battuta tripla*' to faster triple dances, he seems to have been even less thorough about it.

The concept in mensural notation that arithmetical ratios, or proportions, can be applied to note values, appears in *Nobiltà di dame* quite clearly with regard to reduction by half (though there are no mensuration signs to indicate it). A significant number of pieces or balletto movements can only be realized with the text if it is assumed that their note values should be read *alla breve* ($\mathdollar$),[30] rather than the more usual *alla semibreve* (C). The necessity is clearest in the duple dances in which, in the original, the sum of time values in the text is exactly half the sum of the time values in the music for a single playing.[31] In such cases the text is meant to be read normally (in *integer valor*), and the music is meant to be halved. Further evidence appears when comparing the mensural signs in the staff notation of *Nobiltà di dame* with concordant pieces with staff notation in *Il Ballarino*: here we find that most of the $\mathdollar$'s in the earlier book

[25] 'Amorosina Grimana'. The term is not used in *Il Ballarino*, so when it appears in fast triple dances in *Nobiltà di dame* that are taken from the earlier book, it is helpful (e.g., 'Spagnoletta Nuova').

[26] E.g., 'Alta Regina', fifth playing, first sentence.

[27] E.g., 'Celeste Giglio', saltarello, first sentence.

[28] E.g., 'Bassa, et Alta'.

[29] E.g., the 'Grave' in the title of the second movement of 'Barriera', a triple afterdance, is not matched by *grave* or *semigrave* steps; two balletti later in the book call for *grave falling jumps,* but by defining them as 'each to one beat' ('Alta Vittoria') and equating them with semibreves, Caroso appears to be using his earlier terminology.

[30] The term *alla breve* is used cautiously here, because it is not clear that a fixed tactus *alla semibreve* was the norm in *Nobiltà*; in such a case a reading at half value would mean reading exactly twice as fast as in *integer valor,* and there is no evidence that this was indeed the case.

[31] E.g., 'Passo e mezzo', opening figure. In more complex variations, it is not so easy to recognize *alla breve* because of the numerous divisions of the beat by the step patterns.

have been changed to C in the later, with no other change in the musical notation.[32] When the texts to musically concordant pieces are also unchanged or only slightly altered from *Il Ballarino*, they provide additional confirmation that a proportion of 2:1 is intended.

The question as to whether or not a dance notated in triple minims (3♩) is to be read at half value in 3♩ is somewhat more difficult to answer because of the various ways of reading the step values in triple pieces, especially when those step values are subdivided. When a dance in 3♩ is one of a type that is usually notated in 3♩, and when the step values in the text are also typical of fast triple dances (including, for example, a *breve Reverence* rather than a *long Reverence,* and many *broken sequences* or *Sapphic steps*), reading the music at half value seems entirely justified.

As has been said, the involvement of other proportions in the internal temporal relationships of movements in balletti is not certain, but the texts confirm the probability that there was a theoretical fixed ratio of dance movements to each other, for some of the subtitles of the texts of the fast after dances (those usually notated in 3♩) refer to proportion of some sort (e.g., 'Celeste Giglio', third movement: 'This Piece is Played in Triple Proportion, as a Saltarello'). Again it must be stated, however, that the degree to which this evidence of proportional thinking reflects actual practise in Caroso's time is unknown.

The concept of 'resolution', or temporal adjustment of complex step patterns from duple to triple (or vice versa) is essential in correlating choreography with music. Since step values in simple duple dances (in C) are always duple, step patterns used in duple dances but defined in triple in the Rules are probably to be adjusted to duple: for example, a *broken sequence* described as 3 ♩ ♩ ┆ ♩. ┆, may be adjusted to duple as C ♩ ♩ ┆ ♩ ┆.[33] Analogously, step patterns used in triple dances but described in duple in the Rules should be adjusted: for example, the *ordinary sequence* is described as C ♩ ♩ ┆ o ┆, and may be adjusted to triple as 3 o ♩ ┆ o. ┆.[34] Here again, however, one must be alert to the possibility of regroupings in triple dances which might necessitate a duple reading of a step pattern.

As has been said, recognition of the norms described here can assist materially in identifying both unintentional errors in text and music, and

[32] E.g., 'Passo e mezzo'.

[33] The exact rhythm in triple is not clearly stated in the Rules, but is implied by the rhythmic patterns in the music. Supporting evidence for the duple rhythm is given in *Il Ballarino,* I, f.7ᵛ.

[34] In this case, the two *minim steps* in the first bar become unequal, and the last step of the group becomes a triple semibreve.

intentional deviations. Most of the latter consist of phrase- or strain-lengths differing from the normal multiples of four bars; indeed, the astoundingly regular '*Vierhebigkeit*' of much of this collection is perhaps the single most noteworthy aspect of dances from a period in which fluidity of rhythmic structure and temporal length was still a major feature of much of the vocal music performed in the homes of the great families of Italy.[35]

It is sometimes easy to see that the exceptions are due to the special demands of the choreography: a dance for three (such as 'Allegrezza d'Amore') may require each dancer in turn to perform a two-bar step pattern, thereby necessitating a six-bar phrase in the music;[36] or of two almost identical pieces, one may have a normal four-bar strain with fitting choreography, and the other may have a five-bar strain with suitable choreography (for example, 'Ghirlanda d'Amore' and 'Nido d'Amore').[37] In other cases the pre-existent music has clearly prescribed a choreography to fit its unusual length (as in 'Laura Suave', whose music is based on Cavalieri's famous ballo).[38] In still other unusual instances, however, as in 'Altezza d'Amore', third strain, it is not so easy to determine whether the choreography or the music is responsible. Where text and music do not yield to reasonable explanations, special notational devices may sometimes be identified[39] which show that the basic strain-lengths have indeed been maintained. That some mysteries and ambiguities even then remain should, it is hoped, spur further study and elucidation.

[35] For sixteenth-century vocal types that closely resembled the four-bar structures of our dances, see Jack Westrup, with Thomas Walker, 'Aria, Part 1.', *The New Grove*, 1, p. 573.

[36] Second strain.

[37] Third strain of both pieces.

[38] See the Commentary for the concordance; the second strain of 'Laura Suave' is twelve bars, which is less common than four-, eight-, or sixteen-bar strains.

[39] E.g., the notations of some first and second endings at internal cadences, discussed in ch. 7.

7

The Musical Edition

The chief purpose of this edition is to facilitate the correlation of choreography and music without obscuring the original.[1] In addition, then, to correcting obvious errors or attempting to make musical sense of difficult spots, the texts of the dances have been consulted closely and the music revised in their light, where necessary, or possible. Since the choreographic texts include extensive information on rhythmic details which may affect the musical edition, the transcriptions can only be completely understood in relation to the texts. All changes from the original have, of course, been noted in the music and the commentary to each dance.

Some general observations can be made about certain aspects and problems of this edition. Because many of the pieces have unique characteristics, however, their problems of transcription must be solved on an individual basis. They are discussed in detail in their contexts in the critical commentaries, which also cite changes in mensuration or barring, give concordances with *Il Ballarino* or other pieces in *Nobiltà di dame*, and list all editorial corrections, additions, and suggestions.

---

[1] For a more literal modern transcription (of the tablature only) of 30 of the pieces, without commentary, see Helmut Mönkemeyer, ed. *Fabritio Caroso 'Il Ballarino'* (Rodenkirchen/Rhein: R. J. Tonger, 1971); for a review of this publication by Julia Sutton and Charles P. Coldwell see *Notes* XXX (1973), pp. 357-59. An earlier transcription by Oscar Chilesotti is in *Biblioteca di rarità musicali*, Vol. I (Milan: G. Ricordi, 1884). Neither edition takes the texts into accounts.

The principles and problems of mensural notation and tablature during the late sixteenth and early seventeenth centuries, a time of rapid change in notational practices, are reviewed in Geoffrey Chew, 'Notation #III,4, Western from 1500. . . .', *The New Grove*, 13, pp. 373-405 and Howard Mayer Brown, 'Performing practice, part 4, 15th and 16th centuries', *The New Grove*, 14, pp. 377-83.

The following recent studies are especially relevant to a study of mensural notation and late sixteenth-century music and dance: Putnam Aldrich, *Rhythm in Seventeenth Century Italian Monody* (New York: W. W. Norton, 1966); J. A. Bank, *Tactus, Tempo and Notation in Mensural Music from the 13th to the 17th Century* (Amsterdam: Annie Bank, 1972); Michael Collins, *The Performance of Coloration, Sesquialtera, and Hemiolia (1450-1750)* (Ph.D. dissertation, Stanford University, 1963); Carl Dahlhaus, 'Zur Theorie des Tactus im 16. Jahrhundert', *Archiv für Musikwissenschaft* XVII (1960), pp. 22-39; Dahlhaus, 'Zur Entstehung des modernen Taktsystems im 17. Jahrhundert', *AM* XVIII (1961), pp. 223-240; and Helmut Hell, 'Zu Rhythmus und Notierung des "Vi Ricorda" in Claudio Monteverdis Orfeo', *Analecta Musicologica* 15, Studien X (1975), pp. 87-157.

Mensural signs

Since the time values in the original text were designed to fit the time values in the music, and since we do not know for certain whether and how proportional notation is operating in *Nobiltà di dame*, the original mensural signs, time values, and barrings are retained wherever feasible, but modified when deemed necessary to fit the music to the choreography. The only mensural signs at the beginnings of the eight pieces in staff notation in the original are C and 3, standing for any duple and triple barring respectively (duple barring is normally by the semibreve; triple by the dotted semibreve or dotted minim). In all 42 tablatures, the beginnings of pieces in duple have no mensural signs; only the sign 3 appears where appropriate. At internal changes in the tablatures of the balletto suites there is one C,[2] but there are four ₵'s; 3 is frequent, however. There may be several 3's in succession, because many balletto suites have several successive triple movements. How many units there are in a bar (3♩ or 3♪) is clear in context; both the proportional significance and the tempo intended may be more ambiguous, however. Mensural signs of C and 3 only have been adopted for this edition, and the Commentary notes when and how they differ from the original. ₵ has been eliminated because its differentiation from C is not apparent.

Note values: reduction by one half

Because Caroso expresses the duration of many steps and step-patterns in note values (*breve Reverence, semibreve step*, etc.), confusion is likely to arise when the original music is not notated in the same unit of beat as that specified in the text. When this occurs, the music is transcribed so that its time values correspond with those of the choreographic instructions; in all such cases this has required reduction of note values by one half. When this has been done for an entire piece or the first movement of a balletto it can be ascertained from the original note values given on the prefatory staff (e.g., 'Passo e mezzo'); an internal movement has original note values above the staff at the beginning; all changes are also noted in the Commentary. In ambiguous cases, however, the original note values have been retained.

Rebarring; Dances Notated in Duple But Grouped in Triple

Some dances or movements notated in duple mensuration seem to be intended to be grouped in triple, i.e.,

C | ♩ ♩ | ♩ ♩ | ♩ ♩ | ♩ ♩ | to be played as [3] | ♩ ♩ ♩ ꞉ ♩ ♩ ♩ |.[3]

---

[2] In one case—'Barriera'—C actually appears in the tablature simultaneously with ₵ in staff notation. See Chew, 'Notation', *New Grove* 13, p. 383, for a discussion of the early-seventeenth-century shift from ₵ to C, with no change in meaning; see also Brown and Dahlhaus articles listed above.

[3] See ch. 6 for discussion.

If, as seems possible, Caroso is assuming a relatively fixed *tactus,* he may have used the duple barring in these cases as an indicator of tempo. Thus, these movements would be played about one-third slower than those he notates *and bars* in 3♩ (sesquialteral proportion). In the transcription, movements rebarred in triple are noted in the Commentary and the sign [3] appears on the music.

Several galliards, barred in duple but apparently in triple grouping, may constitute a separate case, for choreographically they do not differ from other galliards barred in 3♩ in the original: 'Alta Vittoria' (whose galliard movement calls for a typical 'four-pattern galliard variation'); 'Coppia Colonna' (where there is, incidentally, a hint that triple grouping is intended in the 3 that precedes the galliard *barred in duple*); 'Vero Amore' (the first movement is not termed a galliard, but galliard steps are called for (e.g., *'ripresa sottopiede in Gagliarda'*). They have been rebarred in 3♩, but whether a slow triple is meant (3♩ = 1½t) is doubtful; 3♩ = 1t seems more likely.

Notation of standard dance types: norms in this edition

An examination of the original note values and barring reveals certain norms for dance movements within the balletto suites, as well as for the discrete cascarde. Most of the opening balletto movements are in duple (at real or at half value, as explained above): most galliard movements are in triple (3♩); saltarello movements are equally divided between 3♩ and 3♩ (to be read at half value); canary movements are always in 3♩; and six of the cascarde are notated in 3♩, the other five in 3♩ (to be read at half value). In this edition, these norms are applied to any exceptional cases when it is clear that, in all other respects, a given dance or balletto movement fits the standard category (e.g., 'Alta Vittoria').

The presence of such norms in the notation and texts of *Nobiltà di dame* suggests that Caroso is communicating information about relative tempos this way, and that a *tactus* (normally the semibreve) is operating here, though not rigidly.[4] The normal order of movements in a balletto suite, and their relationships to a possible tactus according to this theory would be:

I [Pavan type]	II Galliard	III Saltarello	IV Canary
𝄴 } = t	3♩ = t	6♪ } =	6♪ } = t

It is recommended that t = MM. 60-70, but that the *tactus* should remain flexible, and be adjusted to the needs of the dance.

---

[4] See anon. article, 'Proportions', *The New Grove,* 15, pp. 306-7: 'the *tactus* may be said usually to have occupied a semibreve, outside proportional time.' See also Hell, 'Zu Rhythmus . . . ', for notational innovations of the time.

Whether these notational norms and their suggested tempos apply to other dances in *Nobiltà di dame* is still an open question. The editors, basing their opinion on empirical experience as well as notation and text, believe in general that the norms do apply outside balletto suites and cascarde, and the edition follows them. A comparison between the original notation and barring and those of the present edition, with suggested relationships to a *tactus*, appears in the following table:

Original notation	Edition	Possible relation to *tactus*

Duple mensuration and barring

a. C | ◊ ◊ | ◊ ◊ | C | ♩ ♩ | ♩ ♩ | [◊ = o = t]
(ex.: 'Laura Suave', 1st movement)

b.:C | ◊ ◊ | ◊ ◊ | C | ♩ ♩ ♩ ♩ | [□ = o = t]
(ex.: 'Passo e mezzo')

Duple barring, triple grouping

a. [C] | ◊◊ | ◊ ◊|◊◊| [3] | ♩♩♩ ¦ ♩♩♩ | [◊ = o = t; o. = 1½t]
(ex: 'Contrapasso')

b. [C] | ◊◊ | ◊◊ | ◊◊ | [3] | ♩♩♩ ¦ ♩♩♩ | [◊. = o. = t, perhaps 1½t]
(ex.: 'Alta Vittoria, Gagliarda')

Triple mensuration and barring

a. 3 | ◊◊◊ | ◊◊◊ | 3 | ♩♩♩ | ♩♩♩ | [◊. = o. = t]
(ex.: 'Barriera, Gagliarda')

b. 3 | ♦♦♦ | ♦♦♦ | 3 | ♩♩♩ | ♩♩♩ | [◊.|◊.| = |♩.|♩.| = t]
(ex.: 'Laura Suave, Saltarello')

c. 3 | ◊◊◊ | ◊◊◊ | 3 | ♩♩♩ | ♩♩♩ | [o.|o.| = |♩.|♩.| = t]
(ex.: 'Alta Regina, Cascarda')

Five dances in triple using *grave* and *semigrave* steps form a special group: 'Alta Gonzaga', 'Bassa, et Alta', 'Tordiglione', 'Cesarina', and 'Vero Amore'. The significance of their similarity in terminology has not yet been determined. Their special notational problems and suggested solutions are discussed in the Commentary to each dance.

Concordances

Of the forty-four pieces in *Nobiltà di dame* thirty are taken from *Il Ballarino*, either repeated exactly, or slightly varied, or corrected and revised. Because examination of the concordant pieces in the earlier volume has helped to define some of the problems of the notation in *Nobiltà di dame,* and assisted in their solution, the concordances between the two volumes are noted in the Commentary, and any major differences are cited. The same holds true for other concordances within *Nobiltà di dame* itself. Whether the solutions adopted here apply to the same pieces in *Il Ballarino* is not explored, but certainly the corrections of identical blatant errors apply to both volumes.

'Repeat' signs

Most of the dances are made up of strains usually separated by the signs ·|· , ‖ , or ⫴ , and retained in the edition as ‖ . They do not carry the meaning of the modern repeat sign, but instead are used to delineate strains or sections which may or may not require repetition. In some pieces Caroso provides rubrics in the music indicating the number of required repetitions (e.g., 'Celeste Giglio'). In others, however, the nature and extent of repetition can only be ascertained from the text. All rubrics given in the original are translated in the edition.

First and Second endings

In the few cases where Caroso gives rubrics indicating how strain endings are to be modified so that they can lead back to a repetition of a strain or dance movement (first ending), or onward to the next strain or movement (second ending), they are shown and followed in the transcription (see, e.g., 'Celeste Giglio'). In most cases, however, the necessary modifications are supplied by the editor, following the models provided by Caroso. When such changes have been made, the original note values are shown either in small notes above the staff or in the Commentary, or both. Where editorial first and second endings may seem to be omitted (see, e.g., 'Alta Gonzaga', bar 8), it is because the editors feel that the choreographic instructions indicate no repetition. It should, of course, be understood that 'first' endings apply to all playings of the music except the last, for which the 'second' ending should be used.

When a strain in one mensuration is followed by another strain in a new mensuration beginning with an upbeat, we have supplied a second ending to the first strain and put it in the new mensuration (e.g., 'Bassa Honorata'). This has been done because of the editors' conviction that the occasional instances of this process by Caroso himself (in, for example, the transition of the galliard of 'Celeste Giglio') reflect a normal practice in which the musicians would have helped the dancers to adjust to a change of mensuration. Thus in this edition the movements in most balletto suites are notated to proceed without pause.

When a strain ending in a complete bar is followed by a new strain in a different mensuration beginning with a complete bar, no adjustment for the new mensuration is shown; it can be made, however, by subdividing the final measure of the old strain in the new mensuration.

Dots in the tablature

Double vertical dots appear in the tablature in several pieces ('Alta Regina', 'Laura Suave', and 'Passo e mezzo'), normally between two identical chords on upper courses. Their exact meaning has not been determined, but it is likely that they imply some kind of right-hand plucking or strumming technique. Similar dots are shown in Giulio Cesare Barbetta's *Il primo libro dell' intavolatura de liuto* (Venice, 1559) and Pietro Paulo Melli's *Intavolatura di liuto attiorbato, libro secondo* (Venice, 1614), only when the thumb is or has just been otherwise occupied. Whether in Caroso they mean something different from the single dots that appear beneath *chords* in some pieces (e.g., 'Bassa, et Alta', 'Vero Amore', 'Il Piantone') is also not clear, for here too it is likely that the dots mean the thumb is not to be used. Such single dots beneath chords appear in French tablatures of the period, as in Adrian Le Roy's *1er livre de tabulature de luth* (1551), with the same meaning (normally, of course, single dots beneath single notes in the tablature signify the first finger). The possibility that two different signs could mean the same thing is not remote in a volume whose musical sources may have been quite varied. In the edition all dots are shown as given.

The Transcription

1.   General Principles; Summary.

   (1) Prefatory staves show the first complete bar of the original notation of each piece. (2) Obvious typographical errors have been corrected and noted in the Commentary. (3) Square brackets enclose all editorial additions or suggestions, except as noted below. (4) Dotted bar lines are editorial; where original bar lines have been omitted, short vertical strokes appear in the top space of the treble. (5) Double bars framed by two or three dots in the original have been standardized as ⦂ , regardless of whether or not they signify repetition. (6) The notation of first and second endings has been made consistent with modern practice. The designation of ⌐⎯⌐ always applies to the endings of all playings of that strain or section before the final playing. The designation of ⌐₂⎯⌐ always applies to the final playing of that strain or section. The few first and second endings that are specified in the original (either in the text or in the musical notation) are noted in the commentary. In those second endings in which the editor has converted a duple-mensuration bar into the ternary mensuration of the following section, or vice versa, the original notation is shown in small notes above the second ending. (7) Bar numbers are given every five bars. Numbering is consecutive throughout each dance, first and second endings being seen as, e.g., '8a, 8b' (when the final bar of the first ending is divided into two bars in the second ending, it is seen as e.g., '39; 39a, 39b'). (8) Original mensural signs that are retained by the editor are shown on the staff. Those supplied by the editor are bracketed, and where they result

in different barring from the original (as when the barring is regrouped from duple to triple), the original mensuration sign and time values are shown above the staff and noted in the Commentary. When note values are halved throughout a dance, the incipit, when compared with the transcription, will make it clear. (9) All galliards are notated in 3 ♩. | ♩ ♩ ♩ | ♩ ♩ ♩ | ;[5] all saltarelli, canaries, and cascarde are notated in 3 ♩. | ♩ ♩ ♩ | ♩ ♩ ♩ | .

2. Transcription of the Staff Notation

G and F clefs only are used. Accidentals in the original are modernized; superfluous accidentals within a bar are omitted; editorial accidentals are printed in square brackets.

3. Transcription of the Lute Tablature

(1) The lute tablature has been transcribed onto two staves. Notes resulting from courses doubled at the upper octave have been omitted. In order to bring out any partwriting implied in the original, a modified polyphonic style has been employed; thus the durations of certain notes may occasionally differ from what would be possible on a lute. (2) G tuning is used throughout with the exception of four pieces which require A tuning in order to accord with the pitches of the mensural notation, and four pieces whose concordances in *Il Ballarino* include mensural notation requiring A tuning. When A tuning has been used, it is indicated above the prefatory staff. When a seventh course is called for, its pitch (*F* or *G,* depending upon the tuning) is shown above the prefatory staff. Sometimes Caroso writes a low *A* (for a six-course lute in G tuning) as a substitute for an unavailable low *F*; on a seven-course lute the *F* (the lowest course) probably would have been played instead; hence an *F* appears in brackets at such points. (3) Key signatures and rests are editorial except where indicated in the Commentary. (4) All right-handed fingering dots and the double vertical dots that appear in some pieces (see 'The Musical Edition') are retained.

Where interpretative differences occurred, final editorial decisions are those of the general editor and are not necessarily those of the music transcriber.

---

[5] For one exception, see the Commentary to 'Laura Suave'.

8

Bibliography

Only works cited in the text are listed. Additional references may be found in the bibliographies to most of the general reference works or other secondary sources.

Primary Printed Sources of Late-Sixteenth- and Early-Seventeenth-Century Dance, with Modern Reprints, Editions, and Translations

Alessandri, Felippo de gli [sic]. *Discorso sopra il ballo.* Terni: Tomasso Guerieri, 1620.

*Arbeau, Thoinot (pseud. for Jehan Tabourot). *Orchésographie.* Langres: Jehan des Preyz, [1588], 1589; reprinted with expanded title, 1596/Facsimile reprint of 1596, Geneva: Minkoff, 1972.

_____. Copy, with an introduction by Laure Fonta. Paris: Vieweg, 1888.

_____. Translated into English by C. W. Beaumont. London: 1925. Reprinted New York: Dance Horizons, 1968.

_____. Translated into English by Mary Stewart Evans. New York: Kamin Dance Publishers, 1948. Reprinted with corrections, a new introduction and notes by Julia Sutton, and representative steps and dances in Labanotation by Mireille Backer. New York: Dover Publications, 1967. This publication includes a list of translations into other languages, p. 8.

*Caroso, Fabritio. *Il Ballarino.* Venice: Ziletti, 1581/Facsimile reprint, New York: Broude Brothers, 1967.

*_____. *Nobiltà di dame.* Venice: il Muschio, 1600, 1605/Facsimile reprint, Bologna: Forni, 1970.

*_____. *Raccolta di varij balli.* Reissue, with a new title page, of *Nobiltà di dame.* Rome: Facciotti, 1630.

de Lauze, F. *Apologie de la Danse.* [London]: 1623/Facsimile reprint, Geneva: Minkoff, 1977. Translated, with original text, additional commentary and music, by Joan Wildeblood. London: Frederick Muller, 1951.

Lupi, Livio. *Mutanze di gagliarda, tordiglione, passo e mezzo, canari e passeggi.* Palermo: Carrara, 1600.

_____. *Libro di gagliarda, tordiglione....* Second edition of the above, revised and enlarged. Palermo: Maringo, 1607.

Lutij [Lutius?], Prospero. *Opera bellissima nella quale si contengono molte partite, et passeggi di gagliarda.* Perugia: Orlando, 1587, 1589.

*Negri, Cesare. *Le Gratie d'Amore.* Milan: Ponti & Piccaglia, 1602. Reissued as *Nuove Inventione di balli.* Milan: Bordone, 1604/Facsimile reprint of 1602, New York: Broude Brothers, 1969; also Bologna: Forni, 1969.

_____. MS translation into Spanish by Don Balthasar Carlos for Señor Conde, Duke of St. Lucar, 1630. Now in Madrid: Bibl. Nacional, MS 14085.

* Contain music for the dances.

Other Primary Sources

Facsimile reprints only are cited. Other editions may be found by consulting secondary sources.

Arena, Antoine. *Ad suos compagnones...* [Avignon: n.p., ca. 1519].

Barbetta, Giulio Cesare. *Il primo libro dell' intavolatura de liuto.* Venice: Girolamo Scotto, 1569.

Beaujoyeulx, Baltassar de (Belgioioso, Baldassare de). *Le Balet-Comique de la Royne, 1581/* Facsimile reprint Turin: Bottega d'Erasmo, 1965.

Besard, Jean-Baptiste. *De Modo in testudine libellus* in *Thesaurus harmonicus.* Cologne: Grevenbruch, 1603/Facsimile reprint Geneva: Minkoff, 1975. (Trans. by John Dowland in Robert Dowland, *Varietie of Lute Lessons.* London: 1610.)

Cavalieri, Emilio de'. *La Rappresentazione di anima e di corpo.* Rome: [ca.] 1602/Facsimile reprint Bologna: Forni, [1967].

Coplande, Robert. *The maner of dauncynge of bace daunces after the vse of fravnce & other places.* Printed at the end of Alexander Barcley, *The introductory to wryte and to pronounce Frenche.* London: 1521/Facsimile reprint in John M. Ward, 'The maner of dauncyng', *Early Music* 4 (1976), pp. 128-9.

Dalza, Joan Ambrosio. *Intabulatura de lauto, libro quarto.* Venice: Petrucci, 1508/Facsimile reprint Geneva: Minkoff, 1979.

Davies, Sir John. *Orchestra, a Poem of Dancing.* London: 1594.

Della Casa, Giovanni. *Il Galateo.* Milan: 1559.

de Maisse, André Hurault. *A Journal of All that Was Accomplished by Monsieur de Maisse, Ambassador in England from King Henry IV to Queen Elizabeth* [1597], trans. G. B. Harrison and P. A. Jones. London: The Nonesuch Press, 1931.

Dowland, Robert. *Varietie of Lute Lessons.* London: Thomas Adams, 1610/Facsimile reprint, with introduction by Edgar Hunt, London: Schott, 1958.

Fabri, Salvator. *Neuw Künnstlich Fechtbuch.* Nuremberg, 1570.

Feuillet, Raoul-Auger. *Chorégraphie.* Paris: [Feuillet], 1700. Facsimile reprint New York: Broude Brothers., 1968.

Florio, John, *Queen Anna's New World of Words,* 2nd. ed. London: Melch, Bradwood, 1611/ Facsimile reprint Menston, England: Scolar Press, 1968, 1973.

Ganassi, Sylvestro dal Fontego. *Opera Intitulata Fontegara.* Venice: Ganassi, 1535/Facsimile reprint Milan: [n.p.], 1934. (German trans. by Hildemarie Peter, 1956; English trans. by Dorothy Swainson, Berlin-Lichterfelde: R. Lienau, ca. 1959.)

Grassi, Giacomo di. *Ragione di adoprar sicuramente l'arme.* Venice, 1570.

LeRoy, Adrian. *Ier livre de tabulature de luth.* Paris: Le Roy, 1551/Facsimile reprint, ed. André Souris and Richard de Moncourt, Paris: Centre National de la Recherche Scientifique, 1960.

MSS of the Inns of Court: Bodleian Library, Rawl. Poet. 108, ff. 10^V-11^r; British Library, Harley 367, pp. 178-9; Bodleian, Douce 280, ff. 66^{av}-66^{bv} (202^V-203^V); Bodleian, Rawl. D. 864, f. 199^V, ff. 203^r, 204^r; Royal College of Music, MS 1119, title page and ff. 1-2, 23^V-24^r; Inner Temple, Miscellanea Vol. XXVII.

Malvezzi, Cristofano. *Intermedii Et Concerti, fatti per la Commedia rappresentata in Firenze Nelle nozze del Serenissimo Don Ferdinando Medici et Madama Christiana di Loreno, Granduchi di Toscana.* Venice: Vincenti, 1591, II. Transcribed and edited by D. P. Walker, *Les Fêtes de Florence: Musique des intermèdes de 'La Pellegrina'.* Paris: Centre National de la Recherche Scientifique, 1963.

Melli, Pietro Paulo. *Intavolatura di liuto attiorbato, libro secondo.* Venice: Giac. Vincenti, 1614.

Mersenne, Marin. *Harmonie universelle.* Paris: Cramoisy, 1636-7/Facsimile reprint Paris: Centre National de la Recherche Scientifique, 1963.

Moderne, Jacques. *S'ensuyvent plusieurs basses dances tant commune que incommunes.* Lyons: ca. 1529.

Monteverdi, Claudio. *L'Orfeo* (Mantua, 1607). Venice: Ricciardo Amadino, 1615/Facsimile reprint, with introduction by Denis Stevens, Farnborough, Eng.: Gregg International, 1972.

Morley, Thomas. *A Plaine and Easie Introduction to Practicall Musicke.* London: Peter Short, 1597/Facsimile reprint with introduction by Edmund H. Fellowes, Oxford: Shakespeare Association Facsimiles 14, 1937.

Navarro, Juan de Esquivel. *Discursos sobra el arte del Dançado.* Seville, 1642/Facsimile reprint Madrid: Publicaciones de la Asociación de Libraros y Amigos del Libro, 1947.

Newsidler, Hans. *Ein Newgeordnet künstlich Lautenbuch.* Nuremberg, Johan Petreius, 1536/ Facsimile reprint Neuss: Junghänel-Päffgen-Schäffer, 1974 (vol. I), 1976 (vol. II).

Playford, John. *The English Dancing Master,* first ed. London: Thomas Harper, 1651/Facsimile reprint, with an introduction, concordances, and lists of references by Margaret Dean-Smith, London: Schott, 1957.

Praetorius, Michael. *Terpsichore.* Wolfenbüttel: [Fürstlicher Drückerei], 1612/Facsimile reprint of text only in *Werke,* ed. Friedrich Blume, Arnold Mendelssohn, and Wilibald Gurlitt, Wolfenbüttel: G. Kallmeyer, 1928-60.

Rameau, P. *Le Maître à danser.* Paris: Jean Villette, 1725/Facsimile reprint New York, Broude Bros., 1967.

Rossi, Bastiano de'. *Descrizione del magnificentissimo Apparato E de' Maravigliosi Intermedi fatti per la commedia rappresentata nella felicissime Nozze degli Illustrissimi Don Ferdinando Medici, e Madama Christina di Lorena, Gran Duchi di Toscana.* [Florence: 1589].

Thibault, Girard. *Académie de l'Espée.* Antwerp, 1628.

General Reference Works

Apel, Willi, ed. *Harvard Dictionary of Music.* 2nd ed. Cambridge, Mass.: The Belknap Press of Harvard University Press, 1969.

Blume, Friedrich, ed. *Die Musik in Geschichte und Gegenwart.* 16 vols. Kassel and Basle: Bärenreiter, 1949-79.

d'Amico, Silvio, and Savio, Francesco, eds. *Enciclopedia dello Spettacolo.* 9 vols. Florence and Rome: Sansoni, 1954-68.

Eitner, Robert, ed. *Biographisch-bibliographisches Quellen-Lexikon.* 11 vols. Leipzig: Breitkopf & Härtel, 1900-4/Facsimile reprint Graz: Akademische Druck- und Verlagsanstalt, 1959.

Fétis, François-Joseph. *Biographie universelle des musiciens.* 8 vols. Brussels: Meline, Cans, 1837-44.

Riemann, Hugo, ed. *Musik-Lexikon,* 12th ed., ed. Wilibald Gurlitt. 5 vols. Mainz: B. Schott's Söhne, 1959.

Sadie, Stanley, ed. *The New Grove Dictionary of Music and Musicians.* 20 vols. London: Macmillan, 1980.

Other References

Aldrich, Putnam. *Rhythm in Seventeenth Century Italian Monody.* New York: W. W. Norton, 1966.

Alford, Violet. 'What Folk Song Says of Folk Dance', *Journal of the English Folk Dance and Song Society* IV (1945), 237f.

Anon. 'Proportions', *The New Grove Dictionary of Music and Musicians,* ed. Stanley Sadie. London: Macmillan, 1980, 15, 306-7.

Bank, J. A. *Tactus, Tempo and Notation in Mensural Music from the 13th to the 17th Century.* Amsterdam: Annie Bank, 1972.

Brainard, Ingrid. *The Art of Courtly Dancing in the Early Renaissance.* West Newton, Mass.: I. G. Brainard, 1981.

———. 'Bassedanse, Bassadanza and Ballo in the 15th Century', *Committee on Research in Dance (CORD)* II (1969), 64-79.

———. *Die Choreographie der Hoftänze in Burgund, Frankreich und Italien im 15. Jahrhundert.* Unpublished Ph.D. dissertation, Göttingen University, Germany, 1956.

———. 'The Role of the Dancing Master in 15th Century Courtly Society', *Fifteenth Century Studies* II, ed. G. Mermier and E. Du Bruck. Ann Arbor: University Microfilms International, 1979.

Brown, Howard Mayer. *Embellishing 16th-century Music.* London: Oxford University Press, 1976.

———. 'Performing practice, part 4, 15th and 16th centuries', *The New Grove,* 14, 380-1.

Chew, Geoffrey. 'Notation, part III, 4, Western from 1500 . . .', *The New Grove,* 13, 373-405.

Chilesotti, Oscar, ed. *Biblioteca di rarità musicali.* Vol. I: *Danze del Secolo XVI trascritte in notazione moderne dalle opere: 'Nobiltà di dame' del Sig. F. Caroso da Sermoneta; 'Le Gratie d'Amore' di C. Negri, milanese, detto il Trombone.* Milan: G. Ricordi, 1884.

Collins, Michael B. *The Performance of Coloration, Sesquialtera, and Hemiola (1450-1750).* Ph.D. dissertation, Stanford University, 1963; University Microfilms 64-1598, Ann Arbor, Michigan, 1977.

Corti, Gino, 'Cinque Balli Toscani del cinquecento', *Rivista italiana di Musicologia* XII (1977), 73-6.

Crane, Frederick. *Materials for the Study of the 15th Century Basse Danse.* New York: Institute of Medieval Music, 1968.

Cunningham, James B. *Dancing in the Inns of Court.* London: Jordan and Sons, 1965.

Dalhaus, Carl. 'Zur Entstehung des modernen Taktsystems im 17. Jahrhundert', *Archiv für Musikwissenschaft (AfM)* XVIII (1961), 223-40.

———. 'Zur Theorie des Tactus im 16. Jahrhundert', *AfM* XVII (1960), 22-39.

Danner, Joseph. 'Giovanni Paolo Foscarini and his "Nuove Inventione"', *Journal of the Lute Society of America (JLSA)* VII (1974), 4-18.

Dolmetsch, Mabel. *Dances of Spain and Italy, 1400-1600.* London: Routledge & Kegan Paul, 1954/Reprint New York: Da Capo Press, 1975.

Fenlon, Iain. 'Music and Spectacle at the Gonzaga Court, c. 1580-1600', *Proceedings of the Royal Musical Association* (1976), 90-105.

Feves, Angene. 'The Changing Shape of the Dance, 1550-1600, As Seen Through The Works of Fabritio Caroso', a paper read at the National Dance Historians' Conference, Harvard University, 1982.

Fischer, Kurt von. 'Variations, part 4: Up to 1600', *The New Grove,* 19, 538-40.

Heartz, Daniel. 'A 15th-century Ballo, *Rôti Bouilli Joyeux', Aspects of Medieval and Renaissance Music: A Birthday Offering to Gustave Reese,* ed. Jan La Rue. New York: W. W. Norton, 1966, 359-75.

———. 'The Basse Dance. Its Evolution circa 1450 to 1550', *Annales Musicologiques* VI, 287-340.

Hell, Helmut. 'Zu Rhythmus und Notierung des "*Vi Ricorda*" in Claudio Monteverdis "*Orfeo*"', *Analecta Musicologica* 15, Studien X (1975), 87-157.

Hudson, Richard. 'The *Folia* Dance and the *Folia* Formula in 17th-Century Guitar Music', *Musica Disciplina* 25 (1971), 199-221.

Kirkendale, Warren. *L'aria di Fiorenza, id est Il ballo del Gran Duca.* Florence: Olschki, 1972.

Little, Meredith Ellis. 'Saltarello', *The New Grove,* 16, 430-2.

Moe, Lawrence. *Dance Music in Printed Italian Lute Tablatures in the 16th Century.* Unpublished Ph.D. dissertation, Harvard University, 1956.

Mönkemeyer, Helmut, ed. *Fabritio Caroso 'Il Ballarino'.* Rodenkirchen/Rhein: R. J. Tonger, 1971. Music only.

Poulton, Diana. 'Notes on the Spanish Pavan', *Lute Society Journal* III (1961), 5-16.

Prunières, Henri, ed. *Oeuvres complètes de J.B. Lully*. Paris: Editions de la Revue musicale, 1930-39/Reprint New York: Broude Bros., 1966.

Reese, Gustave. 'An Early Seventeenth Century Italian Lute MS at San Francisco', *Essays in Musicology in Honor of Dragan Plamenac*, ed. G. Reese and Robert Snow. Pittsburgh: Pittsburgh University Press, 1969, pp. 253-80.

Stevenson, Robert. 'The First Dated Mention of the Sarabande', *Journal of the American Musicological Society* V (Spring, 1952), 29-31.

Sullivan, Mary. *Court Masques of James I*. New York: Knickerbocker Press, 1913.

Sutton, Julia. 'Arbeau, Thoinot', *The New Grove*, 1, 544-5.

_____. 'The Minuet: Durable Phoenix?', paper read at the joint meeting of the New England and New York chapters of the American Musicological Society (1978), to be published in *Dance Chronicle*.

_____. *Renaissance Revisited*. Twelve dances in Labanotation with music and commentary, notated by K. Wright Dunkley. New York: Dance Notation Bureau, 1972.

_____, and Coldwell, Charles P. Review of Helmut Mönkemeyer's *Fabritio Caroso 'Il Ballarino'* (Rodenkirchen/Rhein: R. J. Tonger, 1971), *Notes* XXX (1973), 357-9.

Ward, John. 'Passamezzo', *Die Musik in Geschichte und Gegenwart*, Friedrich Blume, ed. Kassel and Basle: Bärenreiter, 1949-79, 10, cols. 877-80.

_____. *Tudor and Stuart Dance and Dance Music* (in preparation for publication by Oxford Univ. Press).

_____. 'The Vihuela da mano and Its Music (1536-1576)'. Unpublished Ph.D. dissertation, New York University, 1953.

Weidlich, Joseph. 'Battuto Performance Practice in Early Italian Guitar Music (1606-1637)', *JLSA* XI (1978), 63-85.

Westrup, Jack and Walker, Thomas. 'Aria, part 1'. *The New Grove*, 1, 573-4.

Wolf, Johannes. *Handbuch der Notationskunde*, II. Leipzig: Breitkopf & Härtel, 1919.

Wood, Melusine. *Some Historical Dances*. London: The Imperial Society of Teachers of Dancing, 1952.

_____. *More Historical Dances*. London: The Imperial Society of Teachers of Dancing, 1956.

Nobiltà di Dame
DEL S.ʳ FABRITIO CAROSO
DA SERMONETA,
Libro, altra volta, chiamato
IL BALLARINO.
Nuouamente dal proprio Auttore corretto,
ampliato di nuoui Balli, di belle Regole,
& alla perfetta Theorica ridotto:
Con le Creanze necessarie à Caualieri, e Dame.
Aggiontoui il Basso, & il Soprano della Musica:
& con l' Intauolatura del Liuto à ciascun Ballo.
Ornato di vaghe & bellissime Figure in Rame.
ALLI SER.ᴹᴵ SIG.ᴿᴵ
DVCA, ET DVCHESSA
di Parma, e di Piacenza, &c.
Con licenza de' Superiori, & Priuilegi.

In VENETIA, Presso il Muschio, M DC.
Ad instantia dell' Auttore.

Nobiltà di Dame (The Nobility of Ladies)

BY SIGNOR FABRITIO CAROSO
OF SERMONETA

Second Edition of the Book Called
IL BALLARINO (The Dancing Master)

*Newly corrected by its author,
with additional new dances, and fine rules,
now brought to theoretical perfection.*

With the [Rules] of Deportment Essential to Gentlemen and Ladies

*The bass and treble are given in score, as well as the lute
tablature to each dance.*

Decorated with the Loveliest and Most Beautiful Copper Engravings

[DEDICATED TO] THE MOST SERENE AND LORDLY

DUKE AND DUCHESS

of Parma and Piacenza, etc.

With license and privileges granted by the authorities

Venice, il Muschio Press, 1600
Published by the author

Caption to picture of a bear:	*Caption to picture of an hourglass and compass:*
From Imperfection to Perfection	Time/measure

Caption to portrait: Fabritio Caroso of Sermoneta at the age of LXXIIII

(*Left*) The Most Serene Don Ranuccio Farnese, Duke of Parma and Piacenza, etc. (*Right*) The Most Serene Donna Margharita Farnese Aldobrandina, Duchess of Parma and Piacenza, etc.

To the Most Serene and Lordly
Don Ranuccio Farnese,
and
D[onna] Margarita Aldobrandina
Duke, and Duchess of Parma, and of Piacenza,
etc.

In publishing this book (written with whatever God-given talents I may possess, and in which I have set down all I know concerning my profession), I might have been in grave doubt as to its dedication, and from whom to seek protection and support, had I not been an old and most devoted servant of the Most Serene House of Farnese (first and foremost in all Rome), and had I not also been most graciously showered with favours and special honours from the most illustrious House of Aldobrandini (in the various periods of its grandeur, and especially during this most glorious pontificate of Pope Clement VIII). Thus I could have expected that either House would grant me any favour I might desire for my labours. The Good Lord, however, among the many acts He has performed in seeking to comfort the world, has given us the happy marriage of Your Serene Highnesses, and has thus relieved me of any trace of conflict regarding my fervent loyalty to both [Houses], for He has joined together what was [heretofore] divided, and has sheltered me securely under two masters, and provided strong protection under two such magnificent personages, who are indeed the first and foremost now living in this country.

Thus this work of mine comes into the world, presented and consecrated to Your Most Serene Highnesses, and properly so, because in my opinion its title, which is *The Nobility of Ladies*, provides a unique example in this day and age of those qualities which are appropriate to them; and also because the names of Your Most Serene Highnesses appear most felicitously on the first page. I pray that Almighty God will keep your most great and most fortunate Highnesses ever thus for many long years, and at the same time keep me, your most Humble Servant, in the good graces of Your Highnesses, whose hands I kiss with all due respect.

Venice, 25 November, 1600.

Your Most Serene Highnesses'
Most Humble and Devoted Servant
Fabritio Caroso of Sermoneta

[1]
Celeste Giglio [*Heavenly Lily*]
Balletto

*Dedicated to Their Most Serene Highnesses, Don Ranuccio Farnese and
D[onna] Margarita Aldobrandina,
Duke and Duchess of Parma, Piacenza, etc.*

The gentleman and lady stand opposite each other without holding hands (as in the figure),[1] and gracefully make a *long Reverence* together in four beats of music (as you may see in the score) with two *breve continences* in two beats each (the first beginning with the left foot, the second with the right). Then, taking right hands, do one *pulled step* with your left foot, a *limping hop* with the same foot, raising your right foot, a quick *step in the air* with the left, and a *cadence*. After that do a *knot* with your left, two *steps in the air* (one right, the other left), and two *flourishes;* dropping hands, change places, and take two *minim steps* turning to the left, with two more *flourishes,* two *steps,* and one *Sapphic step* (that is, one *reprise* and one *falling jump*), both turning your left hips in. This done, take left hands, and repeat the same actions and movements to the other side, beginning with the right foot. Then facing towards each other, take both hands, doing two *continences,* as above. The gentleman then drops the lady's right hand and takes her by the customary hand, and making a *Reverence* as before, politely conclude this first playing [of the dance].

In the second playing, progress together, doing a *pulled step* with the left foot, a *limping hop* with the same, and two *steps in the air* (one with the right, and the other with the left); then do two *flourishes,* two *steps,* and one *Sapphic step,* beginning with the left; repeat to the other side. Next take two *steps* forward, one *knot,* two *flourishes,* two more *steps* forward, two *broken sequences,* two more *flourishes,* and a *Sapphic step* to the left, making sure to begin all these movements with your left foot. Repeat to the other side, beginning with your right foot. Also take two *minim steps,* and do one *broken sequence;* repeat to the other side, and then drop hands. Finally, do two *scurrying sequences* in the form of an S, facing towards each other at the end (one having gone to one end of the room, the other to the other end), and bending your knees a little in the manner of a *half Reverence.*

---

[1] No figure is given by Caroso.

The Piece is Played as a Galliard

In the first four galliard patterns, do two *steps* toward the left, a *falling jump* (beginning with your left foot), a *foot under* with your right, and one *flourish* with your left; then do one *falling jump* with your right, a *foot under* with your left, and a *cadence* to the left side. Next do a *little bound* to the aforesaid left, and one *foot under* with your right and immediately dropping your [left] foot, do two quick *steps in the air* (first with the right, then with the left), and then two *flourishes* with the same foot; then with your left foot, which is now raised, do a *half Reverence,* and with the same [foot] do a *foot under* and a *cadence.* Repeat the same variation to the other side, beginning with your right.

Continuation of the Piece, in Which You Do a Variation of Eight Galliard Patterns

In the first four patterns do two *ordinary sequences* (one with your left, the other with your right), taking right hands, and at the end of the *sequence*[s] bend your knees a little, dropping hands while kissing the aforementioned hand. Then do two more *scurrying sequences,* turning left and then right in the shape of an S (as has been said above), one going to one end of the room (or other dancing place) and the other to the other end, facing towards each other at the end of this section with your left foot behind, and bending your knees a little at that moment.

In the Next Four Patterns of the Piece Do the Following Four-Pattern [Galliard] Variation

First, do a *falling jump* with your left foot, a *foot under* with your right, and a *flourish* with the left; repeat to the other side, beginning with your right. Then do a *knot,* two *flourishes* forward, two *quick steps* back, two *half Reverences* in the manner of three beats of the *little bell,* a *foot under,* and a *cadence.* All of these abovementioned movements should be done with your left foot, and the *cadence* as well, and you should finish with that foot forward, or else the variation will be wrong (even if it is in time to the music). After this take left hands, and repeat the same variation, each [then] returning to place with the *scurrying sequences,* now beginning with your right foot. Then, having finished these variations, take two *stopped steps* forward (one with your left foot, and the other with your right). This done, take customary hands, and in the usual courteous manner, make a *long Reverence.*

The Piece is Played in Triple Proportion, As a Saltarello

Progressing together, both do two *quick steps,* one *knot,* two *flourishes,* and a *broken sequence* forward, beginning everything with your left foot; repeat to the other side. After this drop hands and do two *broken sequences* turning to the left, with two *flourishes* forward, and one *Sapphic step* (that is, one *reprise* and a *falling jump*) with your left hip in. Repeat to the other side. Then do two *flourishes*, two *falling jumps*, two *quick steps*, and a *broken sequence* to the left, beginning each of these movements with your left foot; repeat to the other side. This done, do one *falling jump*, a *foot under*, and one *flourish* to the left; repeat to the other side. Finally, do two *broken sequences* flankingly forward, with two *stopped steps;* and in conclusion make a *breve Reverence.*

When the Canary Music [*is Played*]

Do eight canary patterns to this canary music, always two for each foot (that is, two with your left foot, and two with your right) and repeat this once for each foot. Then the lady claps the hands of the gentleman once with both her hands; the gentleman repeats this to the lady. Then do one quick *stopped step* with your left and a *half Reverence* with your right, touching right hands at that moment; repeat to the other side. Then turn left with two *broken sequences,* take two *quick steps* forward, and do a *Sapphic step* with your left hip in, beginning with your left; repeat to the other side. Finally, do two *semibreve stopped steps* (that is quick), politely taking each other by the customary hand in the usual courteous manner; and making a *breve Reverence,* finish this lovely, graceful, and exceedingly beautiful dance in time to the music.

[1] *Celeste Giglio*

This minim changes to a
semiminim the second time

The first
ending

The second ending
which begins the
reprise

Canary

Caption to portrait: Fabritio Caroso of Sermoneta at the age of LXXIIII

To the Reader

In the conduct of our lives, honest pleasure and recreation of the spirit are as essential as affliction and travail are harmful. Now to resolve such contradictions, sweet sounds, games, and other pleasant and merry activities have been given to us. Among these we place the custom of dancing, which is no less delectable, elegant, or worthy of esteem than the others; for in human converse and society it rouses the spirit to joy, and when we find ourselves oppressed by our troubles it relieves and refreshes us, keeping away annoying or unpleasant thoughts. Nor is such virtue of little import, for it is joined with poetry and music, whose qualities are the most worthy of all; and it is one of those [arts of] imitation which represent the affects of the spirit through the movements of the body. Moreover, it is so essential to one of good breeding, that when it is lacking it is considered a fault worthy of reproof. As a result of dance many other praiseworthy and honourable qualities may be acquired, for through physical exercise one keeps fit and becomes agile and dexterous; one also learns proper deportment both in giving or receiving courtesies and honours, as well as that comportment required by etiquette and ceremony. In sum, dance conjoins grace, beauty, and decorum in the eyes of the beholder. Now if the excellence and dignity of matters is judged by the esteem in which they are (or have been) held, there is no question that this is no newly important art, but that it was also respected and practised by the ancients, who not only employed it in their comedies, tragedies, and public festivals, but also in their religious rites, to honour their deities. Thus they established the order of the Salic priests to represent the affections of the spirit. In our own time everyone knows in what high esteem [dancing] is held by lords and gentlemen.

Now, having been in this profession for fifty years, and having duly considered that it might be appreciated by anyone who desires [this knowledge], were I to give precise rules for dancing, and were I to present divers dances (such as grave dances, ballettos, or the galliard, cascarde, passo e mezzo, tordiglione, pavaniglia, and canary), I have therefore imitated the mother bear who, upon giving birth, produces a mass of flesh (a thing other rational or irrational creatures have not done), and who, by much licking of it with her tongue, and by drying it with her furry paws, turns what was imperfect and monstrous into a perfect [creature]. So have I imitated her, by searching my wits and studying day and night, correcting that first work which I brought to light many years ago, according to the laws of symmetry and perfect theory. As I will show you clearly, wherever it was imperfect I have here rendered it truly perfect. I have laboured to bring to light this present volume more from a desire to give satisfaction and service to those who wish it than from the hope of obtaining any glory thereby. Enjoy it, then, and may it be helpful to those more noble spirits who can most appreciate it; for I can receive no greater joy than to learn that through the fruits of my labours they have obtained some good training and delightful recreation. Therefore, along with my hope that every noble and illustrious spirit will acquire [my teaching], goes my prayer that our Good Lord will grant that he may be fully satisfied in this regard.

On the Nobility of Ladies

By Signor Fabritio Caroso of Sermoneta

Book One

In Which Are Taught the Rules Whereby May Be Learnt Those Fine Ways, Graceful Movements, and Courtly Manners, Which Are Expected of Both Gentlemen and Ladies When [Practising] the Art of Dancing (and When Not Dancing), Adapted to the Fundamental Law and Made Perfect in Theory.

The Names and Number
of All the Actions and Movements Which Occur
in Any Kind of Dance, and How to Do Them.

I shall treat here of the art of dancing, whether in basse, balletti, or in other types of dances, in the styles of Italy, as well as France or Spain; and also of proper deportment therein, not previously set forth by anyone—those highly praiseworthy and necessary VIRTUES which render beautiful (and are capable of so rendering) any prince or princess, lord or lady, knight or noblewoman, gentleman or lady, or any other well-born and -bred man, woman, youth, or maiden.

Before coming to a description of the rules, however, it has seemed convenient to list the various terms which I customarily give to each of those actions or movements which may occur in all types of balletti, or when dancing the galliard or the canary, so that I may be more easily understood by everyone in the course of my exposition. Therefore, dear Reader, you should know that these are the terms.[1]

There are Three Types of *Reverences* [*Riverenze*][2]

Grave Reverence [*Riverenza grave*] in six beats of music, as in the Bassa, et Alta, and the Tordiglione.

Long Reverence [*Riverenza lunga*] in four perfect beats of music, which occurs in balletti.

---

[1] The Italian terms are shown in square brackets to aid readers who are accustomed to them.

[2] *Half Reverence, [mezza Riverenza]* omitted.

Breve Reverence [*Riverenza breve*] in two beats, as in cascarde, the Pavaniglia, and the Gagliarda di Spagna.

There are Four Types of *Continences* [*Continenze*]

Grave continence [*Continenza grave*] in the time of six beats, as in the Bassa, et Alta.

Semigrave continence [*Continenza semigrave*] in three beats, also as in the Bassa, et Alta, and the Tordiglione.

Breve continence [*Continenza breve*] in two beats, as in basse and balletti.

Semibreve continence [*Continenza semibreve*] in one beat, as in the Pavaniglia, and the Gagliarda di Spagna.

There are Three Types of *Stopped Steps* [*Passi puntati*][3]

Semigrave stopped step [*Passo puntato semigrave*] in three beats of music, as in the Bassa, et Alta.

Breve stopped step [*Passo puntato breve*] in two beats, as in basse and balletti.

Semibreve stopped step [*Passo puntato semibreve*] in one beat, as in cascarde, the Pavaniglia, and the Gagliarda di Spagna.

There are Five Types of *Steps* [*Passi*][4]

Grave step (that is, *semibreve*) [*Passo grave*] in one beat per *step*, as in basse and balletti.[5]

Quick steps [*Passi presti*] in one fast triple beat per *step*, as in cascarde and the galliard.[6]

Wide held steps [*Passi larghi fermati*], as in the galliard.

Little steps in the air [*Passetti in aria*], as in the galliard.[7]

Pulled step [*Passo Trangato*], as in the Conto dell'Orco.[8]

---

[3] Caroso omits the *pulled stopped step* [*passo puntato trangato*], as called for in 'Cesarina'; and the *minim stopped step* [*passo puntato minimo*], as called for in 'Alta Regina'.

[4] Caroso omits *minim steps* [*passi minimi*] (Rule XI), from this list.

[5] In the title of Rule X Caroso calls these *semibreve natural steps* [*passi naturali semibreve*].

[6] Caroso's title in the text (Rule XII) is slightly different: *quick steps* in cascarde and in the galliard, called *minims*. [*passi presti alle cascarde et alla gagliarda, chiamati minimi*].

[7] Caroso's title in the text (Rule XIV) is: *quick little steps in the galliard*, called *semiminims* [*passetti presti nella gagliarda, chiamati semiminimi*].

[8] There is no rule for a step of exactly this name, but it may be the same as the *pulled* [*step*] [*trango*] (Rule XLIV).

There are Twelve *Sequences* [*Seguiti*][9]

Double sequence [*Seguito doppio*] in four beats, as in the Bassa, et Alta.

Grave broken sequence [*Seguito spezzato grave*] in the Tordiglione, in three beats.

Ordinary sequence [*Seguito ordinario*], that is, *Breve,* in two beats, as in basse, and balletti.

Half-double sequence [*Seguito semidoppio*] in two beats, as in Il Furioso and the Ballo del Fiore.

Pulled sequence [*Seguito Trangato*] in two triple beats, as in the Conto dell'Orco.

Feigned sequence [*Seguito finto*] in two beats, as in balletti.

Broken sequence [*Seguito spezzato*], as in cascarde.

Feigned broken sequence [*Seguito spezzato finto*], also in cascarde.

Scurrying sequence [*Seguito scorso*], as in basse and balletti.

Stamped sequence, as in the canary [*Seguito battuto al Canario*].[10]

Double [*stamped*] *sequence,* also *in the canary* [*Seguito doppio al Canario*].

Sliding broken sequence, likewise *in the canary* [*Seguito spezzato schisciato al Canario*].

There are Four *Doubles* [*Doppi*][11]

Grave double in Italian style
  [*Doppio grave all'Italiana*]

Grave double in Spanish style
  [*Doppio grave alla Spagnuola*]

        As in basse, and balletti.

Grave double in French style
  [*Doppio grave alla Francese*]

Breve double, as in cascarde
  [*Doppio breve*]

---

[9] Caroso omits from this list the *altered broken sequence in French style* [*spezzato alterator alla Francesa*] (Rule LXII); *altered double broken sequence* [*spezzato doppio alterato*] (Rule LXIII); *double scurrying sequence* [*seguito doppio scorso*], as in 'Laura Suave', p. 162 *pulled broken sequence* [*seguito spezzato trangato*], as in 'Vero Amore', p. 289, *scurrying broken sequence* [*seguito spezzato scorso*], as in the 'Tordiglione', p. 284, and the *stopped broken sequence* [*spezzato puntato*] (Rule LX).

[10] Caroso often substitutes *canary sequence* [*seguito di canario*] for *stamped sequence* [*seguito battuto*].

There are Two *Falling Jumps* [*Trabucchetti*][12]

Breve falling jump
[*Trabucchetto breve*]

Semibreve falling jump
[*Trabucchetto semibreve*]

As in all types of dance.

There are Four *Flourishes*

Ordinary flourish [*Fioretto ordinario*]

Flanking flourish [*Fioretto fiancheggiato*]

Flourish to the side with feet parallel [*Fioretto à piè pari per fianco*]

Stamped flourish in the canary [*Fioretto battuto al Canario*]

There are Three Types of *Jumps* [*Salti*][13]

Turning jump in the air [*Salto tondo in aria*][14] as in the galliard.

Reversed jump [*Salto riverso*], also as in the galliard.

Jump to the tassel [*Salto del Fiocco*]

There are Six *Capers* [*Capriole*]

Triple caper
[*Capriola in terzo*]

Quadruple caper
[*Capriola in quarto*]

Quintuple caper
[*Capriola in quinto*]

Broken caper in the air
[*Capriola spezzata in aria*]

Cross caper
[*Capriola intrecciata*]

Half caper in the air
[*Mezza capriola in aria*][15]

All of these are done in the galliard,
the Pavaniglia, and the Tordiglione.

---

[11] The *minim double* [*doppio minimo*] (Rule XXVI) is omitted from this list. The *feigned double* [*doppio finto*], as in 'Laura Suave', is also omitted both from this list and from the rules. The *scurrying double* [*doppio scorso*], as in 'Furioso alla Spagnuola', is entirely omitted as well.

[12] There is no rule for the *semibreve falling jump* [*trabucchetto semibreve*], but there is one for a *minim falling jump* [*trabucchetto minimo*] (Rule XXVI), not listed here. There is also no rule for the *grave falling jump* (see 'Alta Vittoria'), but it is equated there with the *semibreve falling jump*.

[13] The *small jump* [*saltetto*], is omitted, as called for in Rule XXIX.

[14] The words, '*in aria*': '*in the air*', do not appear with the rule for this *jump* (Rule XXVI).

[15] No rule is given for the *half caper in the air*.

Other Movements, each with a Different Name

Little bound [*Balzetto*][16] with feet together or disparate, as in the galliard and Pavaniglia.

Foot stamping as in the canary [*Battuta di piè al Canario*][17]

Cadence [*Cadenza*], and *step under* [*Sommessa*] of the foot,[18] as in the galliard and the Pavaniglia.

Changing [*step*] [*Cambio*], or *exchanging step* [*Scambiata*], as in the galliard.

Little bell [*Campanella*], also as in the galliard.

Five steps of the galliard [*Cinque passi in Gagliarda*]

Corinthian step [*Corinto*], as in balletti and cascarde.

Little side stamping step [*Costatetto*], as in the galliard.

Dactylic step [*Dattile*], as in balletti.

Dexterous step [*Destice*], as in balletti and cascarde.

Knot [*Groppo*], as in balletti, cascarde, and the galliard.

Little mill [*Molinello*], as in the galliard.

Turn on the ground [*Pirlotto in terra*], or *twirl* [*Zurlo*] as in the galliard.

Toe and heel [*Punta, e Calcagno*], as in the galliard.

Chasing step [*Recacciata*], as in the galliard, the Pavaniglia, and Rosa Felice.

Reprise with foot under [*Ripresa sotto piede*], in the galliard, cascarde, and balletti.[19]

Mincing reprise [*Ripresa trita*], as in the galliard.

Sapphic step [*Saffice*], as in balletti and cascarde.

Sliding step in the canary [*Schisciata al Canario*]

Spondaic step [*Spondeo*], as in balletti.

Pulled step [*Trango*], as in the dance called Il Conto dell'Orco.

Shake [*Tremolante*], as in any dance.

Tiny minced jumps [*Trito minuto*], as in the galliard.

---

[16] The rule for this step pattern uses the plural form, *balzetti* (Rule L).

[17] No rule is given for this term.

[18] A separate rule is given for each term.

[19] No rule is given for any *reprises.* Caroso may, however, be referring here to the *foot under* [*sottopiede*] (Rule XLVII).

Limping hop [*Zoppetto*] forward, also as in the galliard.

Limping hop sideways, likewise as in the galliard.[20]

I will treat of all these terms at the proper place in the rules, and [show] how they should be learned and inscribed in the memory, so that each at his pleasure may more easily name this or that action or movement; and by dancing it at the same time, he can simultaneously be in thorough possession both of the quality of the term and of its real effect.

[20] The *mincing reprise,* however, is not described, nor is the *reprise with foot under* as in the galliard ('Vero Amore').

Dialogue
Between a Disciple and His Master

How, and according to what rules one may know the terms for [dance] movements; the reasons they are so termed; and how to do them.

D. Please tell me, Master, if I desired to do a dance right now, how I should begin, what movement would be required, and what rules I would follow.

M. You need to know, my dear Pupil, that you begin with a gesture of raising your right arm—this is the first movement; the second is to take your bonnet or hat (which is on your head) gently by its rim (or brim) with the same hand; and once you have done this, straighten your arm, holding the aforesaid bonnet or hat turned toward your right thigh, as I shall explain in the rule wherein I treat of doffing one's bonnet.

D. This doffing of one's bonnet or hat—what does it mean? And why does one doff it with his right hand instead of his left? Kindly tell me.

M. You need to know that the doffing of your bonnet or hat, my Son, means solely that you honour anyone toward whom you feel respect; you pay him honour this way, since you uncover thereby the worthiest and noblest part of man; therefore you must doff it with your right hand, the hand which is the more appropriate for taking or holding anything, for it is worthier and nobler than the left hand.

The Different Methods Employed Both in Doffing One's Bonnet and in Holding It in One's Hand When Doffed; and Which [Methods] Are the Most Attractive and Most Customary

RULE I

D. I must tell you, Master, that I am highly satisfied with the very effective and genuine points you have given me. Now please explain, once I have doffed my bonnet or hat (which, as you have just told me, signifies that one pays a superior due honour), what rule I should follow after removing it.

M. Among those accomplishments of the utmost importance, my dear Son, which occur at the beginning of dances (wherein one practises beautiful and courtly manners), the doffing of your bonnet (or hat) holds first place, for this is the means mankind has devised to honour and revere one another, even when [we are] not dancing. Now before we proceed to demonstrate the actions and movements just mentioned, I would like to tell you something about them. Every day we see that various styles are in fashion, both in doffing one's bonnet, or in holding it in one's hand when doffed. Some are reprehensible, however, while some are praiseworthy. It is reprehensible to doff one's bonnet (whether it be made of velvet or linen or sarcenet) with one's whole hand, or to grasp it by its rim (or brim, if you will), or to follow another fashion of holding it in one's hand after doffing it, whether with one's arm drawn back and turned so that the inside of the bonnet faces up or forward; or with one's arm straight, with the inside facing front or back; all such conduct can scarcely be recommended. For if a gentleman draws his arm back with the inside of his bonnet turned up, he reminds us of one of those poor cripples who beg for alms. If, again, he holds his arm straight and the inside of his bonnet facing either front or back, he reveals to those in front of or behind him the perspiration which normally stains the rim of a bonnet (as it is impossible for all of us to keep it in brand-new condition). Thus, whichever of these methods [one follows] presents an indecent and repulsive sight to one's beholders. For a gentleman, then, to doff his bonnet (or hat) and hold it in his hand with that utter grace and beauty which may render him elegant, he shall do best to take his bonnet (or hat) gently by its rim (or his hat by its brim), doffing it and dropping his right arm straight down. Note, however, that once it is doffed, he should not pretend to kiss his bonnet or to bring it toward the one for whom he has doffed it, for, as I told you before, this appears disgusting both to the person for whom he has doffed it, and to any other observers. Instead he should hold his bonnet (or hat) with the inside facing the same leg which corresponds to the side on which he removed it, and he should pretend to kiss his own left hand. For since this is the hand belonging to the heart, he thus performs an act of cordiality; consider also that by this behaviour he will not only appear attractive and gracious to all observers, but will also escape any appearance of imperfection which could be associated with any of the [other] methods mentioned above.

D. After I have doffed my bonnet (or hat), if I wish to dance a balletto with a lady, what should I do before we begin the dance?

M. Before you come to the point of taking [the hand of] your lady, doff your bonnet with your right hand, and immediately switch it to your left; then pretend to kiss your right hand (but without bringing it into contact with your mouth), while she does the same. Then take her by the customary hand, which means that the gentleman takes his lady's left hand in his right hand (for these are the customary hands). Once you have done this, you then make a *Reverence*. Now this is how and what you should do before beginning a balletto, because by doffing your hat you honour her, and by making a *Reverence*, you revere her.

D. Please tell me whence comes this term, '*Reverence*'?

M. This term derives from 'to revere', since by humbling your body a bit, drawing back your left foot [and] bending your knees a little, you revere that person toward whom you make a *Reverence*.

D. With which foot should it be done—with your right foot, or with your left?

M. Let me say that it should always be done with your left foot.

D. Why with your left, and not with your right? For you have just told me, Sir, that in doffing your bonnet, you must use your right hand, since it is nobler than your left. Please clarify this point for me.

M. You should make a *Reverence* with your left foot for the following reasons. First, your right foot provides strength and stability for your body, and since it is its fortress, you should do this movement with your left foot, because it is weaker than your right; now this is the first reason. The second is that you honour that individual who is close to your heart and toward whom you wish to make a *Reverence*, and since your left foot is the limb corresponding to the side wherein your heart lies, you should always make it with your left foot. Now let me proceed to clarify six points. The first movement is to raise your hand or foot & *sine ipso factum est nihil.*[1] The second is to honour and take with your right hand, and to support and adore with your right foot, for we can readily see that anyone who doffs his bonnet always does it with his right hand (unless he is left-handed, or is hindered for some other reason which is against nature). We may also see that everyone kneels in church first on his right [knee], which is more stable; or if a gentleman prepares to mount a horse he first supports himself with his right foot on the ground (because it is more stable and stronger) so that he makes the first move with his left foot (which is weaker), by putting his foot in the stirrup. Here I have answered your questions about those parts and limbs [of the body] on the right [side]. Now let us proceed to the limbs on the left [side]. Hold your sword still with your left hand, but grasp it with your right. When preparing to cut bread or anything else with your right hand, first hold firmly what you intend to cut with your left hand. When preparing to walk, or to begin a step (or anything else), do so with your left foot, because it is weaker, as I told you before. In like manner, then, always revere with your left foot. Thus, honouring, holding and adoring are done with the right limb; standing still, walking, and revering always with the left limb. Thus these three actions are divided into three equal movements this way, and you should follow this rule.

---

[1] And if you do not do this you have done nothing.

The *Reverences:* First, the *Grave Reverence* [*Riverenza grave*], Which
Takes Six Beats

RULE II

D.   Master, I have never heard anyone teach so interestingly what you have
     [just] given me; I am pleased by this beyond measure; but, on my life, I
     hope you will not leave unexplained so vital a question; therefore, I pray
     you, give me the rule for how to make a *grave Reverence*.

M.   You need to know, my dear Pupil, that the rule for making a *grave
     Reverence* (which appears in a dance called 'Bassa, et Alta', and in another
     dance called 'Tordiglione') is that you make it in the time of six beats [by]
     keeping your body and legs quite straight, with half of your left foot ahead
     of your right to the extent that the toes of the aforesaid right foot are just
     level with the arch of your left foot, the feet being about four finger-
     breadths apart. Be careful that your toes are quite straight and directed
     toward the lady, or toward anyone else to whom you are making it [the
     Reverence], whether dancing or not. And be sure to avoid what most do,
     [which is] to point one foot south and the other north, so that they seem to
     have been born with crooked feet, for this produces a most ugly sight. Now
     because this *Reverence* is made only in these two dances, you must, at the
     beginning of the music, slightly raise the toe of your left foot (which is
     forward), and then move it straight back, in the time of two beats of music;
     then note whether, in moving your left foot back, its toes are even with
     your right heel; now keep it [your foot] flat on the ground, and do not raise
     your heel at all. Do not do this on your toes, nor draw [your left foot] back
     too far, nor separate it, as some do habitually and who, by spreading their
     knees too far apart, appear to be preparing to urinate; nor must you cross
     the aforesaid foot behind your right, because all of this behavior looks
     extremely ugly to those around you. This done, gracefully bend your
     knees a little, and raise your left heel. Now in moving your foot backward,
     draw your body back slightly, spreading your knees a little, and while
     bending them keep your head ever erect; and this takes two more beats of
     music. Third and last, straighten up in two more beats, and return your left
     toe to your right arch, in such a way that it [your left foot] can proceed to
     do the movements of the two *continences.* Now this is the way to make a
     grave Reverence, divided into six beats. Take care not to make this
     Reverence by turning toward the people around you, as if you were
     greeting them, as was done in the past, or to anyone else who is dancing,
     because in this way you appear disdainful toward the lady with whom you
     are dancing (a custom which has remained with the Jews). On the
     contrary, each of your actions should ever honour and revere that person
     whom you intend to so honour and revere; now avoid making the
     Reverence in that other way. All *Reverences* should be made with your left

foot, for that is the door of entry to the palace, and it remains the exit as well. Thus when you, or others, prepare to dance you should begin with a *grave Reverence,* and conclude with your left foot, with all solemnity, and in proper measure. And the same holds true if you make a *long* or *breve* [*Reverence*]; consequently, if you do otherwise the dance will be quite wrong.

The *Long Reverence* [*Riverenza Lunga*]
RULE III

D. How should one make a *long Reverence?* I should also like you to inform me why it is so termed.

M. This *Reverence* is called *long* because it *is* long, and this term of 'long' in music means four beats, and therefore it is named *long.* If you wish to do it you must follow the same order and procedure as in making a *grave Reverence.* In the first beat raise your left foot slightly. In the second beat draw it back. In the third gracefully bend your knees a little. In the fourth beat return your left toes to your right arch, gracefully raising your body. Now this is the way to make this charming *Reverence,* and it is called *long* for this reason.

The *Breve Reverence* [*Riverenza Breve*]
RULE IV

D. I hope you will have no objection to telling me why the *breve* [*Reverence*] is so called, and how the term was derived.

M. To satisfy you, let me say that this *Reverence* is so named because one breve in music equals two beats, and by dividing these two beats one derives four quick ones. Now in one of them raise your left foot slightly. In the second draw it back. In the third bend your knees a little. In the fourth beat straighten up, and join your feet together as you did in the other *Reverences,* and make sure it takes the time of the aforesaid music. This [*Reverence*] is made in the 'Pavaniglia' and in the 'Gagliarda di Spagna'. Now what remains is to demonstrate how to do a six-beat *grave continence.*

How To Do a *Grave Continence* [*Continenza Grave*] in Six Beats
RULE V

D. Master, I desire you to tell me how this term, '*continence*', is derived, Sir, so that should there be an argument about it, I would then be able to explain to anyone discussing it with me, the reasons for all of my movements and actions; and at the same time, please describe how to do it. I pray you, do not fail to favour me with this.

M. I am pleased that you continually pose new questions. You need to know, then, that the reason for the derivation of this term, '*continence*', is the following: the motions of this *continence* contain all the grace and decorum of all those actions and movements required in the art of dancing; and it is exceedingly important for both the gentleman and the lady to know how to do it. Before beginning it, raise your left foot slightly, and [then] move it sideways to your left, with one foot four or five finger-breadths apart from the other. Before moving it bend your left hip a little; be sure to keep your head erect; and do not drop your left shoulder, but give it a touch of grace. And in adding this grace[2] (aside [from the fact] that everything consists in this [grace]), both the gentleman and lady strut a little, and 'contain' themselves; for from this movement of theirs all that follow should take whatever style and grace is required by this noble art; and in this consists the comeliness of dancers. From this self-containment, therefore, the term '*continence*' is derived. Now returning to our discussion, let me say that in order to do it, move your left foot apart with that grace I mentioned above, wait five beats before joining your right foot to your left, and on the sixth [beat] bring your right [to it]; while [thus] joining your feet bend your body slightly, and then straighten up gracefully, strutting slightly toward the side on which you are doing it; this effect is usually obtained by raising your heels a little, and immediately dropping them in time to the music. End the *continence* this way. Now do not follow the custom of some who, neglecting to swagger slightly with that graceful but very slight dropping and raising of their heels, seem to resemble the possessed when [attempting] to exorcise themselves; nor [follow] the custom of still others, who spread [their left leg] in the first movement (which is done with the left foot) so far from their right that it really does seem as if they are about to urinate; and who then join the right [to the left] with feet together, in a most ungainly and abrupt manner, even though it may be in the right time and with proper measure. Therefore [these movements] must be shunned. Thus, this *grave continence* takes six ordinary beats of music, and when you do it, divide it this way, as I have said above. Now this is how to do it, and so it is termed; and this has been enough instruction on this movement. Therefore I will proceed to explain the *semigrave continence*.

---

[2] I.e., embellishment.

How To Do the *Semigrave Continence* [*Continenza Semigrave*]

RULE VI

D. I should like to know, Sir, the reason you no longer call this the *ordinary continence* (as you did in your first work), why you now prefer to call it the *semigrave continence,* and how it acquired this term.

M. I am glad [you asked], so pay attention: as the saying goes, 'One can learn something new every day'. Also, in the *Proverbs of Solomon,* [one can see] an engraving showing him in a light carriage, for since he was no longer able to walk he was carried like a year-old child. Now though he was quite aged (and on in years), it still gave him pleasure to learn, so he said, '*Dum pedes usque ad foveam teneo, oportet me discere*', which means in the vulgar tongue, 'I am very old, and have one foot in the grave, yet I desire to learn'.

Thus everyone should take him as an example and continue to learn until the day he dies.

> Che se dormendo vol'esser da poco,
> Prendon di lui le scimie festa, e gioco.[3]

Let me say, then, that heretofore I did not know as much about this profession as I do now, and that I have since set my mind to work, and have reduced this step to its basic rule and theoretical perfection. For I had [previously] called it *ordinary continence* because it was ordinarily done this way in basse and balletti. Now, after further study, I have learned that it should be termed *semigrave continence,* because it is divided into three ordinary beats of music; it is thus termed *semigrave continence* because it takes half [the time of] the *grave continence.* It is necessary that everyone do it this way and with the actions I have demonstrated above. At this point, however, I shall go on to explain the *breve* and *semibreve continences,* and the derivation of these terms.

Breve and *Semibreve Continences* [*Continenze Breve, Semibreve*]
RULE VII

D. I pray you, Sir, tell me why, with both of these *continences,* one is called *breve* and the other *semibreve.*

M. I am glad [you asked]. Now you need to know that the *breve* should be done with the same grace and style as I told you for the others, but this one

---

[3] For if one lacks ambition and sleeps [the day away],
[Even] monkeys will poke fun at him.

takes two perfect beats of music, which is one breve, [and] it occurs in most balletti. This is the reason it is termed *breve*. Now I will go on to tell you about the *semibreve* [*continence*], which is done the same way, but divided into one beat; therefore it is called *semibreve* (which is half a *breve*). Here I conclude my discussion of the four *continences,* and will go on to treat of the *semigrave stopped step.*

The *Semigrave Stopped Step* [*Passo Puntato Semigrave*] and How To Do It
RULE VIII

D.   Concerning this *step,* Master, I find that in your first work you called it *stop,* and not *stopped step;* and it really does seem to me that you are thus turning all the terms, as well as the dances, quite upside down. Please tell me what caused you to do this, and why you term it *stopped step* and not *stop,* as before.

M.   You will be much more satisfied with my explanation of this matter, my Son, than with any other explanation I have hitherto placed before you, if you will but lend me your ears. You need to know, then, that there are four reasons for [using] the term *stopped step.* [The first reason is that] if a gentleman or lady takes a step, he or she will never stop with [that foot] so far apart [from the other], as you may often see one do who is badly taught, because it is unstable, as you may see by trying it; for if one promenades, or walks (to put it better), he takes a step with his left foot, [but since it is then] necessary to raise, slightly, the heel of the right foot (which follows), he cannot actually stop. You should do it as I now show you, however, so that after having taken a step with your left foot, you join your right to it. The immortal poet Ovid demonstrated this well in his verse (for one calls that joining of feet a *caesura*), so that when scanning one of his pentameter lines we find first a dactyl, then a spondee, and finally a *caesura,* and here we stop a little. Now from this [act of] stopping has come the term *stopped step.* The second reason is that in writing, when one has concluded a thought, one places a period [or full stop] there. Or when one is reading, upon seeing a period one stops there a little, taking a breath there in the course of his reading; this is another reason it is called '*stopped*'. The third reason is that, when we observe people in daily life, we may see that when someone walks (or promenades) along, he may stop at intervals, and those who observe him stopped this way may say (or think) that he is pondering something deeply; for this is just as if he had put a full stop to his walk. They may say, then, 'He has stopped [completely]'. Now were two people to walk together, if they were to stop they would stand still in order to complete the thread of their discourse. The last reason is that (as one may observe daily) an animal or a stubborn horse, upon seeing something disturbing, does not continue on its path, but stops with feet quite together, and not apart; and whoever sees it stopped this way says, 'Oh, that animal has stopped short!' For these reasons, therefore, it should be termed '*stopped step*', and not '*stop*'.

Now let us proceed to the way to do this; let me say that this *semigrave stopped step* occurs in the 'Bassa, et Alta' and not in balletti, that it is done in three ordinary beats of music, and therefore that it is called *semigrave*. Before moving your left foot, use your hip to strut a little (as I said for the *continence*). Then, having done this graceful hip movement, take one step forward with the same foot, thrusting it forward so that its heel passes a little beyond your right toe; it should also be four or five fingerbreadths laterally away from the same foot; then stopping a little, that is, as if taking a breath (which should be done in the first beat), and then moving your right foot with a slight swagger, join it to the left, bowing your body a little and then straightening up gracefully, as in the rule for doing the *continence*. Here then, my Son, is the answer to your question as to why I now call it *stopped step* and not *stop*. Now I will discuss the *breve* and *semibreve stopped steps*.

What the *Breve* and *Semibreve Stopped Steps* Are
RULE IX

D. I pray you, dear Master, describe how to do these *steps,* and also why you do not term them *stops,* as [you did] before.

M. Let me say that previously, in my other work, I in fact did term them *stops.* Now I call the first one *breve stopped step* because it takes the time of two perfect beats of music (which make one breve). Thus it has acquired the term *breve stopped step*. The *semibreve* [*stopped step*] is so termed because it takes one beat, which is a semibreve (half a breve); thus it has acquired this term. Now I will show you how to do them [both]. First, raise your left foot a little, and take one step in one beat of music; then move your right foot, and put it to the arch of your left, lowering [yourself] a little while putting it there, and then immediately raising your heels a little; this movement takes another beat; and finally, at that instant, gracefully lower your heels. Do the *semibreve stopped step* the same way, but in two triple beats. (These two make one semibreve.) Be careful always to move that foot which is to be joined to the other, and this shall suffice about *stopped steps.* Now I shall discourse on *semibreve natural steps*.

How To Learn the *Semibreve Natural Steps* [*Passi Naturali Semibrevi*]

RULE X

D.   Tell me, Master, why you now term this *natural step* and not *grave step*, as it was called before; and please tell me its derivation.

M.   I will answer your question immediately. Let me say that this *step* is taught us by our instincts, as we may see when a wet-nurse, or a nursing (or suckling) mother of a baby boy or girl begins to dress him when he is seven or eight months old; as soon as he is dressed, she stands him on both feet, holding him either under his arms or by his sleeves, whereupon the first move he makes is to raise his foot and then to put it flat on the ground all by himself. This is called a step. Then with the other foot, which he has left behind, he does the same [thing], walking forward. Now this was not taught him before, either by his nurse or his mother, because it is Nature itself which causes him to move like this, and not these women (as is the case in teaching him to talk). As a [further] experiment, if you were to put that baby in a walker, you would see him walk by himself. This movement, then, can legitimately be called *natural step,* and this is how [the term] was derived. It is called *semibreve* because it takes one semibreve beat. These *steps* are done during the passages of cascarde and other dances, and also when not dancing, but just walking. Now this should suffice for the moment, since I have answered your question. Let me go on to describe how to do *minim steps.*

How To Do *Minim Steps* [*Passi Minimi*]

RULE XI

D.   I would like you to tell me how to do the abovementioned *steps.*

M.   The method, or the rule, for learning to do *minim steps* is this. First raise your left foot in one minim, which is half a beat, and then thrust it forward (just as was said for the *semibreve stopped* [*step*]), taking care not to do it exaggeratedly. Then your right, which is behind, follows, and you thrust it forward, just as you did with your left, with a graceful and charming swagger, accompanying [your feet] somewhat with your body. Note that you should raise your toe while rising, for by really stretching the knee belonging to that foot, it is rendered more graceful, and looks beautiful. Also keep your toes parallel, not like some people, who have one toe pointing east and the other west. Now it is necessary that everyone learn to dance for this reason, if only to learn to walk properly so that it will be pleasing to, rather than derided by, one's observers. Now I shall treat of how to do *minim steps* in the gallliard.

The *Quick Steps* in Cascarde and the Galliard Called *Minims* [*Passi Presti Minimi*]
RULE XII

D. Go on, then, for I listen to you with pleasure.

M. These *steps,* which were called *quick* before, I would like to term *minims* now, because each one takes one minim, which is equivalent in the music to half a beat (and this is why they are termed *minims*). Do them by following the rule I gave you for the *semibreve step.* Now I shall describe how to do the *wide held steps* in the galliard.

How To Do the *Wide Held Steps* in the Galliard [*Passi larghi fermati*]
RULE XIII

D. I should like you to tell me how to do these *wide steps.*

M. Do the *wide held steps* in the galliard by drawing your left foot a little farther back than the heel of your right, and sideways from the right about four fingerbreadths, gracefully bending and separating your knees slightly. Do the same [thing] with your right foot, as if in a *cadence,* and give each step one semibreve beat. Now let us go on to the *quick little steps.*

The *Quick Little Steps* in the Galliard, Called *Semiminims* [*Passetti presti*]
RULE XIV

D. I will gladly hear about these *little steps.*

M. The *quick little steps* in the galliard are called *semiminims* because you do them quickly, with your legs quite straight (whether you do them forward, or backward, or even in the air), on your toes, and with agility and dexterity, raising [your body] as in a *cadence* with feet disparate; you [also] do them in cascarde, traveling forward with one triple beat for each *step.*

Sequences [*Seguiti*]: First, the *Grave Broken Sequence* [*Seguito spezzato grave*], As In the Dance Called 'Tordiglione'
RULE XV

D. Now I am anxious, Master, to understand why the *grave broken sequence* is so termed.

M. The reason is that in doing this *grave broken sequence,* one does it for half again as long[4] as for the *ordinary broken sequence.*[5] I want to term it thus now because you should follow the rule for walking, and because in it you break up your walking movement. From this breaking up it has acquired the term *grave broken sequence,* although it is not used in any other dance but the 'Tordiglione'.

D.   Since you have favoured me with instruction in the origin of this appropriate term, I will pray you will also teach me how to do it.

M   To do this *broken sequence,* take one step forward with your left foot in one minim beat, putting your foot flat on the ground; during the other beat thrust your right foot [forward], putting its toe behind your left heel, but raising your right heel; the moment that you place the aforesaid toe of your foot [there], raise your left, which is forward, keeping your knee quite straight; then drop it straight down just where it was originally joined [to the other foot]. Take care that when you put your right toe behind your left foot, you do it as if it is a *foot under.* Now this is the way to do it, and then you continue this way with your right [foot]. Whoever does this should hold his body erect at all times, and this holds true [both] for the gentleman and for the lady with whom he dances. Now everyone should shun that movement which was formerly associated with the first *step,* that is, jutting one's body forward, and then pulling it back, and finally again jutting forward, and then pulling it back, and finally again jutting forward, for this is the most disgraceful and loathsome sight any observer might see, which is all I can possibly say about it. Let me proceed to discuss the *ordinary* (or *breve*) *sequence.*

The *Ordinary Sequence* [*Seguito Ordinario*], Which Can Also Be Termed *Breve*

RULE XVI

D.   Be gracious enough, Sir, to tell me why this *sequence* is called *ordinary* and *breve,* and the derivation of these terms.

M.   Let me say, my Son, that it is called *ordinary sequence* for the following reason: in doing it we follow the natural order with which we move our feet. It is also called *breve* because it takes two beats of music, and from this has sprung the term *breve sequence;* both terms are correct.

D.   How do we do it, what rules do we follow, and what grace and measure accompany it?

M.   Do this *ordinary* or *breve sequence* with two *minim steps* (that is, fast) and one *semibreve* [*step*], at the end of which gracefully raise the heel of your

---

[4] *'Si fà la metà più grave.'*

[5] There is no rule for the *ordinary broken sequence,* [*seguito spezzato ordinario*], though one may assume Caroso means by this term the *broken sequence* [*seguito spezzato*] (Rule XXI).

following foot, as well as your body; these actions and steps take a breve, which is two beats, for two minims and one semibreve make one breve. With respect to this, begin it in the following fashion: first raise your left toe and extend your knee quite well, and then immediately lower it to the ground; be careful not to put it down flatly, but dance on it a little as if doing a *little jump*.[6] Then take another *little step*[7] with your right foot, so that the arch of that foot is level with your left toe. The last *step*, which is a *semibreve*, you thrust forward, making sure it is flat but not forcing it. Do it instead as I have shown you above, and bear in mind that you should add the grace to it that I have described. Thus you may do this [*sequence*] gracefully, and it will look lovely and charming to all who behold you. With this reminder I conclude my talk on this *sequence,* and go on to discuss the *double sequence.*

The *Double Sequence* [*Seguito Doppio*], and the Derivation of the Term

RULE XVII

D. I am extremely delighted and pleased to learn the meanings of the terms for these learned discoveries of yours, and simultaneously the means by which, from now on, others will be enabled to learn this noble virtue of dancing quite easily without any master. But again, I hope you will not mind telling me how to do this *double sequence,* and whence the term is derived.

M. That is exactly what I had hoped; so I would like you to know that the gentleman begins it with feet together every time. Begin with that foot which you have joined [to the other], and continue in the following fashion: Do one *falling jump* backward on your left toe to the extent that this toe is even with your right foot, and at this moment raise your right foot, with which you do the same thing; these are *minim steps.* Then do one *breve* [*step*] with the left foot, which you will find is raised forward. Then take three more *steps* a little more slowly, one beat for each *step,* finally joining your right foot to your left. Note that in doing these *steps* backward you gracefully bend your body a little, with head erect. Thus it is called a *double sequence,* for with the *ordinary* or *breve sequence,* as we said, your feet make three movements, while with this they make six. Note that every time you bring your feet together you should add the grace of bending your knees a little, and then as gracefully rising, as I pointed out in the rules for the *continence* and *stopped steps.* I shall not discuss this further, for it is time to speak of the *half-double embellished sequence.*

---

[6] *Saltetto,* not described in these rules.

[7] *Passetto,* not given in these rules. The term may, however, be an abbreviated form of *quick little steps* [*passetti presti*] (Rule XIII).

The *Half-double Embellished Sequence* [*Seguito Semidoppio Ornato*]
RULE XVIII

D. Thank you for all you have been kind enough to tell me thus far; I pray you to continue no less effectively.

M. I am not going to deny you this (to help you succeed worthily in this science). Let me say, then, that the movement just taught is [now] followed by the *half-double embellished sequence* (so termed by me because it adorns the dance in which it is done, particularly the dances called 'Il Furioso' and 'Ballo del Fiore'), which is performed during two beats of music; that is, first do two *minim steps* in one beat, and then do one *broken sequence* in another beat.

Note that you take the first *step* on your toes and the second flat; and do the *broken sequence* as I have shown you in its rule. The reason, then, that I term it *half-double embellished sequence* is not because it is a half [*sequence*], but because it is embellished; therefore I have termed it thus. Now it will be a good idea to discuss the *pulled sequence*.

The *Pulled Sequence* [*Seguito Trangato*]
RULE XIX

D. If such discourse is not tiring you, please be good enough to proceed with a description of how the whimsical movement termed *pulled sequence* acquired its name, and how to do it.

M. Do not think that this term is so fantastic, for it is quite appropriate; this *pulled sequence* occurs in a dance called 'Il Conto dell'Orco', and in still another called 'La Moresca'. Do it in two beats of music; first raise your left foot in one minim; then put it down, bending your knee gracefully, in another minim; then with your right foot, which at this moment is off the ground, take a *step* forward in another minim. Lastly take another *step* forward with your left foot, and raise your right foot—in this fashion it takes another minim. Thus four minims make two beats, which equals a breve, and you should do it in this order.

The origin of the term is this: that in first bending [your knee] and then raising it [your foot], it seems that you pull away [from something]; that is, it seems you move this way because something has pricked your foot, and therefore you draw it back as you walk, and do not walk as naturally as you would had you not felt [such] a prick. Therefore, from 'to pull back' the term *pulled sequence* is derived, as is the term *pulled step* (the description of which I will set down in its place in the Rules). But no more of this, since what I have told you is enough, and now I will explain the *feigned sequence*.

The *Feigned Sequence* [*Seguito Finto*]: the Derivation of the Term, and How To Do It
RULE XX

D. Master, what causes you to call this *sequence 'feigned'*, and how was the term derived? Also, with what measure and according to what rule should it be done?

M. This question of yours pleases me, so let me say that this movement takes two beats, as was said in the rule for the *breve sequence.* Now raise your left foot, pulling it back, [then] putting it down on your toes, and gracefully bending your body back a little. This takes one minim. Repeat this with your right to another minim. The last *step,* which is now off the ground, you drop flat on the ground in the same place where it was before, to a semibreve. Now do this last *step* so that you put it down in the time of a semibreve, as I said above, so that these two minims and one semibreve make two beats of music; that is, one breve. It is termed *feigned sequence* for this reason: because you pretend to go backward, but you return your foot to the same place where it was originally. It is very attractive to see this in a dance. I think that by now you are well-trained in this movement, so I would like to go on to other *sequences.*

The *Broken Sequence* [*Seguito Spezzato*], and the Derivation of the Term
RULE XXI

D. A question now arises, which does not seem insignificant to me.

M. What is your question?

D. Previously, you explained the *grave broken sequence;* now I would like to know if in your profession there is a movement called *broken sequence.*

M. Certainly there is, and indeed I intended to talk about it before you asked me. You need to know that it has been termed *broken sequence* because the *ordinary* or *breve* sequence (whichever you may care to call it) takes two [semibreve] beats, as I have told you in the appropriate rule. But this one is broken up, and takes two triple beats, which equal one semibreve, so for this reason it is called *broken sequence.* To continue, do it by interrupting your walking motion, as I have told you in the rule for the *grave broken sequence,* which occurs in the dance called 'Tordiglione'. As I said, do this *broken sequence* in two triple beats. First do a *step* with your left foot, thrusting it forward a half step, but flatly, and two fingerbreadths from the right; then put your right toe behind your left heel, and this should take one triple beat; do not put it beside [your heel], as some people do, for if you do you will be wrong, in view of the fact that if you join that foot to the other, you must follow the rule by subsequently moving that [right] foot. Therefore it is correct to put it, as I have told you, to your left heel, and you should do this so it resembles a *foot under* to the foot you removed; raise your left foot gracefully, keeping your leg and body straight, and then let it fall straight down. This raising and lowering should be done during another beat, as above. Be careful not to thrust your body forward nor pull it backward, since this produces a lascivious movement which, you must remember, will disgust any onlookers. I shall not discuss this further, but will proceed to speak of other movements, chiefly the *scurrying sequences*.

The *Scurrying Sequence* [*Seguito Scorso*] and the Origin [of the Term]
RULE XXII

D. I am infinitely grateful, Sir, for all you have told me, and I pray you to show me how to do this *scurrying sequence,* and the derivation of the term.

M. This movement is done with ten tiny and fast *little steps*[8] in the time of a breve, and in the following way. Begin by raising your left foot and taking a half step forward, with the rest following, always with agility and on your toes. Note that when a lady does them, she should make no noise with her chopines, should hold herself erect, and should not pass her left toe beyond the middle of her right foot. Her feet may be no more than two fingerbreadths apart, and she should do this up to the number of the aforesaid ten *little steps*[9]; this is how to do it. Now since these *little steps* are done quickly (running around the hall or any other dancing place), they are therefore termed *scurrying sequence,* since one does them by scurrying.

The *Stamped Sequences,* As *in the Canary* [*Seguiti Battuti al Canario*], and the Derivation of the Term
RULE XXIII

D. Continue, I pray you, to describe all these beautiful kinds of movement.

M. Do each *stamped sequence in the canary* in one triple beat of music as follows: that is, first raise your left toe, sliding and pushing your heel forward a little. Then immediately move the same toe back, sliding it along the same path while keeping your heel raised; lastly, move forward to the middle of your right foot, flattening it completely on the ground, stamping

---

[8] *Passettini,* not defined or listed elsewhere in these rules.

[9] *Passetti,* obviously in this context the same as *passettini.*

once in time to the music (just as you stamp when putting on your shoes). Then do the same [thing] with your right foot. Now in these *sequences* and in any other actions or movements in the canary, be sure to stamp in such a fashion that your observers comprehend the measure and artistry involved. Now these sequences acquired the term '*stamped*' from this stamping of feet. You should know also that you do the *double* [*stamped*] *sequence* twice with the same foot, just as you did the first. I have nothing further to tell you about this, except that the term, 'canary', comes from those who dance in this style on the Canary Islands.

The *Sliding Broken Sequence in the Canary* [*Seguito spezzato schisciato al Canario*]
RULE XXIV

D. I am extremely delighted with what you have said, and since I believe that there is much more, I am ready to listen to you.

M. Little else remains to be discussed, but so as not to keep you waiting, let me say that to do the *sliding broken sequence* you begin with feet together, first moving your left foot without lifting it at all from the ground, but sliding it or (as we say), gliding[10] it along the ground; push it forward so that its heel is almost level with the tip of your right toe, and about one or two fingerbreadths from it. Then move your right foot, pushing it forward, sliding it along the ground on your toe, with your heel raised, in such a way that your right toe goes under the back of your left heel. When it is raised, drop it straight down on the ground in the same place as if you were trying to put on your shoe. Repeat with your right [foot], and continue thus in succession, always holding yourself erect. Note that in beginning the second step you should gracefully raise and lower your body a little. Now these *sequences* are termed *sliding* because in doing them you always shuffle or slide your feet. Now I shall proceed to tell you something of no little importance about the *doubles*.

The *Double in Italian Style* [*Doppio all'Italiana*], and the Derivation [of the Term]
RULE XXV

D. Now I understand it all, so please continue.

M. Do the *double in Italian style* in four beats of music, by taking three *steps* starting with your left foot, joining your right foot to your left at the fourth

---

[10] *Strisciandolo.* Florio: '*strisciare*...to make a trampling noise with one's feet as Canarie dancers use'.

step, and bending your knees a little each time they are brought together, and gracefully raising and then lowering your heels a little. Do the first movement of the first *step* with the grace I have told you of in the rule for the *continence,* swaggering a bit. In taking these *steps,* carry yourself erect with a fine air, taking care to move that foot which is to be joined [to the other], whether forward or backward, in the manner which will be told you in the Second Book, where I will speak of learning to do balli, balletti and other kinds of dances.

It is termed *double* because, when you do a *stopped step,* you take a *step* and then join the following foot [to it]; now here you do three [steps], but then you add the fourth *step* in the same way. Therefore it is called *double stopped step,* and this is the derivation of the term. Now I have nothing further to say about this except that it occurs in balletti.

The *Minim Double* [*Doppio Minimo*]
RULE XXVI

D.   Please, Master, what are you thinking about so deeply?

M.   [I am wondering] whether I should discuss the *minim double,* for it is similar in manner to the *long double in Italian style.* I will just tell you, however, that although you do it the same way, it should be quicker; that is, for each semiminim you take one small *step.* Now this occurs in cascarde. Do you understand? And now I will not withhold from you a description of the *double in Spanish style.*

The *Double in Spanish Style* [*Doppio alla Spagnuola*]
RULE XXVII

D.   I have understood, and I will not forget; do go on to this [*double*] *in Spanish style.*

M.   The *double in Spanish style* follows what I have just told you, which is done in the same way as the *double* [*stopped*] *sequence;* it is called *double* since it follows the same rule in a dance called the 'Bassa, et Alta' from Castille in Spanish Style.[11] It is thus called a *double in Spanish style,* but it should really be called a *double stopped sequence,* for the [*ordinary*] *sequence* is composed of three *steps,* but this one is composed of six, at the end of which you join your right foot [to your left]; and it takes six ordinary beats of this 'Bassa'. Now on each beat take one *step,* in this manner and according to this rule. Now I shall speak of it no more, but will go on to describe the *double in French style.*

---

[11] Caroso calls for a *double in French style* in 'Bassa, et Alta', however!

The *Double in French Style* [*Doppio alla Francese*]
RULE XXVIII

D.   If I am not mistaken, the only one of these *doubles* left to tell me about is the *double in French style*.

M.   That is true. Let me say, then, that you do this *double in French style* this way: that is, standing with feet together, do one *falling jump* backward with your left foot, and [another] one with your right [foot] to the right side. Then walk forward taking three *steps,* and for the last, which will be the fourth, join your right foot to your left. Now in bringing [your feet] together lower and raise your heels a little, and then drop them again, as was said for the *continence,* and this is how to do it. I will say no more about this, but go on to other movements.

The *Breve Falling Jump* [*Trabucchetto Breve*], Which Previously Was Termed *Grave,* and the Derivation of the Term
RULE XXIX

D.   Now that you have talked about these *doubles,* please, Sir, tell me what movements follow them.

M.   The movement I will show you next is the *breve falling jump,* which you do in the following manner: stand with feet either together or apart, depending on circumstances (for you do it both in balletti and in the galliard), and raise the foot you have [just] joined, or the one which is behind, to one side with a *small jump;* that is, [move] your left foot some distance away from your right foot, and the moment your left foot touches the ground, raise your right foot, bringing it within about two finger-breadths of your left. Be careful, however, not to place it on the ground; but move lightly on your toes, keeping both legs quite straight. Now while doing the *small jump,* and in bringing your right foot over in the aforesaid manner, lower your left hip and raise your right [hip] at the beginning of this *falling jump* to be more graceful; then return your right foot to its original place, repeating with your left [foot] the movement you just did with your right. Take note that you should move your hips with a slight swagger in any *falling jump,* and move with bodily agility and nimbleness. Avoid the habit of some people, who, after having jumped onto their left foot at the beginning, join their right foot to it (as I have said) by putting its toe awkwardly behind the left, so that they seem more to be kicking than anything else. Then repeat to the right. Others spread their legs so far apart when doing this *falling jump* that they really seem to be preparing to urinate, a dreadful sight. These effects one must guard against, and whoever has these habits must correct and amend them. Now it is termed *falling jump* for the following reason: in doing the *small jump* and then drawing one foot near [the other] (as I said before), you move as if you were staggering, because when you lean to the left and hold your right foot up, you seem to be falling over; this is the derivation of the term, *'falling jump'*. Now let me go on to tell you about the *minim falling jump.*

The *Minim Falling Jump* [*Trabucchetto Minimo*]
RULE XXX

D. Please, Master, tell me about this other *falling jump.*

M. I will please you, so let me say that you do the *minim falling jump* just as you did the *breve falling jump,* which takes one beat;[12] this one, however, takes half the time. This is enough about *falling jumps.* Now let me pass on to tell you of *flourishes.*

Flourishes [*Fioretti*]: First, the *Ordinary Flourish* [*Fioretto Ordinario*], How To Do It, and the Origin [of the Term]
RULE XXXI

D. You have quickly despatched these *falling jumps,* which indeed are lovely, but now I am ready and willing to hear about these *flourishes.*

M. I shall discuss them now, for they are very beautiful and highly important to this art. Let me say, then, that you do the *ordinary flourish* by raising your left foot, and thrusting it forward beyond your right so that your left heel is two fingerbreadths in front of its toe, one fingerbreadths from it [to the side], and raised two [fingerbreadths], with your knees quite straight and your toe up. Then, raising your body somewhat at the same time, do a *cadence* as in a galliard, so that your left toe is one fingerbreadth from your right heel, and two fingerbreadths apart [from it], and also so that your toes remain pointed straight ahead and not askew (as we may often see people do nowadays). Do this entirely on your toes so you may be more nimble. Then thrust your left foot, which is now in back, up to the arch of the preceding foot, and raise it at the same time. This is how you do a *flourish,* and you should continue this way. Originally one did a *foot under* here, putting it [the left] in place of the right, which was [then] raised in the same way as the left had been at the beginning. Others, when they finish the *ordinary flourish,* lift the left foot, putting it down in place of the right, after having raised it (somewhat forward, as I said before) while joining it to the right in a *cadence.* Also, when doing a *foot under* with feet together, they raise the right foot and end it this way. Again, even if this

---

[12] If Caroso is referring to the semibreve as a beat in this instance, then the term *'breve falling jump'* in this and the preceding rule must be read as *'semibreve falling jump'*.

method looks nice, I must prefer the first, for it renders you more elegant, enabling you to do a *foot under* more easily and more correctly than the other way; also by staying on your toes you can be more agile than if you put one of them flat on the floor. Now the time of each of these *flourishes* is one beat, and it always concludes with one foot raised.

Now let me say that the origin of this term, '*flourish*' (which you do this way in the galliard, or in any other dance you please), arises because without intermingling *flourishes* in your dancing, your movements seem dead; but if you add these *flourishes* such a variation will bloom and be embellished. Consequently the term '*flourish*' derives from the lovely grace of this embellishment. I shall say no more about it, for I would like to discuss the *flanking flourish*.

The *Flanking Flourish* [*Fioretto fiancheggiato*], and the Origin of the Term
RULE XXXII

D. I am certainly satisfied with these teachings, so pray do go on.

M. The *flanking flourish* follows after what I have desribed, and you do it in one beat like the others, except that, while you do the *ordinary* [*flourishes*] straight forward, you do this one to the side. And when you do it to the left, superimpose your right foot on your left in the *cadence,* and then do a *foot under* with your left, raising your right. On the other hand, when you do it to the right, superimpose your left foot on your right, following the same rule. Now the term '*flanking flourish*' is derived from this use of the side, because you continue to move flankingly with each *flourish*. Let me now explain the one with feet together.

The *Flourish to the Side with Feet Parallel* [*Fioretto à piè pari per fianco*], and the Derivation [of the Term]
RULE XXXIII

D. You have taught me quite enough about this; go on now, I pray you, to give me training in what you have just mentioned.

M. Listen, then, for I will not fail to do so. With your body erect, and with your legs quite straight, raise your left foot a little to the side, and one handbreadth away from your right. Then bring it back to its original place (that is, two fingerbreadths away from your other foot), with your toes parallel, and stamp once on that toe; then with the same toe push your right away, putting it in its place as in a *foot under,* and in so doing raise your right foot. Then repeat what you did at the beginning with your left [foot], moving [your right] away from your left. And beginning another time with your left, and then with your right, you may continue thus one after the other.

Now, the term is derived this way, for you always do these *flourishes* to the side with your feet parallel; try to remember this, for I will tell you no more about it, but go on to tell you of the *stamped flourish in the canary.*

The *Stamped Flourish in the Canary* [*Fioretto battuto al Canario*] and Whence it Originated
RULE XXXIV

D. Have no fear, for I will certainly remember this; now please do not continue with such elementary matters.

M. Do the *stamped flourish,* then, by raising your left foot forward, away from, and higher than your right, four or five fingerbreadths; then put it down immediately in the manner of a *small jump,* stamping the ground with this foot, and raising your right at the same time; then put it down in the same place to which it was raised, and stamp rapidly five times. Do the first [stamp] with the same foot when you drop it, as I said above; the second with your right; the third with your left; the fourth with your right; and the last with your left, raising your right the same distance and height as you did before with your left. Then dropping it, stamp five more times, remaining at the end with your left raised, as I have just told you about your right. These two *flourishes* ([the first] with your left, and the other with your right) take two triple beats of music apiece.

Now the term is derived from the fact that it is stamped throughout, and [so is] different from the others. Thus it is called '*stamped flourish*', since it embellishes every variation which includes it. I have no more to tell you about it, however, but will go on to explain the *five steps.*

The *Five Steps of the Galliard* [*cinque Passi in Gagliarda*], a Corrupted Term
RULE XXXV

D. How pleased I am about this, for I have wanted you to explain it for a long time.

M. You need to know that in olden times this term, '*five steps*', was [applied] quite incorrectly, because in fact they number only two. Now I will show you why. First *hop* on the ground with your right foot, lifting your left foot forward; then bring it straight down, and this is one *step.* Do not jump, but have your knee quite extended; and do not do what was customary before, that is, that when you put your left foot down, you would raise your right foot behind at the same moment, for this simply looked as if you were attempting to kick [something], and such a movement appeared ugly to onlookers. Do it this way, then: once you have *hopped* on your right and raised your left, place it flat on the ground; then thrust your right foot (which is now behind) [forward] with a *foot under* (be careful that its toe goes directly behind your left heel), immediately raising your left [foot]. Then drop this [foot] back into place, and raise your right foot forward again; this is termed a *step in the air*. Thus there are, as I told you, two [*steps*] and not five; since the second stays on the ground, and the one on the fourth beat is in the air. At the end do a *cadence* with that one; that is, bring your right foot (which was raised) back, and your left foot forward. Land agilely in this *cadence* (that is, with your left foot flat on the ground and your right on its toe), making it more graceful by separating your knees a little. Be careful when you do this *cadence* that your feet are not placed wrongly, but just far enough [apart] that your right toe is about four fingerbreadths away from your left heel. Keep your legs quite straight, and your toes turned up, for this way you can extend your knees better in doing the aforesaid *five steps* with a *cadence*; therefore your feet should be held straight at all times. Now put one hand (that is, your left) on the pommel of your sword to prevent it from dancing along as well, and keep your right hand straight down, moving it as seems most graceful to you (that is, do not hold it down stiffly, for then you would appear to have fractured or burned your arm; besides, it looks ugly). Nor do I wish you to move your fingers on that hand; but I would like you to hold yourself erect, with your head high. Do not, however, raise your eyes so awkwardly high as to arouse universal criticism, suggesting that you resemble an astrologer gazing at the stars; keep them level instead.

This is the basis of any kind of dance, and the fundamental law; the foot with which you begin must be the same with which you end; and once you have begun and ended the aforementioned *five motions* or *steps* (if you will) with your left foot, it is proper to do the same with your right foot (which is the left's brother). You should do the same [thing] in other dances or cascarde; that is, you should do as many variations (or sections) of a galliard with your left as with your right; and the same holds true for any type of dance, or any kind of action or movement—one foot [must move] as often as the other—or else the dance will be quite wrong. Now remember that if there are two variations in a dance, the same one that you do with your left [foot] must [then] be done with your right; so avoid the usual practise of some who, after performing a variation of four or six galliard patterns with the left, follow it with a different one with the right, though it may have the same number of patterns. Let me say that though such a variation may be correct [in itself] it does not follow the law I have given you, for your movements and actions must be reciprocal. And you should know that those people (however expert they may be considered in the galliard) who begin a variation with the left foot, and end it in time to the music with the right foot forward, are incorrect.

D.   Please, Master, proceed more slowly. It seems to me that such a variation would indeed be good, because it is done in time to the music, and agrees with your terms. For you have said that anyone desirous of being a good dancer must possess three characteristics: rhythm, grace, and measure. [13]

M.   My answer to your question is that this variation may be correct because it is graceful and concludes in time to the music, but let us see whether it is performed in a measured way. Now 'measure' simply means to do all things in a deliberate and orderly fashion, as I explained at the beginning of this rule, when I said that when you begin a variation with your left foot you must end it with that [foot]; this [principle] holds true for the *five motions,* or *steps* (if you will). Why, then, would one end them with the right [foot]? Now this would be a mistake on the teacher's part. To conclude, then, anyone who begins the *five steps* with his left [foot] must end them with the same [foot], and the same holds true for his right. Thus, in any variation, any kind of action, or any movement, whether in this dance (the galliard) or any other type of dance, each foot must have just as many movements as the other; if not, everything you do will be quite wrong. Always begin any type of dance with your left foot, and end it with the same [foot].

D.   If I remember correctly, you have just told me that every movement you do with your left [foot] you must repeat with your right. Why, then, should you begin [a dance] by making a *Reverence* with your left [foot], but are not required to end [by making a *Reverence*] with your right [foot] (thereby ensuring that the actions of one foot will be equalled by the other)?

M.   My answer is that I showed you clearly in the rule for the *Reverence* why you should always make it with your left foot. Now I repeat that a *Reverence* is like the door in the façade of a well-designed palace; anyone wishing to enter must go through that door, but he must also leave through the very same [door]; only the windows and other ornaments are symmetrical on either side. Therefore you do just the *Reverence* with your left [foot], while you do the other variations and actions symmetrically. Now I will proceed to explain *jumps;* and first of all, the *turning jump.*

Jumps [Salti]: First, the *Turning Jump [Salto tondo]*
RULE XXXVI

D.   Now you have certainly freed me of any doubts [I may have had], so please do the same for *jumps.*

---

[13]   *Tempo, Gratia, e Misura.*

M. Let me say that in order to do a *turning jump,* you start with feet together, jumping off both feet, raising your entire body as high as your strength will allow, turning to the left with two complete turns before landing on the ground so that you are facing in the same direction [from] the same spot as when you first began. Land on your toes, gracefully separating your knees a little. Now be careful to keep your legs quite straight as you jump. This is enough [information] about the first *jump;* let me now proceed to tell you about the *reversed jump.*

The *Reversed Jump* [*Salto riverso*]
RULE XXXVII

D. From what you say, I understand that there are various kinds of *jumps;* now what is this *reversed jump?*

M. Because of its nature, begin it as follows: with your feet parallel and somewhat apart, *hop* once with your right foot on the ground and your left foot raised backward; with that [left foot] do a *foot under* to your right foot, instantly raising your right foot forward; then turn your entire body to the right with a *turning jump,* landing on your toes [with feet close together] and knees a little apart to make them graceful. Now since you turn in the reversed direction, it has acquired the term, '*reversed jump*'. Let me now go on to the *jump to the tassel.*

The *Jump to the Tassel* [*Salto del Fiocco*]
RULE XXXVIII

D. How is this *jump* done?

M. Have the tassel held as high as a man—more or less, as one pleases—stand with your side turned toward the tassel; then raise your left foot somewhat (simultaneously lifting your right),[14] and turning your entire body to the left, while jumping as high as you can, crossing your right leg over your left, raising your [right] toe high enough to touch the tassel, and landing on the ground on the same spot as when you began, still with your right foot. I do not know what more I can say about these *jumps.* Now it is time to explain *capers.*

---

[14] '*Inarborando alquanto il piè sinistro, & ad un tempo medesimo levando il piè destro.*'

Capers [Capriole]: Triple, Quadruple, Quintuple, Broken in the Air [spezzata in aria], and Cross [intrecciata]

RULE XXXIX

D. It seems to me that no one can instruct more completely or better [than you]. Please proceed, therefore, and teach me the aforesaid *capers* as well.

M. You may learn the *triple caper* by leaning both hands on a chair, or holding onto a suspended rope. Keep your right foot ahead of your left (or your left ahead of your right), so that your left toe touches your right heel, and then raise yourself by the strength of your arms (which, like your legs, should also be held· quite straight); first pass your left foot (which was behind) [to the front] and then your right. Then pass your left once more; your feet should pass each other three times, as I have said, as quickly as possible, and end with your left foot forward, landing lightly on your toes. The term, '*caper*', is derived from this: that when a man does it he jumps [high], and moves his feet quickly forward and back like a kid.[15] It is termed *triple caper* because his feet pass each other three times. Let us go on now to the *quadruple caper.*

Quadruple and *Quintuple Capers,* and How To Do Them

RULE XL

D. I understand this; go on to the others also.

M. Do *quadruple* or *quintuple capers* in the same way, but now your legs pass each other four times for the *quadruple caper,* so that the last time your left foot, which was behind, is also behind on landing. Thus it is called *quadruple caper,* since your feet pass each other four times. And do the *quintuple caper* the same way, so that your feet pass each other five times. Keep your legs quite straight, letting yourself land, as above, lightly on your toes. If you exercise with this method you will easily learn how to do them without leaning on anything. Remember that your left foot, which has been behind, should be ahead when landing. And here I will conclude the explanation about them, going on instead to speak of *broken capers in the air.*

Broken Capers in the Air

RULE XLI

D. I pray you to discuss these *broken capers* with me.

M. Begin *broken capers in the air* by standing (as has been said) with your right foot a little ahead of your left; then raise your left [foot], and,

---

[15] I.e., young goat.

dropping it immediately, raise your right, drawing it quickly backward a little, and then thrusting it quickly forward. Then dropping your right [foot], repeat the same [thing] with your left. Always hold your body as erectly as possible. Now since these *broken capers* would be imperfect this way, complete them by jumping with a *quadruple* or *quintuple caper,* as seems most fitting, landing lightly at the end, as has been said above, with your feet in the same position as they were at the beginning; anything else would be quite wrong and very bad, which you must not forget. Now having said enough about this, I must still tell you about the *cross caper.*

The *Cross Caper*
RULE XLII

D. You have told me enough, and I thank you, but do go on to tell me about the *cross caper.*

M. Let me say that you can learn the *cross caper* better if you stand the same way as before, supported by your arms or holding onto the rope, as I said above. In leaving the ground, however, cross your left foot very quickly over your right; then, separating your feet a little, cross your right over your left, landing lightly on your toes with your right foot a little behind. Now do not land with your feet wide apart, as some do, for it looks horrible, but make each *cadence* graceful by separating your knees a little. Do it this way, and in no other way. The term comes from the crossing, or interlacing of the feet. Now let me tell you how to do the *changing,* or *exchanging step.*

How To Do the *Changing [Cambio],* or *Exchanging Step [Sciambiata]*
RULE XLIII

D. It seems to me that there is no more to be said about *capers.* Do be kind enough, therefore, to proceed by demonstrating the *changing,* or *exchanging step.*

M. Do the *changing,* or *exchanging step* (as you will) this way. Stand with your feet together, and move your left foot by thrusting it ahead of your right so that its heel is almost in a straight line with your right toe, though laterally half a handbreadth away from it, and keep your left foot quite flat on the ground with your legs straight. Then move your right foot, and put its toe behind your left heel, as in a *foot under,* simultaneously raising your left foot three fingerbreadths from the ground, and thrusting it as well three fingerbreadths directly ahead of your right toe; then bring it back, joining it to your right [foot], at the same time bending and separating your knees a little, and ending gracefully with feet together. Now it is called *changing* or *exchanging step* because it changes the movement with which it is done. Note that it is not possible to do more than one of these. Enough of this, so let me proceed to describe the *pulled step,* and the derivation [of the term].

How To Do the *Pulled Step* [*Trango*]
RULE XLIV

D. Please begin to tell me about this *pulled step.*

M. Do the *pulled step* by moving your left foot, thrusting it almost in a straight line one handbreadth ahead of your right [foot], yet flankingly; in putting it down, bend both knees simultaneously, separating them a little; and conclude by raising your right heel somewhat, in the course of one semibreve beat of music (now this occurs in 'Barriera'). Then immediately raise your right foot and your left heel, putting it down in the course of the same beat. Having done this with your left, thrust your right foot forward in the same way, continuing to repeat what you just did with the other foot. Thus you do every *pulled step* in the course of the aforesaid perfect beat of music. Nothing more is required, so let us now proceed to speak of the *limping hop.*

The *Limping Hop* [*Zoppetto*]
RULE XLV

D. Please do not omit an explanation of how to do this.

M. Do it this way: begin with your feet together or in some other position (depending upon the context in which it occurs in balletti or the galliard), and raise both feet, one a little off the ground and the other going ahead of it. Do as many [*limping hops*] as the variations call for, whether in the galliard or balletti. Now do them this way, keeping the one foot raised forward, and similarly raised to the side. The term, '*limping hop*', comes from this impression that you really are limping, for while one foot is raised forward, you rise, or hop along with your standing foot. Thus the name, '*limping hop*', is quite appropriate to it, for in truth, when you do this movement, it looks just exactly like someone limping. Thus I have shown you how to do this *hop,* and why it is so termed, so let me say no more about it, but go on to speak of the *little mill.*

The *Little Mill* [*Molinello*]
RULE XLVI

D. Now I will listen to what you promised to tell me about the *little mill*.

M. Perform the *little mill* by doing the *five steps of the galliard* twice, once turning left and once turning right, and always returning to your original position, facing [your partner]. One has termed these movements *little mill* from these full turns in *five steps,* or *five stamps* (as you will). Now let me go on to an explanation of the *foot under.*

The *Foot Under* [*Sottopiede*], and the Origin of the Term
RULE XLVII

D. Please do not postpone an explanation of the *foot under,* for I am quite eager to know about it.

M. The *foot under,* or *to the side,* is always done this way. First take one *step* or *falling jump* to the left with your left foot, and when landing on it lift your right (which was behind) and put it in place of your left foot (which is on its toe with its heel raised), simultaneously raising your left. And with [the left] you continue, repeating more of these *foot unders.* Now the name, *'foot under'*, is derived from this act of putting one foot behind the other, which you should do as I showed you. Now let me go on to teach you how to do the *step under.*

The *Step Under* [*Sommessa*]
RULE XLVIII

D. I am anxious to hear whatever it pleases you to say about this *step under.*

M. Do the *step under* as follows: with one foot flat on the ground (that is, your left) put your right toe under your left heel, as described above for the *foot under.* Now the name of *step under* derives from this placing under of your foot, which you must do in the manner I have described. And since I have nothing else to say about it, let me proceed to speak of the *tiny minced* [*jumps*].

The *Tiny Minced* [*Jumps*] [*Trito minuto*] in the Galliard and the
Origin of the Term[16]

RULE XLIX

D. You have been very brief; please do go on now to tell me something about
the *tiny minced jumps.*

M. Do the *tiny minced jumps* with your feet a little disparate, sometimes to
the right, and sometimes to the left, depending upon what is required in a
given variation. Starting with the front foot, do three *little bounds* to the
side very quickly and with very tiny [movements], with your feet a little
disparate and close together. If you do them to the left, your left foot
should be set down a little ahead of your right. Keep your toes pointed
straight ahead, however, with your heels up, and [see to it] that your legs
are kept quite straight also, and that they move with agility. If you do them
to the right, do them to the other side (that is, as stated above). Now this
movement is termed *tiny minced* [*jumps*] because your feet move in this
minutely minced and quick way, of which I now complete my discourse in
order to tell you about the *little bounds.*

The *Little Bounds* [*Balzetti*] with Feet Together
RULE L

D. I have understood this last rule very well indeed, and have a like desire to
understand whatever you would care to teach me about [the rule] for the
little bounds.

M. Begin these *little bounds* by standing with your feet together (you may also
do them with your feet slightly apart from each other by one or two
fingerbreadths), and jump about two fingerbreadths off the ground with
both feet, landing instantly, and keep them in the same position as when
you began, but at some distance from where you were originally. Now this
jumping [movement] by *little bounds,* now to the left and now to the right
(as need be), resembles large bounds,[17] and therefore has been termed *little
bounds,* which you do this way. Now let us speak of the *knot.*

The *Knot* [*Groppo*], as Done in Galliard Variations
RULE LI

D. Tell me whatever you choose about the knot, for I should like very much
to learn it.

M. Begin by standing with your left foot behind, and do a *falling jump* to the

---

[16]. This rule does not agree with the definition of the term given in, e.g., 'Spagnoletta Nuova'.

[17] Large bounds, or *balzi,* are not described by Caroso.

left, with this foot. As soon as you land cross (or, to say it better, knot) your right foot beind it. Then do another *falling jump* to your right with that [foot], crossing your left [foot] behind your right. Then do another *falling jump* to your left with the left foot, crossing your right behind it, as you did the first time, [but now] putting it in place of your left, do one *step under* with your right, simultaneously raising your left foot somewhat forward. This is how to end the *knot*. You do this in three galliard beats. Now the term is derived from this foot-crossing or knotting, and you must perform it with your feet properly knotted and close together. Now let me go on to an explanation of the *turn*.

The *Turn* [*Pirlotto*], or *Twirl* [*Zurlo*] *on the Ground,* and the
Derivation of the Term
RULE LII

D.   Master, I most heartily wish you would tell me how to do this *turn,* and the derivation of the term.

M.   Stand with your feet together and thrust your left [foot] half-a-foot forward. Then join your right foot to your left, and turn rapidly to the left, lifting both heels and keeping only the ball of your left foot on the ground. Make it more graceful by moving your right elbow out a little, turn around two or three times (or as many more times as you can), hold yourself erect, and end facing the same way [on the same spot], concluding gracefully by separating your knees a little. Be sure not to lean to either side as you do the *turn* (as some people do). Now it is termed thus because you turn like a top (also called 'spool' or 'ball of yarn') which turns as it unwinds.

The Shakes [*Tremolanti*]
RULE LIII

D.   I am waiting for you to tell me about the *shakes.*

M.   *Shakes* may be employed with any kind of *step,* and take the same [length of] time as a *grave step.* Do them this way: raise your left foot and move it extremely fast three times, shaking it both left and right, and put it down on the ground the last time. Then raise your right [foot] and repeat with it what you did with your left. Now the term, 'shakes', comes from those foot-shaking movements, and you do them this way. Let me say no more about them, but go on to speak of the *little side stamping step.*

The *Little Side Stamping Step* [*Costatetto*]
RULE LIV

D.   Please, Master, tell me about this as soon as possible, for it will please me immensely.

M.   Begin with your feet together, and move your left foot half-a-foot sideways from your right, which will come up as you raise yourself with a *little jump*. Then repeat this by moving your right foot to the [other] side, returning to the place where your left foot was originally. Now always do it on your toes and in this manner. Now the term for this movement, '*little side stamping step*', has been taken from these sideways stamps from side to side. Now I will tell you about the *little bell*.

The *Little Bell* [*Campanella*]: How To Do It, and the Derivation [of the Term]
RULE LV

D.   Do go on, and I shall listen eagerly.

M.   Begin the *little bell* by drawing back your left foot (which was forward) and at the same time hopping on your right with a *limping hop*. Now this requires one beat of the *little bell*. Then thrust your left [foot] forward, and do another *limping hop* simultaneously on your right; and this is another beat. Thus you may gracefully continue to practise it. In the same manner, you can do this while turning, taking care that the beat [of the *bell*] begins and ends in back. Thrust your foot backward and forward in a straight line this way, like the clapper which rings a bell. Do the first beat to ring it [the bell] in back, and when you wish it to stop ringing, ring it in back to finish. Thus this term, '*little bell*', was derived, for any other term it might be given would be wrong. Now this should be enough to enable you to learn it, so let me therefore go on to speak of the *chasing step*.

The *Chasing Step* [*Recacciata*]: How To Do It, and the Derivation of the Term
RULE LVI

D.   How delighted I am! Please do go on.

M.   Do one beat of the *little bell* backward with your left foot, which was forward; then, with the same [foot], do a *step under* (that is, a *foot under*) to the right, and these two movements take one musical beat. This is the way to do the *chasing step,* and then you should continue the same way with your right foot. Now the term, '*chasing step*', is derived from the effect of one foot chasing the other away. I cannot refrain, now, from discoursing on how to do those movements for the *toe and heel*.

The *Toe and Heel* [*Punta, e Calcagno*]
RULE LVII

D. I wish to learn these lovely steps very much; therefore I am prepared to listen to you.

M. These movements are executed with one *limping hop* on the ground with your right foot, at the same time touching the ground with your left toe four fingerbreadths from your right. Then do another *limping hop,* again with your right, touching the ground with your left heel, holding your [left] toe up four or five fingerbreadths from the ground. Finally, put your left foot down flat as in a *limping hop,* and repeat another *toe and heel* this way with your right [foot].

These movements have been given the term *toe and heel* from the way you touch one of your feet thus to the ground, alternating toe and heel. And now let me go on to explain the *sliding step.*

The *Sliding Step in the Canary* [*Schisciata del Canario*]: How To Do It, and the Derivation [of the Term]
RULE LVIII

D. I am waiting for you to tell me, Sir, why this movement is termed *sliding,* and how to do it.

M. Slide your heel forward, or push it forward with each *step,* shuffling forward on your heel and backward on your toe. The term has been applied from this manner of shuffling, or sliding, your feet. Now since nothing further occurs to me to tell you about it, the *cadence* remains to be explained.

The *Galliard Cadence* [*Cadenza in Gagliarda*]
RULE LIX

D. You dispatched that very quickly, so do let us go on to the *cadence.*

M. First raise your left foot forward, drawing yourself back and simultaneously rising somewhat off the ground, and then come down, landing with both feet on the ground (that is, with your left foot backward and your right forward). This movement has been termed 'cadence' from this way of landing with both feet at the same time. Now, when you come to the end of [performing] a certain variation, you should conclude it by doing this cadence with the foot which is already up. Since this is all I have to say about it, let me go on to explain the *stopped broken sequence.*

The *Stopped Broken Sequence* [*Spezzato Puntato*][18]
RULE LX

D.   If this movement is not too difficult, I should like to learn it immediately.

M.   Do this [step] just as I showed you in the rule for the *broken sequence,* except that in this case, when you do it with your left [foot], join your right foot [to your left] at the end of the *broken sequence.* This movement has been termed, '*stopped broken sequence*', from the act of stopping [the movement] with your [other] foot during the aforesaid *broken sequence* (which is not so difficult as you thought). Now let me tell you of the *feigned broken sequence.*

How To Do the *Feigned Broken Sequence* [*Spezzato finto*], and the Derivation of [the Term]
RULE LXI

D.   Be courteous enough to tell me, Master, if it is necessary [to know] this *feigned broken sequence.*

M.   Very necessary indeed, especially in cascarde and other dances where the sciolta occurs in the music for the dance (as, for instance, in 'Alta Vittoria'). For [there] one does two *broken sequences* backward (one with the left foot, and the other with the right); and with his left foot, which is now forward, he moves forward the same way. Now this is against the rule, and this movement is quite wrong indeed (as I told you in another of my rules), because the forward foot cannot step forward (for such a movement would be unnatural). Therefore one should learn [the *feigned broken sequence*], for it is very necessary indeed. Do it as follows: draw your right foot (which is forward) back on its toe; then do a *falling jump* with your left foot, and drop your right foot, which is now raised, straight down in the same place. It has been so termed because you pretend to go backward, but then return immediately to the same place. Now I have nothing further to say about it, but will go on to describe how to do the *altered broken sequence.*

The *Altered Broken Sequence in French Style* [*Spezzato Alterato alla Franzesa*], and the Derivation [of the Term]
RULE LXII

D.   Please, Sir, describe this *altered broken sequence* to me as soon as possible, for I would really like to learn it, especially since it is a movement in the French style.

---

[18]   *Spezzato puntato.* Caroso consistently shortens the term, '*seguito spezzato*' to '*spezzato*'.

M. We do this [type of] *broken sequence* in the dance [dedicated] to the
Queen of France,[19] and it can also be done in cascarde, because it is a most
graceful movement. Now to do this, it is necessary to do one *limping hop*
with your right foot flat on the ground, at the same time raising your left
[foot]; then, do an *ordinary broken sequence* with your left foot, and you
continue this way, one after the other. Because it is altered at the beginning
by doing the *limping hop*, it is called *altered broken sequence*. Now let me
not forget to explain the *altered double broken sequence*, which is a very
charming movement.

The *Altered Double Broken Sequence* [*Spezzato Doppio alterato*], and the
Derivation of the Term

RULE LXIII

D. I have enjoyed these steps so much, but this one has stood out, to my mind,
from the others. Now, however, please describe how to do this other
[step].

M. Let me say that in this *altered double broken sequence,* you do a *limping
hop* as explained above, and then drop your left foot (which is now raised),
putting it down as in a *step,* and immediately doing a *foot under* with your
right foot. Then repeat this by taking another *step* with your left foot, and
another *foot under* with your right. This is how to do it; and note that it
requires two triple beats. And if, instead of doing two *reprises* and two
falling jumps in a cascarda, you do two [of these steps] with the same foot,
observers will find you quite admirable and most graceful, for this is a new
step. It is called *altered double broken sequence* because it is changed and
is double the other one. Now I want to discuss the *dactylic, spondaic,
Sapphic, dexterous,* and *Corinthian steps.*

The *Dactylic Step* [*Dattile*]: How To Do It, and the Derivation of the
Term

RULE LXIV

D. Please, Master, describe and explain the derivation of this *dactylic step,*
and how to do it, for since in your other work there were no *dactylic,
spondaic, Sapphic, dexterous,* or *Corinthian steps,* I would like to know
about them.

M. Your desire pleases me immensely, so I will not refrain from making you
expert in these movements, nor [from giving you] the derivation [of these
terms]. Let me begin first with the *dactylic step,* and tell you that this is a

---

[19] 'Nuova Regina'.

Latin term, and that [the *step*] is done to the verses of Virgil or Ovid which, when scanned, consist of one long foot and two short [feet]. To do it, then, thrust the first *step* forward on your toe, as in a *falling jump,* in one musical beat, and do the next two *steps* quickly (that is, one minim for each, which will equal another beat), but with your feet flat on the ground, and adding grace to the first *step.* Now this is really the true *sequence,* [20] and this is how it should be termed and also how to do it, especially in the 'Ballo del Fiore' and the 'Contrapasso'. Thus, my Son, I have answered the question you asked of me, 'What is the derivation of this term?' by giving you the rule for how to do it. Now let me say that the term *dactylic step* derives from 'digit', which in the vulgar tongue comes from the second finger; that is, the one next to the broadest finger. This is indeed so, for that finger has three joints, and of the three, one is long and the other two are short (that is, smaller), so that the length of the one is equalled by the length of the other two, as you may easily see and measure right now. Now this is the reason for the derivation of the term from 'digit'. Enough of this, and remember it well, for you have never heard it from anyone else, as it is my own invention. Let me continue in like manner to describe the other four [*steps*] to you; but most importantly, the *spondaic step.*

How To Do the *Spondaic Step* [*Spondeo*], and the Derivation [of the Term]

RULE LXV

D. You have given me much joy, Sir, by letting me know about the *dactylic step.* Now I ask, since I am a student, that you do me the favor of teaching me how to dance this *spondaic step,* and then that you will deign to tell me the derivation of this term.

M. I shall be delighted to show you this, and will also tell you how [the term] was derived. You should know how gratified I am to understand that you are a [real] student, [21] for now I am even happier to instruct you. Now then, when you read Ovid or Virgil and scan their lines, you are quite aware that there are dactyls and spondees in them. I have [just] described how to do the *dactylic step* and the derivation [of the term]. Let me tell you now that the *spondaic step* contains two long feet, so that to dance it you do two *semibreve steps* (that is, one beat of music for each foot), and this is how to do it. The term, then, is derived from the broadest finger of the hand because it has two joints of equal length, as you can [see when you] measure them; and since this finger borders on the other fingers, the name,

---

[20] In Rule XVI Caroso gives the rhythm for the *ordinary sequence* as ♩ ♩ ○ , while here he reverses it. See also rhythm given on the diagram for the 'Contrapasso', p. 243.

[21] I.e., a serious university student versed in the classics.

'*spondaic step*', was derived from it.[22] Notice that in Ovid's first line, which says:

Hanc tua Penelope, lento tibi mittit Ulisses,[23]

there are four dactyls and two spondees. Remember, therefore, that in order to dance properly and according to the fundamental law, you must make as many movements with your left foot as with your right; that is, two *dactylic steps* and one *spondaic step* for each foot. By thus following my rule, all your dancing will be quite correct, and none will criticize you; on the other hand, if you allow one foot more movements than the other during any balletto, you will be absolutely wrong in every case (as I have mentioned elsewhere, in the rule for the *five steps* in the galliard). Now it remains for me to tell you how to do the *Sapphic step*.

How To Do the *Sapphic Step* [*Saffice*], and the Derivation [of the Term]
RULE LXVI

D. Master, this term, '*Sapphic step*', seems very suggestive[24] to me; nor have I ever heard any other master speak of it. Therefore I pray you, if you truly love me (as I believe you do), teach it to me, and tell me how it was given this term.

M. Willingly, my Son. For this *Sapphic step* you should do one *reprise with foot under* with your left foot to the left, and a *falling jump* with the same foot, and then repeat to the right. [Do these *steps*] where a *broken sequence* was done formerly, which on occasion turned out to be problematic in certain dances (especially in cascarde), because one's feet would end up in the wrong position. If you do it this way, however, you will be quite correct in any dance (and also in cascarde). Now let me go on to clear up the question of the derivation of the term, '*Sapphic step*': *idest* [*sic*] *ad sufficientiam rei, & motorum.*[25] Or, to speak plainly in the vernacular, this *Sapphic step* completely suffices for all difficult movements, and by using it you may bring any dance to true perfection. From this sufficiency, therefore, it has acquired the term, '*Sapphic step*', which seems so indecent to you. In addition to all this, however, I shall not fail to show you how to do the *dexterous step*.

---

[22] Caroso treats '*spondeo*' and '*sponda*' as the same word.

[23] This is the first line of the first poem of Ovid's *Heroides*, 'This thy Penelope slowly sends to you, Ulysses'.

[24] The Disciple seems to imply here a derivation from Sappho.

[25] . . . it is entirely adequate for everything and every moment . . .

How To Do the *Dexterous Step* [*Destice*], and Why It Is So Termed
RULE LXVII

D. How grateful I am for the evidence you have given me, Sir, which has made me expert in the fundamental law you have formulated. I wish, however, that you will not hesitate to show me this *dexterous step,* nor [to tell me] its derivation.

M. These questions of yours thrill and delight me, and I absolutely glory in them, for now I know that you are a [serious] student and want to learn in detail the first and last names of all the movements appropriate to all types of dances. I shall not be ungracious in showing them to you, therefore, so that you may be thoroughly in possession of them. To do this *dexterous step,* then, follow the same rule as for the *Sapphic step,* except that in this *step* it is necessary to do two *reprises with foot under* and a *falling jump* with your left side in, by moving your body agilely. And move the same way and do the same things with your right side in. Now follow this rule to do it, for it is an extremely necessary [*step*], whether in balletti or in cascarde. The derivation of the term now remains to be told. Let me say that when you do it you *dexterously* [manoeuvre] your body (first one side and then the other), which appears very graceful to any bystanders; from such dexterity, then, the movement has acquired the term *dexterous step.* Let me not fail, however, to show you how to do the *Corinthian step.*

How To Do the *Corinthian Step* [*Corinto*], and the Derivation [of the Term]
RULE LXVIII

D. You should know, Sir, how charmed I am at your having explained your rules so clearly, and answered, I do confess, so many questions so perfectly and correctly. Last of all, teach me how to do this *Corinthian step,* and then tell me the derivation [of the term]; for among the five orders of architecture, the Corinthian is the fourth. I hope, then, that you will not wait to speak of this, which is so highly important to me.

M. Let me respond to this last question that it is quite true that in architecture there is a Corinthian style belonging to the fourth order, and I admit that this architecture is most accurate. You should know, then, that I have imitated it; for as you can see in the frontispiece to this work, everything is executed according to true architectural law. Thus, for illustrating one of the two mottoes are a compass and a timepiece,[26] and the motto around them says, 'Rule, Time and Measure'.[27] Let me say, then, that should an

---

[26] *Oriolo.* The frontispiece shows an hourglass.

[27] See frontispiece. '*Regola*' (Rule) is omitted.

architect who is less than first-rate plan a beautiful palace and complete it, it may contain sundry defects. Despite this, and though it will always be subject to criticism for such defects, it will not cease to be termed a palace. [True perfection, however,] requires one to be as supremely excellent in his work as the great Michel Angelo Buona Rota, who, whether in painting, sculpture, or architecture, was unique in all the world; in Rome [for example] you may see the beautiful grand palace [of] the Most Serene Duke of Parma, as well as the façade of the Church of Jesus (one of the great wonders of the world). There you may see that all is truly ordered, even the letters which are equidistantly inscribed on the aforementioned façade. Thus, though many [practitioners] in all sciences may be called masters, few are truly perfect. Therefore, in this profession, all who follow it must do so according to basic laws and theoretical perfection, and not just because of [common] practise. Now to do this *Corinthian step* do three *reprises* with your left foot, and one *falling jump* sideways, and repeat with your right foot. This term is derived from the way these graceful movements pull at the heartstrings, causing onlookers to become enamoured of them, so I have termed it thus. Now I have given you all the rules and answered all your questions about [dance] movements.

Dialogue
Between a Disciple and His Master, on the Conduct Required of Gentlemen and Ladies at a Ball and Elsewhere

How a Gentleman Should Wear His Cape and Sword at a Ball, and
Elsewhere Than at a Ball

NOTE 1

D. Now that you have completed the discussion of the [dance] movements,
Sir, I would be delighted if you would teach me that attractive and
chivalrous conduct that is fashionable today, both in dancing and
otherwise, since it appears to be of such great importance.

M. This honest desire of yours pleases me, so I shall not fail to gratify it. Let
me say, then, that [whether] in balletti or grave basse [dances], you wear
your cape or riding cloak[1] with its edges down, and equal [in length]; then
with your left arm lift half of its left side, putting it over your left shoulder.
Be careful not to cover the hilt of your sword, and clasp [your cloak] with
your left arm so that it will not drop, placing its edge behind your
swordhilt; for if you wear it with both sides down, without raising it [the
left side], you look like a pedant; furthermore, if the cape is made of
sarcenet or light cloth, it may easily fall off, which is inappropriate for a
gentleman, especially when dancing the galliard, or the 'Pavaniglia',
'Tordiglione', cascarde, and other heightened[2] dances. Wear your cape or
riding cloak, then, as shown in the figures for the 'Pavaniglia' and
'Tordiglione'.[3] Now if you do dances in which one takes both hands [of his

---

[1] Florio: *'Ferraiolo,* . . . a riding-cloake'.

[2] *'alterato'.* All of these dances are lively, consisting of a series of variations 'breaking up', or
dividing the note values by means of combined hops, kicks, and jumps and rapid steps, i.e., all
movements are off the ground.

[3] There is no figure for the 'Tordiglione' in this volume or *Il Ballarino*. The 'Pavaniglia' in this
collection is 'Amorosina Grimana', p. 102, the figure for which shows a short cloak worn almost
evenly on both sides, and not wrapped around as described. This illustration is identical for the
'Pavaniglia' in *Il Ballarino*. See the figures on pp. 346, 347, & 352 for the long cape treatment
Caroso seems to be describing. See figures on pp. 350 & 351 for uneven wearing of the short cape.

partner], wear it as shown in the figure for the dance called 'Contentezza d'Amore'.[4] Be careful never to dance without your cape, because this looks most unsightly, and is not appropriate to the nobility. When a gentleman wears a sword while dancing these lively dances, he should hold it with his left hand, so that it will not wave around wildly; also if he finds himself dancing in a very small space, he should hold it [still] with his left hand, turning it a bit by that hand so that the point will hang forward in order to avoid offense to those seated behind him. If you have space, however, allow it to move as usual. Be careful not to push down on your sword hilt to such an extent that the tip points skyward, for if you do so, you resemble a Spanish Captain playing his part in the Commedia,[5] and you will be mocked at and ridiculed, rather than appreciated, by any onlookers. After you have taken leave of your lady, and as you return to your seat, pay due respect to those near where you will be sitting with a small salutation; and with your hat in your right hand, and your left hand turning your sword toward the front.

How Gentlemen Should Conduct Themselves When Attending Parties

NOTE II

D. Please, Master, I pray you to teach me the gentleman's comportment at a party.

M. I will do so, if you are patient. Let me say, then, that there are some gentlemen who go to parties wearing gloves so tightfitting that, upon being invited to dance by the ladies, and preparing to take hands, they must take more time than an 'Ave Maria' to remove [them]; and if they do not succeed with their hands, they even use their teeth! When they do this, some accidentally drop their capes (or riding cloaks). This also pays little honour to the lady who has invited one, by making her wait so long. It is better, then, to wear gloves that are fairly loose rather than too tight, for on occasion I have seen [a gentleman], on trying to remove them with his teeth, who has had one finger of the glove left in his mouth, while all in attendance at the party laughed at this behaviour.

D. Is there anything else you wish to advise me of, Sir?

M. Yes, of course. Let me say, then, that there are others who, while dancing a grave dance, or promenading with a lady, take one side of their cape in their left hands and put it over their left shoulders, leaving the other [end] hanging down so far that it trails along the ground, which is awkward and doesn't look well; for though ladies are permitted to trail their dresses, or

---

[4] See page 353.

[5] 'che recita in comedia'. [sic] This refers to the stock character in the Commedia del'Arte.

trains (if you will), this is not suitable for a gentleman. There are still others who wear their [cloaks] even more improperly while dancing, for they wrap themselves up as if swaddled, which has two unfortunate consequences: first, that they cover their swordhilts; and the other is that the swords are so obstructed that if they should be needed, they could not be [got at], thereby endangering their lives, which is a bad and perilous habit. So I advise you to wear your cape, or any mantle with which you cover yourself, in the style I have shown you above, and always to shun this bad behaviour since it displeases everyone, and could cause the entire company to ridicule you.

Another Way to Wear the Items Mentioned Above
NOTE III

D. I am quite pleased with this excellent information, but now please tell me, if you will, whether the mantles of which we have spoken are not worn differently on certain ceremonial occasions.

M. Yes they are, but since this is a matter outside my profession I had not planned to discuss it with you; now that you have asked me about it, however, I feel constrained to give you my opinion. You need to know, then, that should a prince or gentleman be required to approach a great king to kiss his hand, the sides of his cape or mantle (whichever it is) should be of equal length, for aside from the fact that [any unevenness] looks quite ugly, it is also necessary that he reveal the front of his body, and keep his hands down, holding both ends of his cape or riding cloak with them, so that the king will have no reason whatsoever to suspect him of carrying something beneath them that could harm him (as we have seen occur in our own day, and not too many years since). It is good, therefore, to reveal your hands and to wear your cape or riding cloak as I have said above. Moreover, you should doff your bonnet (or hat) as I have taught in the rule for doffing the bonnet; you should doff it with your right hand, changing it to your left hand as soon as you have removed it, and turning the inside of your bonnet toward the thigh corresponding to the hand in which you hold it. Upon appearing in the hall (or room) where the king is, immediately make a *grave Reverence;* then take four or six steps forward, and make another [*Reverence*]; and when you are a short distance from His Majesty, make the last one very low, so as almost to touch the floor with your knee, pretending to kiss the king's knee. Then look up and kiss your petition, accompanying this act with another *Reverence,* and presenting it to him. After this, having achieved your purpose, or a suitable answer from His Majesty, take leave of him, once again pretending to kiss his knee. You ought to know that in making the last

Reverence you should not face His Majesty, but [should face] a little to the side, so that the king is on your right; if the king is seated, however, and you are standing, face him directly. Should the king walk along with you, stay a step behind him at all times. In turning, follow the commendable Spanish fashion of falling back three steps, always keeping His Majesty on your right. When taking your leave, make a *Reverence* by bowing so low that your knee almost touches the ground (as I have said above); and upon rising, retire by making three more *Reverences* without ever turning your back upon the king. Now I have nothing more to tell you about this.

How a Gentleman Should Be Seated
NOTE IV

D. Master, please do not fail to tell me how a gentleman should be seated, since this is important to know.

M. Sit with your left arm completely stretched out on one arm of the chair, and your right (which has the simple but joint duties of commanding and of learning) resting similarly on the other arm, but in such a way, that your right hand drops from your wrist. Now you may also lean your elbow [on the chair arm], so that from that point on your arm faces your right thigh. Both styles are commendable. [You may] be more graceful still by holding a handkerchief, gloves, or a flower, in that [hand]. Be careful that when you lean back you do not lean too far, because then your feet will necessarily have to come off the ground, and this, besides appearing ugly and disgusting to those present, is more tiring than relaxing, since your feet are not resting on the floor. In order, then, that as a gentleman you should not be universally criticized, you should sit halfway on the chair, because by so doing your feet will reach the ground (or paved floor), equally. Make sure that your feet are almost together, and not crossed, or wide apart, as is the habit with some. Now in this fashion you will sit like a true gentleman, according to all the rules, with absolute decorum, and with greater repose. Take care also that you do not wear your bonnet (or hat) so low that your eyes are just barely seen, nor that you wear it on one side of your head, as some do, for this looks ugly to those around you.

How Gentlemen Should Comport Themselves at a Ball
NOTE V

D. Master, will you not give me some instructions on the conduct of gentlemen at a ball?

M. Of course I will, although from what I have already said here, everyone may learn how to pay court, and what etiquette is fashionable and required at a ball. So let me just say that when a prince or a gentleman who has come to a ball is invited [to dance] by a lady, it is improper for anyone else to take his [seat], and should you do so, it would be reasonable to return it with good grace when he has stopped dancing; and if, out of excessive modesty, he desires you not to rise, pretend at least to do so, in order to return his seat to him, as is your duty. If the aforementioned seat is a stool, and the other will not consent to your rising, [then] offer him half of it, so that he will not be constrained to remain standing. Now, by doing this (in addition to being praised and loved by all), you will have acted as befits a well-bred gentleman, and have given no cause for picking a quarrel (though often enough one may see the contrary come to pass), for the company has gathered to be gay.

It is the custom to invite cardinals to parties of importance (that is, for the nobility), and to seat them according to precedence; dukes, princes, marquises, counts, lords, and knights should take the places assigned them in the same way, for this is required by the chivalric code. Do not follow the current habit whereby, if one person is already seated (having arrived first at the ball), another will have a chair brought for him (whether high or low), and have it placed in front of the prince who was already seated there; then others follow suit, putting themselves directly in front of cardinals, lords, or ambassadors, and finally encroaching on the dancing place. They do this only so as to be invited to dance by the ladies, and knights and gentlemen follow their example, also placing themselves in front and creating an uproar. Sometimes when there is no room to dance, or when the gentlemen are seated [too] close to the ladies, the sponsors of the ball call it off much sooner than they would have otherwise; even worse, it has happened on occasion that quarrels have arisen from this [situation]. Thus it is good to observe the rules of decent and honourable conduct, for by so doing, one will be welcomed and beloved by ladies as well as by gentlemen.

Further Recommendations to Princes, Lords, and Gentlemen
NOTE VI

D. You would do me a favour, Sir, by giving me some advice on the manner in which princes, lords, and gentlemen should dance.

M. Some of those mentioned above may choose to do the dance called 'Il Furioso', for six, twelve, or even eighteen people, depending upon the capacity of the ballroom (or [dancing] place) to handle such a group (or number) of people. Such a prince (or gentleman), who would like to begin this dance, should choose nine ladies, and place them in a line at one end of the hall (or dancing place); then he should invite eight princes (or gentlemen) [to dance], and after having been chosen they should place themselves at the other end [of the room]. [Now sometimes] when the master of ceremonies commands the instrumentalists to play this balletto, the aforementioned lords and gentlemen take longer than [the time] to recite the 'Credo' to get into place, simply because there are two or three very beautiful women with whom each of them would like to dance; so that the leader who initiated the dance ends up by not dancing with the lady he chose first (and with whom he should, properly, remain to dance upon the conclusion of 'Il Furioso'), but instead is left by this disorder to dance with another lady—and as a result the gentleman indeed pays her no favour, but rather demeans her. Now, then, to avoid the scandals that might ensue at this point, it would be proper for the prince (or gentleman) who leads the dance and invites the ladies, to think carefully about claiming the one he considers the most beautiful [lady] at the ball (or she who best suits his taste), and to place her at the head of the line, so that she remains to his right. After having chosen the gentlemen, he must certainly place himself opposite her, and the others will follow suit one after the other. Thus scandals will be avoided, and she who was first will remain to dance, and the gentleman [who leads] will never have to dance with any 'plain Janes'.

When Dancing the Balletto Called 'Contrapasso', or The 'Ballo del Fiore', Follow the Same Procedure, or Rule
RULE VII

D. There are some who are of the opinion, Master, that when dancing the 'Ballo del Fiore', the prince (or gentleman, whichever it may be) is free to give the flower to any one of the ladies he likes who perform this dance. Is this so, or not?

M. Let me say in answer to this that in this dance it is unseemly to give the flower to anyone other than the lady he invited first, for she deserves this honour since she took precedence over all others as first choice; one should do this also in the balletto called 'Contrapasso in a Circle', as well as in the dance called 'Il Furioso'.

How Superfluous Formalities Should be Shunned
NOTE VIII

D. I should like to know whether or not it is a fault to be extremely formal.

M. You need to be aware that unnecessary, empty and precious courtesies are scarce-hidden flatteries; on the contrary, [they are] so clear and obvious to all that those who make too many *Reverences* (by sliding their feet, kissing their hands or doffing their bonnets while bowing and scraping before their favourite ladies) lose just as much [favour in the eyes of others] as they think to gain, for their blandishments only displease and bore them. Those who strive to behave so affectedly and unsuitably do so from thoughtlessness and vanity, like men of little worth, as the *Galateo* says.[6] Others are too verbose and overly polite in order to compensate for the defects of their base and lowly natures; be advised, that were they as brief and sparing with words as they are in deeds, none could suffer them, and that's the truth.

Appropriate Conduct for Ladies When Attending Weddings and Festive Occasions
NOTE IX

D. Up to this point you have taught me the comportment for gentlemen; now I would like to know that for ladies.

M. I was about to do so. Let me say, then, that it is more essential for ladies to learn good manners and how to comport themselves honourably than anything else; and this is even more true for those who are of noble or princely [blood]. For if they do not know how to behave, all who observe them will say, 'This woman acts the great lady, but she is unworthy', as they will not perceive that this is [simply] the result of ignorance. Thus it is necessary, first, for a lady to learn how to make a *grave Reverence* and when to bow, and how to do these gracefully; then [second] she should learn to wear her chopines [properly]; third, how and according to what principles to walk and move gracefully; fourth, how to salute a princess or another lady; fifth, how to be seated; sixth, how to arise from a seated position, and how to take her leave; seventh, proper style and rules of etiquette when she calls upon a new bride; eighth, what to do before taking a gentleman's hand when she has been invited to dance; ninth, how to take her leave [at the end] of the dance; tenth, how to comport herself at a ball when she has not been taken out to dance; and finally, how to make her departure.

How to Learn the *Grave Reverence*
NOTE X

D. Please go on to describe each of the abovementioned headings, so that I shall know how to teach them to my womenfolk.

M. First of all, [a lady] should learn how to make a *grave Reverence* thus: that is, beginning with feet together, she draws her left foot back three or four

---

[6] Book of etiquette by Giovanni Della Casa (Milan: 1559). Caroso's Note VIII is a paraphrase of Della Casa's passage on *'le cerimonie vane, isquisite & soprabondanti',* p. 21.

fingerbreadths, keeping it completely flat; then she bows, inclining her body a little before bending her knees [but] with head erect. Now as soon as she has bowed, she should slowly straighten up, joining that [left] foot [to the other] in place. Be careful not to adopt the habit of some who first draw their bodies back while bending deeply, and then thrust their bodies forward (a movement so unseemly that were I to say what it resembles, everyone would die laughing). Still others bend so very straight down and then rise, that they truly resemble a hen about to lay an egg.

How a Lady Should Walk, and How To Wear Chopines Properly
NOTE XI

D. With regard to the first [recommendation] you have satisfied me completely; now let us go on to the second.

M. Some ladies and gentlewomen slide their chopines along as they walk, so that the racket they make is enough to drive one crazy! More often they bang them so loudly with each step, that they remind us of Franciscan friars.[7] Now in order to walk nicely, and to wear chopines properly on one's feet, so that they do not twist or go awry (for if one is ignorant of how to wear them, one may splinter them, or fall frequently, as has been and still is observed at parties and in church), it is better for [the lady] to raise the toe of the foot she moves first when she takes a step, for by raising it thus, she straightens the knee of that foot, and this extension keeps her body attractive and erect, besides which her chopine will not fall off that foot. Also, by thus raising it she avoids sliding it along [the ground], nor does she make any unpleasant noise. Then she should put it down, and repeat the same thing with the other foot (which follows). In this way, and by observing [this rule], she may move entirely with grace, seemliness, and beauty, better than the way one walked before; for a natural step is one thing, but a well-ordered step is another. By walking this way, therefore, even if the lady's chopines are more than a handbreadth-and-a-half high, she will seem to be on chopines only three fingerbreadths high, and will be able to dance *flourishes* and galliard variations at a ball, as I have just shown the world this day.

---

[7] Florio, p. 616: '*Zoccolanti,* certain Franciscan friars that goe on high wooden pattens or startops'.

The Manner in Which a Lady Should Greet a Princess and Other Ladies at a Party
NOTE XII

D. Since I am now quite expert in this as well, please go on to the third point.

M. In general, all princesses are extremely courteous in giving to and receiving honour from the ladies who come to call, but some callers may misbehave, either because they do not know proper deportment, or because they are too arrogant to observe good manners. Those who are ignorant of them should learn them willingly, so that when they find themselves at an aristocratic ball, and are invited to dance, they will not be treated with scorn by the other [ladies]. Now as soon as a lady espies a princess or noblewoman (whichever the case), she should step out and go toward her; and before approaching her, she should make a *half Reverence* (that is, a little bow), and when she has come close she should kiss her own right hand (without, however, bringing it near her mouth, but holding it at some distance), bending it a little, and not holding it so rigidly that it appears to be crippled. While moving this way, she should make a *grave Reverence,* as indeed I showed you, pretending to kiss the princess's right hand. If she is not the equal of that particular princess or great lady, however, she should pretend to kiss the [princess's] knee. Then the princess should make a *Reverence,* making the same [gestures] as if she were her equal; if [she is] not she should pretend to raise her with her [own] hands, taking the visitor's left hand in her right hand. This is even more appropriate if she is her equal, for anyone who is paid a visit should always receive the caller most warmly and affectionately. Should the hostess wish to put the caller on her own right to honour her, however, the visitor should never permit it.

How a Lady Should Be Seated, Whether At a Ball or Elsewhere
NOTE XIII

D. Do go on now to show me how a lady should be seated at a ball, for this will be very important to me.

M. There are many and various ways of seating oneself, or even after being seated, or (to say it better) while sitting down. Those who tend to seat themselves without regard to any mannerly or formal standard, sit down carelessly, leaving their trains outside their chair (either toward the left or right, depending upon how they have seated themselves). Once seated, they then seek to draw them [the trains] close to themselves with their foot, exactly as cats do (to speak disrespectfully), in a most unsightly style. Others habitually take the backs of their dresses in their right hands before seating themselves, raising them so that their trains will not remain outside the chair [legs], but this too is a disgraceful habit, resembling that which modesty forbids me to mention! Should a lady desire to seat herself, then, with the utmost grace, beauty, and charm with which she may flatter her own person, she would do well if, before she were seated, she would turn her face and body toward the princess, or other noblewoman she is calling upon, gracefully turning her hip slightly and strutting a little. [Then she should] employ the farthingale (or hoop skirt) under her dress, to assist her in putting her train in the space between the legs of her chair. To do this, she should approach the chair (or seat, if you will) with her back directly to it, and from about half an arm's-length away, whence she should make a *Reverence* to the princess, or anyone else sitting there, acknowledging her before she seats herself. Then she should turn to her right, graciously acknowledging the other lady. When seating herself, she should not raise her train at all (which would be ill-mannered), but should approach and place her train under the chair. Now approaching [the chair] more closely, she should seat herself halfway [back] on it; for if she were to seat herself [all the way] back, her farthingale would raise her dress so high in front, that those facing her might see as much as half her legs, but if she were to sit (as I have said) halfway on her chair, her feet would touch the floor equally, and so would her farthingale and dress. Be careful that chopines are never revealed. When ladies raise their dresses the other way, however, the poor things must beat on them with both hands as if they were shaking out dust or fleas to lower them and keep them down properly, but even so their farthingale strings will not allow their dresses to be lowered. Now all of this is most unseemly conduct. Others, while seating themselves, raise their farthingales to the waist with their right hands, and then let them fall, and I believe they do this ostentatiously to show off their beautiful underdresses (or petticoats) to their observers. Let me say that this too is quite unseemly. Sometimes (as master of ceremonies), I have seen some who, though expecting to raise only their farthingales, accidentally grasped their petticoats too, thus revealing such things as modesty will not permit me to mention! By following the rule and procedure I have just demonstrated, however, they may look most charming. Now, after having seated herself, the seated lady should turn her head to her left and acknowledge the lady on her left, resting her left arm completely on the arm of her chair, with her right elbow resting [on the other arm], and her right hand toward her lap. At times she may handle a handkerchief or fan, if it is summer, or she may hold a muff, or snuffkin (as some call it) if it is winter. Take note that she should not sit [as still] as a statue, but from time to time should move in one way or another, whether by putting on her gloves, or (if it is summer) gracefully fanning herself, or by doing her best to maintain a conversation with those sitting nearby. Above all, however, her eyes should be modest and should not rove here and there, or she may not be esteemed as a lady of discretion and worth, but deemed one of vanity instead.

How To Sit on a Low Chair Without Arms
NOTE XIV

D. You have spoken in general terms about how one should be seated; I would like you to go into detail.

M. Let me go on to say that a lady should proceed the same way when she prepares to sit on a low chair; but since it has no arms, she should keep her hands in her lap, her left hand under her right; and her dress should in like manner remain touching the floor.

The Conduct of a Lady When Dancing
NOTE XV

D. It seems to me that you have said enough about the good manners required of a lady when seating herself; now I would like you to tell me something about those she should use when dancing.

M. When a lady dances backward, she should never use her hands to lift her train or the trail[8] of her dress, for this looks most unseemly, except when she finds herself in such a narrow space that she cannot do otherwise. Instead she should dance the first step backward with grace (whether a *reprise* or a *Sapphic step*), strutting a little and moving in a snakelike way with a slight swaying of her dress and the farthingale underneath it, thus obtaining the same effect much more gracefully than by lifting it in the other way. She should also remember not to raise her eyes too high while dancing, as some do, nor to turn her head hither and thither in order to look at this or that gentleman, for this is a thing of vanity.

What a Lady Should Do When Attending a Wedding, and Her Conduct When She Calls Upon the Bride
NOTE XVI

D. You have satisfied me greatly on this matter; do proceed now to other manners.

M. When a lady attends a [wedding] festivity, especially if she is a lady of rank, she should go directly to the bride, and make a *Reverence* upon

---

[8] '*strascino*.' Florio, 'the traile . . . of a . . . Ladies garment'.

approaching her, kissing her own right hand; at that moment, the bride [who is] with the other ladies seated at this party should rise from her chair, and should also gracefully kiss her own right hand; then taking hands and making a *Reverence,* they should exchange pleasant words. Then that lady should also salute the other ladies who have paid her honour. Now keep in mind that one should not be seated by the bride's side (if there is room), unless invited to do so by the bride (or unless her family gives her a seat), for that would be unmannerly. When the bride is seated, all the others should then be seated. In addition, when elsewhere than at a ball, if a lady or gentlewoman calls upon a lady who is with child, she should apply the same [rules of] etiquette.

The Comportment of a Bride Who Has the Honour To Receive a Princess at Her Wedding
NOTE XVII

D. Now I should like to know the proper conduct of a bride who has the honour to receive a princess at her wedding.

M. When a duchess or princess appears in the hall, the bride should rise to her feet, as well as the others who are seated, and she and her mother, or sisters, or relatives should approach her, and make a *grave Reverence* upon nearing [the great lady], pretending to kiss their own hands. Then [the bride] should take the princess's left hand in her right hand, giving her precedence even though she may not wish to accept it, conducting her to her own [the bride's] seat, and making another *Reverence* to her before [the bride] seats herself. The princess should repay the honour to the bride before being seated. Now those ladies who have paid honour to her by making a *Reverence* together to her, will not be seated ahead of the princess. Then the bride should engage the princess in pleasant and delectable conversation, as is the custom among women.

Etiquette for a New Bride When a Princess Chooses to Depart Before the Ball is Over
NOTE XVIII·

D. Now that you have taught me the proper and good manners for a bride who has the honour to receive a princess at her wedding, it will not be such a difficult matter to teach me how she should conduct herself when the same princess departs.

M. Most willingly. Upon noticing that the princess has risen, she should rise immediately, and so should the other ladies; then, should the princess make a *Reverence* to her, it behooves the bride and the others to do the same. The bride should turn her head towards the others, paying her respects to them, as if excusing herself, as she must accompany the noblewoman. Then the bride should place herself to the left of the lady, and if, out of modesty, she does not wish to be so accompanied, the bride (and her relatives) should not hesitate to attend her to the door of the hall, kissing the princess's hand, making a *grave Reverence,* and expressing gratitude that Her Excellency deigned to favour her with her presence. Upon returning to her seat, [the bride] should then make another *Reverence* to the other ladies, and they should all be seated simultaneously. When another lady departs, the bride should rise to her feet, and make a *Reverence* to her, thanking her, kissing her own hand, and touching the other's; then she should be seated again, and so on.

A Lady's Conduct When Inviting a Gentleman To Dance
NOTE XIX

D. You have fully satisfied me as to what I wished to know; I pray you now to describe the comportment for ladies when asking gentlemen to dance.

M. [Sometimes] during a dance, some new brides and other ladies cast their eyes so low that the gentlemen cannot tell which one of them has been invited [to dance], so that one rises to his feet rather than the other. Or sometimes, in their great eagerness to dance, they [all] give her their hands, with the result that she does not know which one to take. It would be better, then, for a lady to keep her eyes level, and when she chooses to invite some gentleman, to look at him [directly], so that those sitting near to or behind him will not need to rise, thus avoiding any ensuing scandal. Now as he rises, the gentleman whom she has invited should remove his right glove (if he is wearing it) at the same time as she makes a *Reverence* to him, and she should pretend to adjust her dress, making it sway, strutting slightly, and turning a bit sideways toward the one she has just invited. On occasion a gentleman may wear his gloves so tightly that removing his right glove takes longer than saying an *'Ave Maria',* as I have said above. It is not proper, however, for the lady to remain directly facing [the gentleman], for it would look as if they were making love; therefore gentlemen should wear their gloves a little loose rather than tight.

Other ladies invite a gentleman [to dance] while he is talking with another; then someone [else] seated behind or near that one who is seated may rise to his feet, and the lady may insult him, saying that she has invited that other and not him. This is unseemly, for once he has risen to his feet, she should respect his honour by dancing with him.

Still other ladies invite gentlemen to dance who are seated or standing toward the back by beckoning [to them] with their hands or their heads, or occasionally even calling them by name, all of which is unseemly behaviour. It is instead appropriate for ladies to dance with discretion, modesty, grace, and good manners; should they do otherwise, they will be taxed by all those present (and by the ladies as well), with poor breeding.

Further Good Manners for Ladies When Taking Leave
NOTE XX

D. I am waiting, Sir, for you to tell me also how ladies should behave when they take their leave at the end of a dance.

M. I would like to satisfy you, so let me say that once a dance is over, the lady should turn gracefully and make a *Reverence* to her partner, without kissing her hand at all. I would also not want to fail to mention that there are ladies so incautious that, when one [of them] is invited to dance, another who was seated nearby will take the seat of the one who has gone to dance; thus, when the lady [who has been dancing] takes her leave of the gentleman and goes to her seat, she finds that it has been taken; to follow proper etiquette, therefore, it would be suitable for her to find a seat elsewhere. Now this is also wrong, for the proverb says, 'Do unto others, as you would have them do unto you'.

There are other [ladies] who prevent a lady who has taken her leave after a dance from returning to her seat, because they are seated in such a great crowd. Now the others should draw aside and make room for her, so that she may return without being constrained to raise her farthingale up to her girdle (for which she would be universally criticized). If she raises it very little, however, while dipping her body a bit, she should be able to pass through the space the other ladies will have made [for her], and then she should drop her farthingale when she seats herself; [should] she do this, she will ever be praised by all.

How Ladies Should Be Groomed Before Leaving Home
NOTE XXI

D. Tell me if you have any further and essential recommendation for ladies.

M. They should take great care, when preparing for a ball or other event, properly to fasten their farthingales, stocking strings, and other items which I am loathe to mention for modesty's sake, [but] which with my own eyes I have seen them drop and [have to] recover (a most shameful thing). Now to save their own honour they should attend to this before leaving the house. Also, they should keep their handkerchiefs in their great sleeves[9]

---

[9] '*Manicone*'. Caroso may be referring here to false sleeves of the type shown in the figures to 'Alta Regina', 'Passo e mezzo' or 'Bassa, et Alta' (note, however, that in the latter illustration the lady holds her handkerchief in her hand).

(half in and half out) when dancing, to be more attractive. Be careful not to drop a glove while dancing, because that is wrong, and causes many gentlemen to bestir themselves, running like a flock of starlings to pick up the aforementioned objects, just to show a lady favour, and thus ladies can cause a disturbance; now this behaviour should be eschewed, for it is unseemly.

[The Behaviour of] Ladies Who Are Not Invited To Dance
NOTE XXII

D. These recommendations of yours are good; therefore, do go on.

M. Frequently at balls there are some ladies who are never invited to dance; they should not be melancholy or dejected, however, but should disguise their feelings by pretending to be as happy as possible, and by conversing with other ladies sitting nearby.

It is also unseemly for gentlemen to show excessive favour to some [particular] lady; instead, [they should] invite and show favour to one or another who has never been asked. If they do this they will be appreciated and loved by those [ladies], their relatives, and everyone at the ball.

D. Please slow down, Master, for I wish you to comment on a question that I have heard raised on occasion; that is, whether not just a gentleman, but a lady also, who fails to return an [invitation to] dance, is praiseworthy rather than blameworthy.

M. This question requires consideration, so let me say that it is proper to return an [invitation to] dance the first time but not again and again, as some do without consideration; for when they do this, they generate not a little suspicion in the hearts of those in attendance at the ball, that the gentleman or lady in question loves the one thus favoured beyond normal decency. Now you should eschew anything that [might] raise even a suspicion with regard to a lady's virtue, as much as the act itself. In conclusion let me say that if [only] four or five people dance all the time, while the others watch, this is certainly not good. Also, should a prince or two honour the festivities with their presence, yet remain seated well over an hour without ever being asked to dance by a lady, then the husband of one [lady] (annoyed by such discourtesy) may send someone to tell his wife that she should invite that prince [to dance]; now she may answer that she cannot, because she is obliged to return another invitation. As far as I am concerned, however, after having returned one invitation to dance, everyone should invite his favourite (or the one who is most on his mind) [to dance]; if they conduct themselves in this fashion, everyone will take part in the ball. This is not solely my opinion, but that of many wise men who have come to the same conclusion on this point; that is, that it is better to behave this way than what has been the custom heretofore.

The Conduct of a Lady When Dancing 'Il Piantone'
NOTE XXIII

D. You have certainly answered this unusual question very well; now please go on to tell me how a lady should comport herself in the dance called 'Il Piantone'.

M. When a lady participates in the dance called 'Il Piantone', which is more popular than any other dance, she should never move either hand about more than usual as she dances, as is the custom and unseemly behaviour of many (for they resemble peasants scattering seed at sowing time). It is good style, however, if she moves her right arm gracefully a bit (just as she does her body), while she dances, keeping her palm facing her thigh, while she keeps her left arm down and quiet, and also close to her left side. [She should] also turn the palm of this hand toward her dress, being careful not to hold it [her hand] with its underside (or palm) facing back, as do some who appear [thereby] to be maimed [in some way]. It would also be good [for the lady] occasionally to put on a glove as she promenades, or to put her hand to a necklace (should she be wearing one around her neck), or to some ornament or slit (if she wears an overdress) to appear more graceful. Then, when inviting or taking leave of a gentleman by making a *Reverence,* she should drop both hands in a completely graceful, decorous, and beautiful fashion. Here let me say that when a lady takes a gentleman's hand in the course of a dance, she should not do so with her glove on (as I have seen some do), because if she does, she will be derided and gibed at by all. Now when performing such dances as 'Il Furioso', 'Il Contrapasso', or 'Il Ballo del Fiore', she should remove her gloves and put them in her long sleeve before the moment when one takes hands, for by comporting herself thus she will be well received by all in attendance at the ball.

The Comportment for Ladies When Unmantled, and Seated In Public Among Others in a Hall (or Elsewhere) Where a Ball is Being Held
NOTE XXIV

D. If you please, Sir, discuss with me the conduct or comportment of a lady when seated among others at a ball, for I would be delighted to know this.

M. Let me answer your question by saying that on occasion a lady may be seated unmantled among others at a ball, yet resist an invitation to dance from a prince or other person, obstinately refusing to honour the fellow who has invited her to dance, even if he or others beg her to do so. Let me say that this is not correct, for it is an affront that sometimes results in the ball coming to an end with little satisfaction to anyone. It would be correct, then, when a lady is invited to a wedding or festive occasion where she knows there will be dancing (and should she not feel inclined to dance), that after she has arrived at the salon where the bride is, she make a *Reverence* to her, in the usual courteous and ladylike manner, without removing her bordered scarf (or veil)[10] from her head. Even if the bride's relatives should press her forcefully to remove it, she should not consent for any reason whatsoever, but should go instead into a private chamber. Now if she prefers to remain in the hall where the others are seated, she should not remove her mantle, [however], since it is not permissible to refuse an invitation from anyone who invites her to dance, for that is quite ill-bred. Note that if she should be pressed for quite some time [to dance] by one of her blood relatives, she must on no account dance [with him], so as to avoid the scandal which could ensue; and if she so comports herself all will praise her. Nor is it appropriate for anyone to invite a [lady] to dance who is seated and mantled at the aforementioned ball; thus, if she does not accept the invitation it is not her fault, but that of the person who has invited her.

---

[10] '*panno listato, o velo*'.

On The Nobility of Ladies

By Signor Fabritio Caroso of Sermoneta

Book Two

Containing Instructions for Various Kinds of Balletti, for
Cascarde, Tordiglione, the Passo e Mezzo,
Pavaniglia, Canary, and Galliards
As Performed in Italy, France, and Spain

WITH THE BASS AND SOPRANO OF THE MUSIC,
And With the Lute Tablature For Each Dance

[2]
Nuova Regina [*New Queen*]

Balletto

Dedicated to the Most Christian Madame Maria de Medici,
Queen of France, etc.
(Fig. I)

We have now spoken enough about the rules in the first book, whether in giving the terminology or the effects of all the actions or movements required of gentlemen and ladies in the dances, or in describing those manners that are suitable to both in the dances. Now what remains to be done in this second book is to begin to teach the way these dances may be learned most easily.

Let me say, therefore, that to do this balletto, begin it as shown in the figure, making a *Reverence* together in four triple beats; then do two *Sapphic steps* (that is, one *reprise* and one *falling jump*, first to the left and then to the right). After this progress with four *altered broken sequences,* one *knot,* two *flourishes,* two *falling jumps,* two *minim steps* (that is, fast), and conclude with one *Sapphic step,* beginning all movements with the left foot; repeat to the other side, beginning from the *knot* and going on to the other movements.

In the second playing, progress once more with six *altered broken sequences* and two *Sapphic steps* (one to the left, the other to the right). Then repeat the *knot,* with all the above-mentioned movements, beginning them with the left foot; repeat to the other side, as I said in the first playing.

In the third playing take right hands, with two *ordinary broken sequences,* and two *Sapphic steps;* [then] dropping hands, do two more *broken sequences* turning to the left; [then] opposite each other, do two *minim steps* and one *Sapphic step* turning your left hip in. Note that these movements should begin with the left foot. After this turn a little to the right, and do a *stopped step* with the right foot, and a *half-Reverence* with the left; repeat to the other side, turning left. At the end do one *knot,* two *flourishes,* and two *Sapphic steps,* beginning with the right. Now in doing these *Sapphic steps,* do the first turning your right hip in, and after that [turn] your left hip; begin these movements with your right foot (that is, from the *knot* to all the others that follow).

In the fourth playing, take left hands, repeating the same movements to the other side.

In the fifth (and last) playing, do two *altered broken sequences* turning left, and facing each other, do two *flourishes,* and one *Sapphic step* with the left hip in; turn right, and follow the same order, beginning these movements to the other side. Then do one *reprise with foot under* to the left and one *flourish;* repeat to the right with the right foot. Finally do two *Sapphic steps* flankingly (first with the left hip in, then with the right), with two *minim stopped steps* forward. Conclude by taking customary hands again, making a *Reverence* in four triple beats, as at the beginning, and gracefully finishing this lovely dance called Nuova Regina in time to the music.

[2] *Nuova Regina*

7th course = F

5   10   ①

[3]
Alta Regina [*Great Queen*]
Cascarda

Dedicated to The Most Serene and Catholic Donna Margarita of Austria,
Queen of Spain, etc.
(Fig. II)

Begin the first playing of this cascarda by standing as shown in the figure, and making a *breve Reverence* in the time of four triple beats of music. After this move in a circle with four *ordinary broken sequences*, two *Sapphic steps*, two *minim stopped steps* (one forward, the other back). Conclude with four *stamped sequences in the canary*. Note that all the preceding movements are begun first with the left foot, and then with the right. Therefore this is called a Symmetrical Passage, because the left foot does exactly as many movements as the right, and this is the way to do it to be perfect in theory.

In the second playing circle with four *broken sequences*. After this turn left, doing a *minim stopped step* with the left foot, and a *half Reverence* with the right; repeat the same *stopped step* and *half Reverence* to the other side, [turning] to the right. Then do one *minim stopped step* forward, and another back (that is, one with the left, the other with the right); and make a *Reverence* at the conclusion of the music.

In the third playing the gentleman alone does one *knot*, two *flourishes*, two *falling jumps*, two *minim steps*, and one *Sapphic step* forward with his left hip in; repeat to the other side. Then both together do two *minim stopped steps* (one forward, the other back). Now conclude with a *Reverence*.

In the fourth playing, the lady alone does the same [as the gentleman just did]. Then do the same movements together (that is, the two *stopped steps* and the *Reverence*).

In the fifth playing, both do two *flourishes*, two *falling jumps*, two *minim steps*, and one *Sapphic step* with the left hip in; repeat to the other side. Then repeat the abovementioned *stopped steps* (one forward, and the other back). Conclude this playing with a *Reverence*.

In the sixth (and last) playing, do two *reprises* to the left, two *falling jumps*, two *minim steps*, and one *Sapphic step* with the left hip in; repeat to the other side. Then, by taking one *minim stopped step* forward, and another back, gracefully finish this cascarda, making a *Reverence* at the end of the music.

[3]   *Alta Regina*

7th course = F

[4]
Amorosina Grimana [*Beloved Grimana*]
Pavaniglia

Dedicated to the Most Serene Lady Moresina Moresini Grimani,
Princess of Venice
(Fig. III)

In the first playing of the Pavaniglia stand as shown in the figure, and make a *breve Reverence* together, in four triple beats of music (as I said in the cascarda Alta Regina), with two *semibreve continences* in two triple beats, which equal one semibreve beat. Then do one *falling jump* with the left foot, one *foot under* with the right, and one *flourish* with the left to the left; repeat to the other side. Note that with the right foot, which is now on the ground, you then do one *limping hop,* a *step in the air* with the same foot, and a galliard *cadence,* ending with the left foot forward. Then with the same foot do another *limping hop,* one *step in the air,* and a *cadence* at the end of the music, as stated above, but landing with the right foot forward. Now because this part [of the dance] in which there are so many beautiful movements, takes one playing [of the music], I call it a Symmetrical Section, just as, when dividing a piece of land between two brothers, one marks the boundaries so that each will know his own section; thus, since both feet are brothers, I have arranged for each foot to do just as many movements as the other (since this occurs while one section of the piece is played through, I call it a Symmetrical Section) so that it is correct in theory, and is not what was done before, which was quite wrong.[1] Therefore I have corrected it and brought it to absolute perfection; now aside from the correctness of these movements, they will appear very graceful to those present.

In the second playing, progress without dropping hands, taking two *minim stopped steps* in one perfect musical beat of the music for this dance, which is two triple beats. Then do one *falling jump* with the left foot, and one *foot under* with the right (but do not make a *half Reverence,* as was done before). Now as soon as you have done these movements, do two *ordinary steps,* two *flourishes,* two more *steps* with two more *flourishes,* and a *cadence,* landing with the left

---

[1] The reference here, and in all subsequent references to what was done before, is to *Il Ballarino.*

foot behind. After this do one *limping hop* with the right, with the left foot raised. Then take one *step in the air* with the right foot. At the end of the music conclude this passage by doing a *cadence,* landing now with the left foot forward. Note that this is called a Well-Ordered Passage, because one ends it with the same foot with which one began the first step, as I can demonstrate by doing the *five steps* (or movements, if you will), in which one ends with the same foot with which one began.

In the third playing, once again take two *stopped steps,* as above (with the right [foot] first), with all the subsequent movements. Note, however, that in place of the two *steps* which were taken forward, you should do two *falling jumps,* and continue backward with all the succeeding movements I gave for the second section.

In the fourth playing, take two *stopped steps* forward, as above, then immediately make a *half Reverence* with the left, and with that foot do a *foot under* to the right, and a *cadence,* turning to face each other. Now the lady should note that when taking these *stopped steps,* she should begin with one backward with her right foot (which will have been forward), and then take the other forward with her left, and this is so that she may move along with the gentleman; and she should do all the other steps to the right, continuing to face him, and beginning them all to the right, in opposition to the gentleman. After you have done the aforesaid *cadence,* do two *little bounds,* one *foot under* with the right, and one *step in the air* with the left. Then do one *cadence,* one *little bound,* one *foot under* with the right, dropping the left immediately, and another *step in the air* with the right, one *flourish* with the same foot, one *chasing step* with the left, another with the right, and a *cadence.* After this do the following codetta this way: one *limping hop,* one *step in the air,* and a *cadence* at the end of the music. Note that, in this dance, whenever I tell you to do the Codetta, I intend you to do it as above.

In the fifth playing, both repeat to the other side; and although the gentleman has his right foot behind, he takes one *stopped step* forward with that foot and another back with his left, and this will be quite correct. Note that whenever the Codetta is done you should face towards each other, as when you began this dance. Now should the lady not know how to do the variation described above, instead of the two *little bounds* and the other movements done by the gentleman, she may do two *reprises,* and two *falling jumps* twice. Then she does two more *reprises,* a *knot,* and a *cadence;* and to conclude she should do the Codetta, as I described above.

In the sixth playing, do the aforesaid *stopped steps* forward, a *half Reverence,* and a *cadence,* beginning with the left foot, and bending your knees a little. Then do a *little jump* to the left, a *foot under* with the right, a *knot* with the left, two *flourishes* forward, two *chasing steps,* and a *cadence.* Then do the Codetta as above [beginning] with the left foot.

In the seventh playing, repeat the same variation to the other side, beginning with the right foot.

In the eighth playing, take two *stopped steps,* and dropping hands, do two *flourishes* turning to the left, and a *sequence* forward facing each other. Then turning to the right, do the same *flourishes,* and a *sequence* forward (beginning, however, first with the left and then with the right). Note that when doing the last *sequence* with the right, you gracefully bend your knees a little; and at the same time do a *limping hop* with the right foot, a *step in the air,* and a *cadence;* repeat the *limping hop, step in the air,* and *cadence* to the other side. Now this is called a Symmetrical Section, as I said for the first playing [of this dance]; if it were done otherwise the dance would be completely wrong.

In the ninth playing, do the abovementioned two *stopped steps* forward, one *falling jump,* and one *foot under.* Then turning your body a little to the left, do two *quick minim steps,* a *foot under,* beginning with the left foot, and immediately one *limping hop* with the right; repeat to the other side, turning a little to the right. Then, facing towards each other, do a *knot,* two *flourishes* forward, a *cadence,* and the Codetta at the end of the music.

In the tenth playing, do everything to the other side, that is, beginning all these steps with the right.

In the eleventh playing, do the two *stopped steps* again, one *falling jump* with the left foot, and one *foot under* with the right. Then do one *flourish* to the left, one *limping hop* with the left foot, and one *step,* dropping the right foot to the ground. Then thrust the left foot forward, and immediately draw it back in the manner of a *half Reverence.* Then with the same foot do a *falling jump* with the left and another with the right; [then] turning to the right, do a *flourish,* one *limping hop* with the same foot, a *step* dropping the left to the ground, and a *half Reverence* with the right, as above. Then do two quick *falling jumps* (one with the right foot, the other with the left), a *foot under* with the right, and a *cadence.* At the conclusion of the music do the aforesaid Codetta [beginning] with the left foot.

In the twelfth [playing], repeat to the other side.

In the thirteenth [playing], do the two *stopped steps* again, with a *half Reverence,* a *foot under,* and a *cadence,* beginning with the left. Then with the same [foot] do one *limping hop,* crossing the right in the air behind the left, and at once with the same [foot] do one *step* forward, and one *foot under* with the left. Then do two *quick steps* (one with the right, the other with the left), and a *foot under* with the right. Then turn to the left, with four *flourishes,* and a *cadence* facing towards each other, beginning with the left, and with the same [foot] do the Codetta.

In the fourteenth [playing], repeat the same variation as above, but to the other side.

In the fifteenth [playing], do the same Symmetrical Section as given in the eighth section.

In the sixteenth (and last) playing, do the aforesaid two *stopped steps* forward, one *falling jump* with the left, one *foot under* with the right, and one *flourish* with the left; repeat to the other side. Then do two *Sapphic steps* flankingly forward (first with the left hip in, then with the right), concluding by taking each other gently by the customary hand, and making a *Reverence* in the same number of musical beats as at the beginning, gracefully bring this dance to an end.

[4] *Amorosina Grimana*

[5]
Laura Suave [*Gentle Laura*]
Balletto

Dedicated to the Most Serene Madame Christena Lorena de Medici,
Grand Duchess of Tuscany
(Fig. IV)

To begin this balletto stand as in the figure (that is, the lady at one end of the hall and the gentleman at the other end of the hall or any other dancing place). When the music begins, in the usual well-mannered fashion make a *long Reverence* in four beats of music, with two *breve continences* in two beats each. Then do two *minim steps* and one *Sapphic step* to the left, beginning these movements with the left foot; and with the right, which is now raised, do a *falling jump* with the right hip out; now with the left foot, which is raised, do one *dexterous step* (that is, two *reprises* and a *falling jump*) with the left hip in; repeat the same *steps* and all the other movements to the other side. Then do two *ordinary broken sequences,* and two *Sapphic steps* flankingly toward each other, concluding by taking each other by both hands in the usual well-mannered fashion, with two *continences*. The gentleman kisses his left hand, dropping the lady's right and politely doffing his bonnet (or hat) with that hand, making a *Reverence* in the same time as above.

In the second playing, still holding hands, progress with one *pulled step* with the left foot, and a *limping hop* with the same [foot], raising the right. Then do one *step in the air* with the left foot, and a *cadence* with the right forward; repeat to the other side, beginning with the left.[1] Then take one *minim step* with the right, and one *Sapphic step* with the left to the left; repeat the same movements to the other side, beginning with the right. After this continue to progress by doing two *half double sequences* (that is, two *quick steps* and a *broken sequence* for each one). Then do a *knot*, two *flourishes*, two *minim steps* forward, and a *Sapphic step,* beginning with the left; repeat to the other side. Once again do two more *half-double sequences,* concluding by dropping hands in the usual well-mannered fashion. Now the lady goes to one end of the room and the gentleman to the other, with two *double scurrying sequences,* facing towards each other at the end, and making a *half Reverence* at the end of the music.

---

[1] *Sic.*

The Sciolta of this Entire Piece as a Galliard

If the gentleman knows how to dance the galliard, he does a solo variation (or division, if you will) of four patterns, concluding with his left foot forward after having done a *cadence* (it would be quite wrong if done otherwise, for, as I said in my Rules, if one begins a variation with the left foot forward, one must also end it with the same foot forward, and not the way many do, who begin a variation with a *cadence,* and when ending it do a *cadence* with the right foot forward, which is improper). Let me say, therefore, that if a gentleman wishes to do this variation of mine, he first does one *knot,* two *flourishes,* two *minim steps* (that is, quick) backward, two quick *half Reverences,* beginning each movement with the left [foot]; then one *falling jump* with the same [foot], another with the right, a *foot under* with the left, and then two *flourishes* with the right, two *minim steps* back, and a *cadence* ending with the left foot forward, as he began.

Lady's Variation

The lady should note that when the gentleman does his variation, and while he dances, she should not stand still, but should make a good pretense at adjusting her train, swaying gracefully, donning a glove or, should it be summer and she has a fan, moving it prettily so as not to resemble a statue; when used, these lovely and honest gestures appear most graceful, and will meet with approval and endear her to all who are present. Now let me say that she should do the same variations as the gentleman has just done; but if she does not know the *knot* or *flourishes,* she may do the [following] graceful variation: that is, one *sequence* flankingly to the left with the left foot, and another to the right with the right [foot]. Then she should do two slow *falling jumps,* and one *feigned sequence* with the left foot, concluding by bending her knees a little in the manner of a *half Reverence.*

When the lady has concluded her variation, the gentleman once again does the same variation as before, beginning and ending it with his right foot. Note that one must not do a different four-pattern variation composed of different movements, for even if it is in time to the music this does not make it right, as I said in my Rules.

The lady does the second variation similarly to the first, beginning with her right foot.

In these four patterns the gentleman does a symmetrical [variation] (that is, two patterns for each foot), in the following manner: two *limping hops* with the left foot raised and the right limping, two fast *half Reverences* with the left (which will have been raised), two *falling jumps,* one *foot under* with the left, and a *cadence* with the left forward; repeat beginning with the right. The lady does two *doubles in French style* (one to the left, the other to the right). Then do two *double scurrying sequences* together, turning first to the left and then to the right in the shape of an S; and approaching each other, take customary hands.

The Sciolta of this Piece as a Saltarello, in Triple Beats

In this sciolta movement of this piece, do two *broken sequences*, two *stamped sequences in the canary*, and one *Sapphic step*, beginning with the left; repeat with the right foot to the other side. Now release hands, turning first to the left and then to the right, and doing two more *ordinary broken sequences* and one *Corinthian step* (that is, three *reprises* and a *falling jump* with the right hip in); repeat to the other side. After this do two *reprises*, two *falling jumps*, and a *feigned double*, beginning with the left. Repeat to the other side. After this do two *stopped steps* (one forward with the left, the other backward with the right), and at the conclusion of this section of the music do a *breve Reverence* in the time of four triple beats.

When the Canary Music [is Played] Do a Pedalogue

The gentleman does one *double stamped sequence in the canary* with his left foot, the *tiny minced jumps* (that is, stamping his feet quickly three times) beginning with his right, and concludes with a *stamped sequence,* which ends with his left foot forward as at first (now these are *tiny minced jumps*). The lady does the same, and this is done four times by each person. Then do a *stopped broken sequence* with the left foot, and a *half Reverence* with the right, touching right hands; repeat to the other side. Then the gentleman does two *falling jumps* and one *Sapphic step* flankingly backward; the lady does the same after this; and you do it four times per person. When you have completed this pedalogue do two *broken sequences* beginning with the left foot and turning to the left, two *minim steps* forward, and one *Sapphic step* flankingly, with the left hip in; repeat beginning with the right. Then conclude this balletto by doing two *stopped steps* forward, and taking customary hands, make a *grave Reverence* with the utmost gentility, gracefully concluding at the close of the music.

So that everyone should know how this term 'pedalogue' is derived, let me say that, just as we say that when two people converse they are engaging in a dialogue, so here, when the gentleman dances one group of steps (or one variation) with his feet, and the lady answers the same way, this foot conversation leads me to term it 'pedalogue'.

[5] *Laura Suave*

Play this part of the
piece twice and then
begin the Galliard

7th course = F

Repeat once more

Galliard

Saltarello

[6]
Alta Gonzaga [*Great Gonzaga*]
Balletto

Dedicated to the Most Serene Donna Leonora de Medici Gonzaga,
Duchess of Mantua, Etc.
(Fig. IV)

Stand opposite each other as shown in the figure, beginning this balletto with a *grave Reverence* in six ordinary beats, in the usual courteous manner. Then do two *semigrave continences,* each in three beats of music. After this do a *knot,* two *flourishes,* a *stopped step* (beginning all of these movements with the left [foot]), and a *half Reverence* with the right; do the same *knot* and the other movements to the other side. Then take right hands and do one *double sequence* to the left; taking left hands, repeat to the other side. Then take both hands and do two *breve continences,* each to two beats. This done, the gentleman drops the lady's right hand and they make a *Reverence* as above, in the usual well-mannered fashion.

In the second playing do a *knot,* two *flourishes* forward, two *semibreve steps,* and two *broken sequences* and a *Sapphic step,* beginning with the left foot; repeat the same movements to the other side. Then do two *doubles in Spanish style,* two *semibreve falling jumps* to one beat of music apiece, and a *dexterous step* (that is, two *reprises* and a *falling jump* to the left); then repeat the same *falling jumps* and *dexterous step* the other way to the right, beginning with the right foot.

In the third playing do two more *doubles* as before, a *falling jump* with the left [foot], a *foot under* with the right, and a *flourish* with the left; repeat the same movements to the other side. Then do two *semibreve steps* forward, and four *ordinary sequences,* concluding by bending your knees a little in the manner of a *half Reverence,* and dropping hands in the usual well-mannered fashion. This done, the gentleman goes to one end of the room (or dancing place), and the lady to the other and, both turning first to the left and then to the right with two *scurrying sequences* in the shape of an S, concluding by facing towards each other. At the end do two *stopped steps* and a *Reverence.*

Symmetrical Variation to Do Together

In the fourth playing, do a *falling jump* with the left, a *foot under* with the right, and a *flourish* with the left; repeat the same movements to the other side. Then do a *minim step* in the manner of a *half Reverence*, a *foot under*, and a *cadence*, beginning and ending with the left foot forward; repeat to the other side. Then do a *knot*, two *flourishes*, one *stopped step*, and a *half Reverence* with the right; repeat to the other side. After this do two *semibreve steps*, a *falling jump*, a *foot under*, a *flourish*, and a *cadence*, beginning with the left; repeat to the other side. Finally do two *falling jumps* as above, and a *dexterous step*, both turning left hips in and beginning with the left [foot]; repeat to the other side.

In the fifth (and last) playing, take right hands and do two *sequences*. Now dropping this hand, take two *minim steps* turning to the left and changing places, beginning with the left foot. Now with the same [foot] do a *falling jump* with the left hip out, and one *broken sequence* with the right [foot] with the right hip in, and at the end another *falling jump* with the left, turning the left hip in; taking left hands, repeat to the other side, turning to the right, beginning with the right [foot], each returning to your own place. Then do two *semibreve steps,* and one *breve sequence* to the left; repeat to the other side. This done, conclude this dance with two *stopped steps* forward and a *Reverence* as before, not omitting, however, the usual courtly manners.

[6] *Alta Gonzaga*

7th course = F

[7]
Passo e mezzo [*Step and a Half?*]

Balletto

Dedicated to the Most Serene Signora Donna Livia Dalla Rovere,
Duchess of Urbino
(Fig. V)

To perform this Passo e mezzo, begin by standing as shown in the figure, making a *long Reverence* together in four beats of music, with two *breve continences* in two beats apiece. Progressing to the left, do two *reprises,* two *falling jumps,* and one *breve sequence* of two beats, beginning all the above-mentioned movements with the left foot; then repeat the same *reprises, falling jumps,* and *sequence,* beginning with the right. Now this is called a Symmetrical Passage, because the left foot has exactly as many movements and actions as the right, which is quite proper.

The Gentleman's First Variation

In the second playing, while the lady does a passage both to the left and the right, the gentleman does the following variation: two *limping hops* thrusting the left foot up and forward, and with the same [foot] two quick *half Reverences* (in the manner of three beats of the *little bell*), and a *knot,* beginning these movements with the left foot. Then immediately do one *step in the air* with the right, and a *cadence* with *tiny minced jumps* (that is, with this cadence do three *little jumps* to the left, called *tiny minced jumps*). Then do a *foot under* with the right, a *falling jump* with the left, and another *foot under* with the right, two quick *steps in the air* (one with the right, and the other with the left), and with the same [foot] do a *flourish,* another [*flourish*] with the right, two *minim steps* backward, two more *half Reverences,* two *falling jumps,* a *foot under,* and a *cadence* at the end, landing with the left foot forward as you began. After this repeat the same variation with the right foot, which remained in back, and conclude with the same foot; and by thus doing this variation it will be correct, and in time to the music.

The lady's passage is as follows: two *semibreve steps* (each to one beat), and a *half-double sequence,* beginning with the left, an *ordinary broken sequence* with the right, two *minim steps,* and a *breve sequence* (that is, *ordinary*) to conclude, beginning with the left. Repeat the same passage to the right, beginning, therefore, with the right foot. This passage is also done by the gentleman while the lady does her variation.

The Lady's First Variation

In the third playing, she does a *knot,* two *flourishes* forward, two *quick steps* backward, two more *flourishes* forward, two slow *steps,* and four *flourishes* turning to the left, concluding with a *cadence.* Then do the Codetta as in the Pavaniglia: that is, a *limping hop* with the left [foot] forward, a *step in the air* with the right, and a *cadence,* landing with the left foot forward. Repeat this variation to the other side. The gentleman does the same passage [as above].

The Gentleman's Second Variation

In the fourth playing, the gentleman does the following second variation: first do a *falling jump* to the left with the left [foot], and a *foot under* with the right twice. Then do two quick *steps in the air* (one with the right, the other with the left), two *flourishes* forward, and a *knot.* Then turn with two slow *steps,* and facing your partner do two *flourishes,* two *quick steps* backward, two quick *half Reverences* as above, two *falling jumps,* a *foot under,* concluding with a *cadence,* always landing with your toes straight [ahead]. Begin these movements with the left [foot], thus landing at the end with the left foot forward, as I said above. Repeat to the other side.

The lady does the same passage, both to the left and the right.

The Lady's Second Variation and the Gentleman's Passage

For the second variation the lady does two *reprises with foot under* and a *flourish* to the left side. Repeat these movements to the right. Then do a *knot* with a *cadence,* two slow *steps,* two *flourishes* turning to the left, and two *quick steps* backward and a *cadence.* To conclude do the Codetta (that is, a *limping hop,* a *step in the air,* and a *cadence,* as I described in the first variation). Repeat to the other side.

Do This Passage Together in a Circle

To do this passage the gentleman begins with two *flourishes,* two *minim steps,* two *flourishes* and two *steps,* and two more *flourishes;* [then] two *steps* forward, and a *cadence.* Then do the Codetta as above (that is, a *limping hop,* a *step in the air,* and a *cadence*). Note, however, that in doing this circular passage the lady begins with two *steps* followed by two *flourishes,* the opposite of what the gentleman just did. After this repeat everything to the right side, reversing parts (that is, the gentleman begins with the *steps* and the lady with the *flourishes*), each returning to your own place.

The Gentleman's Third Variation and the Lady's Passage

He does one *semibreve stopped step* with his left hip in, beginning with his left foot, and two *flourishes* forward, beginning with his right; repeat backward to the other side. Then do two *steps* turning to the left, with two *flourishes* forward, and a *cadence*. After this do the Codetta (that is, a *limping hop,* a *step in the air,* and a *cadence*), as I said above. Repeat the same variation to the other side, beginning with the right [foot].

The Lady's Third Variation, and the Gentleman's Passage

She does the same variation the gentleman did, both with her left foot and her right.

The Gentleman's Fourth Variation and the Lady's Passage

The gentleman begins this last variation by doing two *reprises with foot under* to the left, two *semibreve steps* forward, another *reprise* as before, and a *cadence* with his right [foot] forward. Then he does a *little jump* to the right, a *foot under* with his left, two *flourishes* forward, two quick *minim steps* backward, two *half Reverences,* two *falling jumps* and a *cadence,* beginning from the *flourishes* backward[1] with his right [foot]. Then he does the Codetta (that is, the *limping hop, step in the air,* and *cadence*), landing with his left forward. He repeats this in exactly the same order to the other side.

The Lady's Fourth Variation, and the Gentleman's Passage

She does a *Corinthian step* (that is, three *reprises* and a *falling jump* with her left hip in); repeat to the other side. Then facing towards her partner, she does two slow *steps* turning left, two *flourishes* forward and two *minim steps* (that is, quickly backward), and a *cadence*. After this she does the Codetta as above. Repeat the same variation to the other side, beginning with the right foot.

The Coda for Both to do Together

Progress together, with two *reprises with foot under,* two *falling jumps,* and a *feigned sequence* facing towards each other, beginning with the left foot; repeat to the other side. After this do two *breve stopped steps* forward (one with the left, the other with the right). This done, conclude this balletto gracefully by making a *Reverence* in time to the music, in the usual courteous and well-mannered fashion.

---

[1] *Sic.*

[7] *Passo e mezzo*

[8]
Barriera [*The Barriers*]

Balletto

Dedicated to the Most Serene Donna Verginia Medici d'Este,
Duchess of Modena, etc.
(Fig. V)

In my other book, when doing this Barriera the gentlemen stood to the lady's right, holding hands (as you see even now in the figure[1]), for I knew that all princes, noblemen, and gentlemen should always give the full honours appropriate to ladies, whether at a ball or elsewhere. But was it therefore proper for him to stand to her right? And then, after doing two *sequences* passing behind [the lady] at the end of this playing, was it [proper] for him to use whichever foot happened to be in back to make a *Reverence?* Now because this is against the rule and in bad style, everyone must eschew it. If one wishes to do it in a way [which is] correct in theory, and in a properly symmetrical fashion, it should be done in the following manner.

Begin this Barriera by standing opposite each other without holding hands, as in the figure to Nuova Regina de Francia[2], with a *long Reverence* in four beats of music, and two *breve continences,* each in two beats. Then do two *Corinthian steps* flankingly in (note that for every *Corinthian step* one does three *reprises* and a *falling jump,* as I said in the rule for the *Corinthian step*), and having done these *Corinthian steps,* take each other by the customary hand and make a *Reverence* again, in the usual courtly manner.

In the second playing, progress together, with two *breve stopped steps* (each in two beats), four *semibreve steps* (each in one beat), and an *ordinary sequence* (in two beats), beginning all these steps with the left foot. Then do two *Sapphic steps* (each in one beat), and finally two *continences* (with two beats per *continence*), beginning these *Sapphic steps* and *continences* with the right foot.

---

[1] The figure given here does not show this, however, as it is identical to Fig. V; the figure to which Caroso refers in *Il Ballarino* (fol. 64v) shows the gentleman to the right of the lady, holding her right hand in his left.

[2] I.e., Nuova Regina, dedicated to the Queen of France.

In the third playing, do the same passage to the other side, beginning with the right foot. Note that before, when dancing this Barriera, one progressed to three repetitions of the music, always beginning with the left foot, and always doing the *reprises* to the right and never to the left. Let me say, however, that whatever dance one does, and whatever the movements may be, it will always be completely wrong unless each foot has an equal number [of steps] as the other. Therefore, when one does two passages, it is suitable to begin the first with the left; and the second with the right; and by thus making reciprocal movements one will perform each dance correctly, according to the rules, and according to the true beat of the music. And, in order for this to be correct, there are sixteen perfect beats to each part of the music for the Barriera. Note, then, that in the second playing [of the dance] the two *stopped steps* are worth four beats (two [beats] each); the four *semibreve steps* take four more beats, making eight; [there are] two for the *breve sequence,* making ten; one for each *Sapphic step,* making twelve; and four for the two *continences,* making the number of sixteen perfect musical beats. Thus I have clarified this [matter], and therefore it is necessary to do two passages (not three), the left foot having the one and the right foot having the other.

In the fourth playing, take right hands, and do a *stopped step* with the left foot and a *feigned sequence* with the right, bending your knees a little as in a *half Reverence.* Then dropping hands, do four *steps,* each to one beat, turning to the left and changing places; [and] taking plenty of space, do a *sequence* as above to the left, beginning with the left. After this do two *Sapphic steps* and two *continences,* beginning with the right.

In the fifth playing, take left hands, and do the same actions and movements, beginning to the other side with the right, each returning to his place. Note, however, that in place of the *continences* you make a *Reverence.* Now do not perform it as before, when you took each other only by the right hands, and never by the left, which was not fitting and was wrong.

In the sixth playing the gentleman alone does four *semibreve steps* flankingly forward (each in one beat), and to begin them place the right edge of your cape under your right arm (as is shown in the figure for Nuova Regina); note that this movement must be done gracefully, gripping it with your left arm (that is, above the elbow) without covering the hilt of your sword. After this turn to face towards the left, and do a *stopped broken sequence* with your left, and a *half Reverence* with your right; repeat, turning to face towards the right (that is, to the other side). Note, however, that when making a *half Reverence* it is necessary to bring your feet together [again] immediately, for if you do otherwise (as some do who leave that foot behind with which they have just made a *half Reverence*), then you will be unable to do the four *broken sequences* retreating backward; for, as I stated in my Rules, that foot which remains behind cannot move backward yet again. By moving this way, however, you will be quite correct. Therefore, do four *pulled steps,* or four *broken sequences,* flankingly backward. After this make a *Reverence* together in four beats of music, as above.

In the seventh playing, the lady alone does exactly what the gentleman just did.

The Grave Sciolta of this Piece, Played Twice

Progress together, doing two *doubles in French style* (one to the left, and the other to the right). After this take two *stopped steps* flankingly backward. Then do two *scurrying sequences,* taking hands, concluding by bending your knees a little as in a *half Reverence,* joining the left foot [to the right], and with it repeating the above-mentioned *steps* (or *broken sequences,* if you prefer). Then do an *ordinary sequence,* beginning these movements with the left. Thereupon do two *Sapphic steps* (one with the right, and the other with the left foot).

Repeat this passage once more, beginning with the right foot. Now if you do it this way, the dance will be quite correct, for one passage will begin with the left, and the other with the right.

The Sciolta of this Piece as a Saltarello, Played Just Once

Both do four *broken sequences* flankingly forward. Then the lady, pretending to kiss her hands, strikes the gentleman's hands once, and he then does the same [thing]. Then both do a *falling jump* to the left, striking right hands; and another *falling jump* to the right, striking left hands. After this take hands, with two *continences* (one with the left, and the other with the right), and make a *Reverence* at the end of the music.

The Sciolta of this Piece as a Galliard

Dropping hands, both do four *ordinary sequences* flankingly backward. Then take two *steps* turning to the left, and do one *sequence* forward, beginning with the left; repeat to the other side. Finally do two *stopped steps* flankingly forward, at the end of which take each other by the customary hands, and conclude this dance by gently making a *Reverence* in four beats of music.

[8] *Barriera*

Play this [part of the] piece seven times

7th course = F

Galliard

Spagnoletta Nuova [New Spagnoletta]

In the Style of Madrid

Dedicated to the Most Illustrious and Excellent Lady,
The Vice-Regent of Naples
(Fig. VI)

Begin this Spagnoletta by standing as shown in the figure, making a *breve Reverence* in four triple beats in time to the music. Then progress, holding hands, with four *ordinary broken sequences*, two *Sapphic steps*, two *reprises* to the left, two *flourishes* forward, two *minim steps* and a *Sapphic step*, beginning everything with the left foot; then do the abovementioned *reprises* and other movements to the right to the other side. After this do two *broken sequences* flankingly backward (that is, one *ordinary* [*broken sequence*] with the left foot, and another *feigned* [*broken sequence*] with the right). Finally do a *stamped sequence in the canary*, with the *tiny minced jumps* (that is, after the *sequence* do three quick *stamps*, beginning and ending with the right), and immediately do another *stamped sequence* with the left, as above, concluding with two more *stamps*, one with the right foot, and the other with the left. Repeat the same *broken sequences* and all the other movements to the other side.

In the second playing, progress the same way, doing four more *broken sequences*, two *flourishes*, two *minim steps*, and two *Sapphic steps* (one to the left, the other to the right). Then do one *knot*, two *flourishes*, two *minim steps*, and one *Sapphic step*, beginning with the left foot; repeat to the other side. Finally, do one *reprise with foot under* and a *flourish* to the left, the same to the right, and a *Corinthian step* to the left. Repeat to the other side.

In the third playing take right hands and do two *broken sequences*, two *falling jumps*, and a *Sapphic step*, progressing to the left. Then take left hands and repeat to the other side. Releasing hands, do one *knot*, two *flourishes* facing each other, and one *stopped broken sequence* to the left, beginning everything with the left foot; at the end of these *broken sequences* make a *half Reverence* with the right; repeat to the other side. Then do two *broken sequences* flankingly forward, two *minim steps* turning to the left, and at the end do one *Sapphic step* with the left hip in. Repeat to the other side.

In the fourth (and last) playing, take both hands round, progressing to the left, and doing two *flourishes,* two *falling jumps,* two *minim steps,* and one *broken sequence,* beginning with the left foot; repeat to the other side. Then drop hands, doing one *knot,* two *flourishes,* two *minim steps* turning to the left, and one *Sapphic step* with the left hip in; repeat to the other side. This done, do two *broken sequences* flankingly backward (one *ordinary* [*broken sequence*], and the other *feigned,* as I said in the first section), with two *Sapphic steps* flankingly forward. Finally, do two *minim stopped steps* forward towards each other. Then take each other once more by the customary hand, in the usual courtly manner, and with a *Reverence* in time to the music as at the beginning (having joined the left foot to the right), gracefully end this beautiful Spagnoletta. Note that it must be done symmetrically.

[9]   *Spagnoletta Nuova*

Gagliarda di Spagna [Spanish Galliard]
Balletto

*Dedicated to the Most Illustrious and Excellent Donna
Anna Cordua Cardona, Duchess of Sessa*
(Fig. III)

This Gagliarda di Spagna begins with the couple standing as shown in the figure. During the first playing make a *breve Reverence* in two beats, and two *continences,* with one beat per *continence.* Then do one *reprise with foot under* to the left, two *flourishes,* and one *half-double sequence* (that is, two *steps* and a *broken sequence,* pausing for half a beat); repeat to the other side. This done, immediately do a *reprise with foot under* to the left, one *flourish,* one more *reprise with foot under* to the right, and with the same foot do a *limping hop,* raising the left forward, one *step in the air* with the right, and a *cadence;* repeat to the other side. Note that whenever I say the Codetta should be done in this dance, begin from the *reprises, flourishes,* and subsequent movements, which must always be performed symmetrically.

In the second playing do two *breve continences,* each in two beats. Then progressing through the ballroom, do a *knot,* two *flourishes,* two *steps* forward, and one *Sapphic step* (in which there is a half-beat pause); then repeat the *knot* and other movements to the other side. Now at the end do the abovementioned Codetta with both feet (that is, one Codetta with the left, the other with the right).

In the third playing, drop hands, and taking right hands do two *breve sequences* (that is, *ordinary*), after which you make a *half Reverence;* drop hands, turning to the left with two *steps,* two *flourishes,* and one *ordinary sequence* forward, changing places and pausing for half a beat. Then taking left hands, repeat to the other side. This done, do the abovementioned Codettas.

Gentleman's First Variation

In the fourth playing both do two *sequences* as above, at the end of which gracefully bend your knees a little in the manner of a *half Reverence.* The lady, having done the two *sequences,* stands still. The gentleman does the following variation: first he does two *semibreve stopped steps* (each in one beat), and one *reprise with foot under* to the left (that is, one *falling jump* and a *foot under*). Having done the *reprise,* do a *flourish;* repeat the same *reprise* and *flourish* to the other side. Then facing [your partner] do one *knot,* two *flourishes* forward, two *minim steps* backward, two *half Reverences,* a *foot under* and a *cadence,* beginning these movements with the left foot; repeat everything to the other side, beginning with the *knot.* Finally do the two Codettas, both to the left and to the right ([first] with one foot and then with the other, as I said above). Now this is a Symmetrical Variation, for one foot has as much to do as the other.

Lady's First Variation

In the fifth playing the lady repeats what the gentleman has just done.

Gentleman's Second Variation

In the sixth playing, the gentleman does two *breve stopped steps* forward (each in two beats), pausing at the end for half a beat. Then do two *limping hops* with the left raised forward, and immediately with the same foot two *half Reverences,* one *knot,* one *step in the air* with the right, two *flourishes* forward, and a *cadence.* After these movements, pause for another half beat, having begun these movements with the left foot; repeat to the other side. This done, conclude this variation by doing the two Codettas as above.

Lady's Second Variation

In the seventh playing, the lady repeats the same variation the gentleman has just done.

Variation to do Together

In the eighth playing, both together do two *breve stopped steps,* at the end of which you pause for half a beat. Then do two *reprises with foot under* to the left, two *flourishes* forward, and one *dexterous step* flankingly, beginning with the left; repeat the *reprises* and subsequent movements to the other side. Note that at the conclusion of the *dexterous step* you pause for half a beat. Then immediately, without waiting any longer, do the two Codettas as above.

In the ninth playing, do two *breve stopped steps,* pausing for half a beat. Then do two *flourishes* forward, two *minim steps,* and one *Corinthian step* (that is, three *reprises* and a *falling jump*) flankingly forward; repeat the *flourishes* and the other movements to the other side. This done, do two *semibreve stopped steps,* each in one beat. Finally, observing the same standards of courtly etiquette, take each other by the customary hand, and conclude this Gagliarda di Spagna with the *breve Reverence* in two beats, as you did at the beginning. Now all of this balletto should be done according to the Rule of Symmetry, and it will be quite correct.

[10] *Gagliarda di Spagna*

[11]
Bassa, et Alta [*Low and High*]

Balletto

The gentleman stands somewhat opposite the lady and takes her by the customary hand, as you may see in the figure, making a *grave Reverence* in six ordinary beats, and two *continences* in three beats each. Then progress with two *stopped steps,* also in three beats apiece, and four *feigned doubles in French style.* Note that in this dance, as in others, you move that foot which joins the other, as I have said in my Rules. After the four *doubles* do two more *stopped steps,* as above, two *continences,* two *reprises* to the left and two to the right, and one *grave continence* in six beats, beginning all the movements in this passage first with the left foot and then with the right. Then do two *reprises* to the right and two to the left, two *stopped steps,* two more *doubles* in the same fashion [as above], and, similarly, two *stopped steps,* two *reprises* to the right, two more to the left, and after that another *grave continence* to the right, beginning these movements with the right foot. Then do two more *reprises* to the left, and two to the right. At the conclusion of the music to this Bassa do two *continences,* as above (one to the left, and the other to the right). Note that the Bassa does not end here, however, but continues where it says, 'The finale to the Bassa [music]'. Now since our predecessors incorporated the Alta and the Gioioso here, we do not make a *Reverence* to [this part of] the Bassa; but after you have done the Gioioso you will do the [real] finale to the entire Bassa. Thus, at the end of all the movements in the finale section, you [then] make a *Reverence* (also in six beats).

Here the Alta Begins

Begin the Alta by making a *Reverence* (also in six beats). Then progressing through the ballroom, do six *ordinary* (that is, *breve*) *sequences,* at the end of which the gentleman describes a half-moon with his hand, guiding the lady so that he is facing her; bend your knees a little as in a *half Reverence,* and drop hands.

The gentleman alone does two *ordinary sequences,* and two *semibreve falling jumps,* concluding with a *feigned sequence* in the manner of a *half Reverence,* doffing his bonnet (or hat) from his head. Note that you must not do this as before, for the dance was quite wrong.

The lady does the same.

The gentleman repeats the same variation to the other side, following the same order [of steps].

After this she does the same as the gentleman has just done.

The Giogioso[1]

To do this Gioioso[2], the gentleman does two *dexterous steps* flankingly forward, in place of the two *stopped steps* which were done before. Then, facing towards your partner, do two *continences,* two *stopped steps* flankingly backward, and two *doubles in French style* as above (one to the left, and the other to the right). Then do two *continences,* one *dexterous step* to the left, and one to the right. This done, do two more *stopped steps,* either forward or back, as the case may be. Then doff your bonnet (or hat), and make a *Reverence* together. The lady does the same [solo]. Note that while the gentleman is dancing this Gioioso, she should not resemble a statue, but should move gracefully in some fashion, as I said in the Notes on the deportment of a lady when standing still during a dance. And note also that you do no *scurrying* [*steps*] as was done before.

The Finale, Done to the Bassa

For the finale, do one *dexterous step* together to the left, and one to the right, two *breve stopped steps,* and two *ordinary sequences* somewhat flankingly, at the end of which the gentleman doffs his bonnet, and [bending both your knees] in the manner of a *half Reverence,* both kiss your own customary hand. After this do two *scurrying sequences,* the gentleman guiding the lady by the hand into a half-moon position. Then do one *dexterous step* to the left and one to the right, with two *stopped steps* either forward or backward, as the gentleman thinks best. Finally, doffing his bonnet and making a *Reverence,* gracefully concluding this Bassa, et Alta, with the left foot joining the right at the end of the music. Now if you do it this way, it will follow the proper rules and be perfect in theory.

---

[1] *Sic.*
[2] *Sic.*

Note

People did this dance before with five *doubles,* and the *reprises* always to the right. Similarly, the *grave continences* were always done with the left foot. Then, in the middle of the Gioioso a *Reverence* was made without following any rule or order. Those who did it were satisfied to say that it was correct, as long as they moved that foot which they joined [to the other]. Also, the gentleman went to take the lady [by the hand] while she was still *scurrying,* which was incorrect. Instead let me say, that everyone at a ball who wishes to do this dance should do it this way, for if so he will never open himself to criticism, but will meet with approval and endear himself to everyone.

[11]   *Bassa, et Alta*

[11] *BASSA, ET ALTA*

Altezza d'Amore [*The Grandeur of Love*]

Balletto

*Dedicated to the Most Illustrious and Excellent
Donna Flavia Peretti Orsina,
Duchess of Bracciano*
(Fig. I)

To begin this balletto, the gentleman takes the lady by the customary hand, as shown in the figure, making a *long Reverence* in four beats, and two *breve continences,* each in two beats. Then progressing, do one *knot,* two *flourishes,* and one *half-double sequence,* beginning all these movements with the left [foot]; repeat the same *knot* and other movements to the other side. Then do two *minim falling jumps* and one *broken sequence,* beginning with the left; repeat to the other side. Note that at the end of the *broken sequence* with the right, you drop hands in the usual well-mannered fashion. Then do four *scurrying sequences* in the shape of an S (that is, first you turn toward the left, and then toward the right), at the end of which you will be facing towards each other, and do the Codetta of this first section with two *falling jumps* (one with the left foot, the other with the right).

The Gentleman's First Variation

Do a four-pattern galliard variation, beginning with the left foot on the first beat of the music, and finishing likewise with the same foot forward; to do otherwise would be unfitting and quite wrong.

The Lady's First Variation

Do two *reprises with foot under* to the left, and one *flourish,* beginning with the left foot; repeat to the other side. Then do one *knot,* two *flourishes* forward, a *half Reverence,* one *foot under,* and a *cadence* at the end of the music, beginning and ending this variation with the left foot forward.

The Gentleman's Second Variation

The gentleman repeats the same variation as above, beginning and ending with the right foot. Note that it should not be done in any other way, for even if he begins and ends in time to the music, and with the right foot forward, it will not be correct in theory, as I have said in my Rules.

The Lady's Second Variation

The lady also repeats [what she did] before, beginning, however, with the right foot forward, and ending with the same foot.

The Sciolta of this Piece as a Saltarello; that is, in triple beats.

Progress with two *altered broken sequences,* two *flourishes,* and one *Sapphic step,* beginning with the left; repeat to the other side. Then do two *ordinary sequences* turning to the left, and three *canary sequences* opposite each other, with two *stamps* (one with the right, the other with the left); repeat to the other side, turning to the right. This done, immediately do a *knot,* two *flourishes,* and one *stopped broken sequence,* beginning with the left, and a *half Reverence* with the right; repeat to the other side. At the end of this Saltarello do two *falling jumps* (one with the left, the other with the right). Now all of this single playing [and section] is symmetrical, which is quite correct.

The Canary is Done as a Pedalogue

Opposite his partner, the gentleman does two *stamps* and a *canary sequence,* beginning with the left, and three more quick *stamps,* beginning with the right, and ending with another *sequence* with the left; the lady does the same. The gentleman repeats this variation to the other side, and the lady does the same. After that do one *minim stopped step* together with the left foot, and a *half Reverence* with the right; repeat to the other side. The gentleman does two *falling jumps,* and one *Sapphic step* with his left hip out; the lady does the same. The gentleman repeats this to the other side, beginning with the right; the lady does the same. Then both do two *broken sequences* turning to the left, with two *minim steps* forward, and one *Sapphic step* with the left hip in, beginning with the left. Repeat to the other side. Finally both do two *minim stopped steps* flankingly forward. Then take each other by the customary hand, and in the usual well-mannered fashion, gracefully conclude this balletto with a *breve Reverence* in four triple beats, in time to the music.

[12] *Altezza d'Amore*

[13]
Coppia Colonna [*The Colonna Couple*]
Balletto

*Dedicated to the Most Illustrious and Excellent Lady
Giulia Colonna Colonna*
(Fig. IV)

To begin this balletto, stand as shown in the figure (that is, the lady at one end of the room, and the gentleman at the other end), and when the music begins, make a *long Reverence*, completing it in four beats, with two *continences* in two beats per *continence*. Then do a pedalogue, the gentleman beginning by taking one *stopped step* in two beats, with his left hip in; [and then] the lady does the same. Then he takes another with the right; and again she does the same. The gentleman then does two *ordinary sequences;* and the lady too, beginning with the left. Then in the usual well-mannered fashion take hands, and do two *semibreve falling jumps* (each in one beat), with one *Corinthian step* to the left; repeat to the other side. The gentleman then drops the lady's right hand, kissing it,[1] immediately and politely doffing his bonnet with the same left hand, and make a *Reverence* together as before.

In the second playing progress together, doing two *stopped steps,* each in two beats, two *semibreve steps,* each in one beat, and one *ordinary sequence* in two beats beginning with the left foot; repeat to the other side from the beginning. Note that at the end of the *sequence* to the right you drop hands in the usual courteous manner, and then turn to the left with two *steps* and one *sequence* as above; repeat to the other side turning to the right, but doing the last *sequence* in the manner of a *half Reverence*. Then do two *falling jumps* and one *Corinthian step* flankingly with the left [hip] in, beginning these movements with the left foot; repeat to the other side. Finally, do two *continences,* each in two beats, and the *Reverence* as before.

In the third playing, take right hands, doing two *breve* (that is, *ordinary*) *sequences,* concluding in the manner of a *half Reverence*. Then dropping hands in the usual courteous manner, and turning to the left, do two *semibreve steps* and one *ordinary sequence* forward, changing places. After this do two *breve*

[1] *Sic.*

stopped steps flankingly forward; and these done, do two *steps* turning to the right, and one *sequence* forward facing towards each other, beginning with the right; repeat the same *stopped steps* and the following movements to the other side. Opposite each other, do two *falling jumps* and one *Corinthian step,* beginning with the right; repeat to the other side, adding two *continences* as at first (one with the right, the other with the left).

In the fourth playing, take left hands and repeat everything you did in the third section to the other side, each therefore returning to your original place.

The Sciolta of this Piece is [Played as] a Galliard

In the fifth (and last) playing, do two *breve stopped steps* flankingly forward, and two *dexterous steps* (that is, two *reprises* and one *falling jump* per *dexterous step*), one to the left, and the other to the right. Then do two *ordinary sequences,* at the end of which bend your knees a little in the manner of a *half Reverence,* and do two *scurrying sequences* forward in the shape of an S, passing each other and changing places. Then do two *double sequences in Spanish style* (one to the left, the other to the right). Finally do two *stopped steps,* and then the gentleman takes the lady by the customary hand in the usual courteous and well-mannered fashion, gracefully ending this balletto by making a *Reverence* in time to the end of the music.

[13] *Coppia Colonna*

Galliard

Rosa Felice [Happy Rosa]

Balletto

Dedicated to the Most Illustrious and Excellent Lady,
My Highly Respected Patroness and Benefactress,
Donna Felice Maria Orsina Caetana, Duchess of Sermoneta
(Fig. I)

To begin this balletto, the gentleman should first doff his bonnet (or hat), and immediately after doffing it, take the lady's left hand with his right in the usual courteous fashion, as you see in the figure, both making the *long Reverence* together, and two *breve continences,* as I have said for the dance of the Grand Duchess of Tuscany.[1] Then do one *reprise with foot under,* and one *flourish* to the left; repeat to the other side. After this is done, immediately do a *limping hop* with the left foot raised (limping on the right), a *step in the air* with the same foot, and a *cadence* (this is the Codetta); do another Codetta to the other side, ending with the right foot forward. Now this first playing is called a Symmetrical Section.

In the second playing, progress with two *breve stopped steps.* Then do a *reprise with foot under* to the left, two *flourishes,* two *quick minim steps,* two more *flourishes,* and a *cadence.* Then immediately do one *knot,* two *flourishes,* two *minim steps* backward, and a *cadence* with the left foot in back. Now with the same foot begin and end the Codetta, beginning all movements with your left foot. This is called a Well-Ordered Passage.

In the third playing, once again do two *stopped steps* (one forward, the other backward). After this repeat these movements to the other side, beginning with the right foot, but dancing backwards a little, and always side by side.[2]

In the fourth playing, do two *reprises* to the left, two *falling jumps,* and one *feigned sequence,* beginning with the left foot; repeat to the other side. Then do one *reprise with foot under,* with one *flourish* to the left; repeat to the other side. This done, once again do the abovementioned Symmetrical Codetta, as I said in the first section.

In the fifth playing, take right hands in the usual well-mannered fashion, and do two *breve* (that is, *ordinary*) *sequences,* at the end of which drop hands and bend your knees a little in the manner of a *half Reverence.* Then do two *broken sequences* turning to the left, facing towards each other again at the end, and

---

[1] I.e., 'Laura Suave'.

[2] 'sempre al pari'.

then do two *Sapphic steps* (one to the left, the other to the right), changing places. Then do one *reprise with foot under,* and one *flourish* to the left; repeat to the other side. Finally, do the two Codettas as above.

In the sixth playing, do one *breve stopped step* with the left foot, one *feigned broken sequence* with the right, one *reprise with foot under,* two *flourishes* forward, one *knot,* two more *flourishes,* two *quick minim steps* backward, one *half Reverence,* one *step in the air* with the left, and a *cadence.* Then do another *knot,* two *flourishes* forward, two *minim steps* backward, and a *cadence.* Finally, do one Codetta only with the left foot.

In the seventh playing, take left hands and repeat the same movements to the other side that you did in the fifth playing with the right foot, thus returning to your original places.

In the eighth playing, both repeat the same variation you did in the sixth playing, to the other side.

In the ninth playing, do two *breve* (that is, *ordinary*) *sequences,* concluding in the manner of a *half Reverence,* and taking customary hands in the usual courteous fashion. Then do two *broken sequences forward,* two *flourishes,* and two *semibreve falling jumps,* each in one musical beat. This done, do one *Sapphic step* to the left, and another to the right. Finally do the above-mentioned two Codettas.

In the tenth (and last) playing, do two *breve sequences* forward. Then do two *breve continences.* After this do the *long Reverence* in four beats, and in the usual courteous way, politely conclude this lovely and graceful balletto.

[14] *Rosa Felice*

Barriera Nuova [New Barriers]

To Be Done By Six [Dancers]

Dedicated to the Most Illustrious and Excellent Lady,
Princess Colonna
(Fig. II)

To begin this Barriera, the gentleman who has just danced the Ballo del Piantone remains on the floor, choosing three ladies, one at a time. Then he selects two gentlemen, and all six form a circle (that is, one gentleman and one lady, and so on), with a *long Reverence* in four beats of music, and two *breve continences,* each in two beats. After this turn to the left with two *semibreve steps,* each in one beat, and do one *ordinary sequence* in two beats facing towards each other. Repeat the same *steps* and *sequence* to the other side.

In the second playing, do two *breve stopped steps* forward, then progress with four *semibreve steps,* one *sequence* turning to the left, beginning with the left, and another facing towards each other with the right. Then do one *breve continence* with the left, one *Sapphic step* to the right, and one *dexterous step* to the left.

In the third playing, progress a second time with the aforementioned movements that were done before, beginning, however, with the right foot, and ending with that foot as well. Note that everything that is done with the left foot must be repeated with the right, except for the *Reverence.*

In the fourth playing, each gentleman takes the right hand of the lady on his right, and both do one *breve stopped step,* and one *half-double sequence.* Then, dropping hands in the usual courteous manner, turn to the left with four *semibreve steps,* one *half-double sequence* facing towards each other, beginning with the left foot, and three *reprises* to the right. Then do one *continence* with the left, one *Sapphic step* to the right, and one *dexterous step* to the left.

In the fifth playing, take left hands, and do all the movements you did in the fourth playing to the other side.

Gentleman's Symmetrical Variation

In the sixth playing, each gentleman does four *semibreve steps,* as above, or four *broken sequences* flankingly forward opposite his lady. After this, turn your bodies a little to the left with one *stopped broken sequence* (beginning these movements with the left foot), and immediately make a *half Reverence* with the right, doffing your bonnet (or hat); repeat the same *stopped broken sequence* and *half Reverence* to the other side. Then, with the left foot, which will now be in back, do two *falling jumps,* and one *Sapphic step* flankingly backward, beginning with the left; repeat to the other side. Note that [at this point] you should not do [either] four *broken sequences,* or *pulled steps,* for since the left foot is in back, it cannot do a *broken sequence* (or *step*) backward, because that would be quite wrong, and against the rule. Then, finally, the gentlemen and ladies make a *long Reverence* together.

In the seventh playing, the ladies repeat the same.

The Piece is Varied, and Played Twice

In the first playing of this [varied] piece, progress to the left, doing two *semibreve steps* and one *half-double sequence,* beginning with the left foot; repeat to the other side. Then do two *breve stopped steps* (one forward with the left, the other backward with the right), and facing towards each other do one *double scurrying sequence* forward, taking hands in a circle without doffing your hats. After this drop hands, doing four *Sapphic steps* (or *broken sequences*) flankingly backward, one *continence* to the left, one *Sapphic step* to the right, and concluding with one *dexterous step* to the left.

In the second playing, repeat everything to the other side, beginning, therefore, with the right foot.

The Sciolta of this Piece as a Saltarello, [Played] Only Once

In this playing, everyone does four *broken sequences* flankingly forward. Then everyone strikes hands four times, beginning by first striking the [hand of the] lady on the right with the right hand, then striking the [hand of the] lady on the left with the left hand, and repeating this once more, until you have struck four times. Now this is called the Melee[1]. Finally, do two *breve continences* (each in two beats), and a *Reverence* in four [beats].

The Sciolta of the Piece as a Galliard

In this playing, progress in a chain (or braid, if you will) in a circle. That is, each gentleman simultaneously takes his lady by the right hand, and everyone (gentlemen and ladies equally), does one *half-double sequence* at each taking of hands. Then, dropping right hands, take left hands, changing ladies (similarly, the ladies change gentlemen). Now this chain lasts until each gentleman meets

---

[1] *Folla:* 'crowd'. As this is the figure which most closely resembles a mock tournament, the technical term in English for this action in a tournament has been used in the translation. See Florio, '*Folla*, a course in the field where many horsemen or tilters after they have runne single one to one they runne pell mell altogether'.

his lady again, which will occur after having done six *half-double sequences.* After this do two *continences* and two *breve stopped steps,* at the end of which each gentleman takes his lady by the customary hand in the usual courteous manner, gracefully completing this Barriera with a *long Reverence.* But the gentleman who invited all the ladies [to dance] should note that he and his lady must remain in order to continue with the Ballo del Piantone, while the other gentlemen must return their ladies to their places, taking their leaves in the usual courtly manner.

Play the same music as for the Barriera on p. 185.

[16]
Doria Colonna

Cascarda

Dedicated to the Most Illustrious and Excellent Lady,
D[onna] Giovanna Colonna d'Oria, Princess of Oria
(Fig. VII)

This cascarda is divided into five sections. Standing opposite each other, as shown in the figure, and taking right hands, do one *stopped broken sequence* with the left foot, and a *half Reverence* with the right; repeat to the other side. Then do two *flourishes*, two *falling jumps*, and two *Sapphic steps* (one to the left, the other to the right). After this do four *ordinary sequences* gracefully, and two *half-double sequences,* circling to the left. Then do the Codetta to the Pavaniglia twice, the first with the left foot (that is, one *limping hop,* one *step in the air,* and a *cadence);* repeat to the other side, with two *flourishes* and two *falling jumps* besides. Then do two *minim steps* turning to the left, two more *flourishes* forward, with two more *minim steps,* one *Sapphic step* with the left hip in at the conclusion of the music.

In the second playing, repeat everything from the beginning to the other side.

In the third playing, do the two Pavaniglia Codettas. Then do two *reprises with foot under* to the left, and one *flourish;* repeat to the other side, concluding with two *falling jumps.* After this take right hands, doing one *half-double sequence* with the left foot, two *flourishes* forward, and a *Sapphic step* to the right, beginning with the right foot. Then drop hands, and do two *minim steps* turning to the left, two *flourishes* forward, two more *minim steps,* and conclude with a *Sapphic step* with the left hip turned in, beginning these movements with the left foot.

In the fourth playing, repeat everything you did in the third section to the other side.

In the fifth (and last) playing, do one *knot,* two *flourishes,* two *falling jumps,* and a *Sapphic step* with the left hip in, beginning these movements with the left foot; repeat to the other side. Then do two *broken sequences* turning left, two *minim steps* forward, and a *Sapphic step* with the left hip in; repeat to the other side. After this do two *reprises,* two *falling jumps,* two *minim steps,* and a *Sapphic step* to the left, beginning with the left foot; repeat to the other side.

Then do one *reprise with foot under* to the left, and a *flourish;* repeat to the
right. Do two *broken sequences* flankingly forward, and two *semibreve
stopped steps.* Finally take customary hands in the usual gentle and courteous
manner, and gracefully conclude this cascarda with a *breve Reverence* in time
to the music.

[16]   *Doria Colonna*

Alta Colonna [Great Lady Colonna]

Balletto

Dedicated to the Most Illustrious and Excellent Lady
Arsilia Sforza Colonna, Princess of Pellestrina
(Fig. VIII)

To begin this dance, the couple take hands, as shown in the figure, with a *Reverence* and two *continences*. Then do two *sequences* (one to the left, the other to the right), two *grave falling jumps*, and one *dexterous step* to the left, beginning these movements with the left foot; repeat the abovementioned *sequences*, and all the following steps, to the other side. Finally do two *continences*, and when these are done, the gentleman drops the lady's right hand, doffing his hat with that hand, and both make a *Reverence* together. Now this is termed a Symmetrical Section.

In the second playing, progress with two *semibreve steps* and a *breve sequence*, beginning with the left foot; repeat to the other side. Then immediately do two *flourishes*, one *knot*, two *flourishes*, two *minim steps*, two more *flourishes*, and one *dexterous step*, beginning with the left foot; repeat to the other side. After this do two *breve stopped steps*, and a *long Reverence* to conclude. Now this is similarly called a Symmetrical Passage.

In the third playing, take right hands, and do two *steps* and a *sequence;* repeat, beginning first with the left foot, and then with the right, at the end of which drop hands in the usual courteous fashion, bending your knees a little, therefore, in the manner of a *half Reverence*. Then immediately turn to the left with two *steps* and two *flourishes;* and facing each other do one *knot*, two more *flourishes*, two *steps*, and one *dexterous step*, beginning these movements with the left foot; repeat the same *steps* and all the other movements to the other side, except that in place of the *dexterous step* you do a *Sapphic step*. Finally do two *stopped steps* (one forward, the other backward), two slow *falling jumps*, and a *Corinthian step*, beginning with the left.

In the fourth playing, take left hands, and do everything you did in the third section to the other side. Note that these two sections are called Well-Ordered Sections.

In the fifth (and last) playing, do two *breve sequences,* concluding in the manner of a *half Reverence,* and take customary hands in the usual well-mannered fashion. Then progress with two *breve stopped steps,* two *steps,* and a *sequence,* beginning with the left foot. Then do one *Sapphic step* to the right, and one *dexterous step* to the left; repeat to the other side. Then do two *stopped steps* as above, and making a *long Reverence* in four beats, conclude this graceful balletto in time to the music.

[17] *Alta Colonna*

Allegrezza d'Amore [*The Joy of Love*]

Cascarda

Dedicated to the Most Illustrious and Excellent Lady
D[onna] Margarita Gonzaga Carafa, Princess of Stigliano
(Fig. IX)

To begin this cascarda, the gentleman who remains after the Ballo del Fiore invites two ladies (one at a time) who know how to dance it. Then arrange yourselves in a circle holding hands, as shown in the figure (even though the picture in the figure cannot show the circle), and make a *Reverence,* as described in Alta Regina. After this drop hands with all due courtesy, and all do two *Sapphic steps* flankingly backward (not as before, when two *broken sequences* were done, so that the left foot, which was in front, was the same used to walk forward, which was wrong). This done, do two *minim doubles* (one to the left, the other to the right), and the gentleman alone does two *stamped sequences in the canary;* the lady who is on his right does the same, and the other lady does the same. This done, all do two *broken sequences* flankingly forward, one *reprise* to the left, and one *flourish;* repeat to the other side. Finally do two *falling jumps* and one *Sapphic step* to the left; repeat to the other side, beginning all these movements first, to be sure, first with the left foot, and then with the right.

In the second playing, all do two *flourishes,* and two *falling jumps.* Then the gentleman who leads the dance passes between the ladies with a *double scurrying sequence,* all changing places (that is, the gentleman goes to the ladies' place, and they go to the gentleman's place); repeat to the other side, beginning, therefore, on the opposite [foot], and everyone returning to place. After this the gentleman does two *stamped sequences of the canary;* the ladies do the same, one at a time, as I said above. This done, do two *broken sequences* turning left, two *minim steps* forward, and a *Sapphic step* flankingly; repeat to the other side.

In the third playing, do eight *broken sequences* in a chain: the gentleman who leads moves between the ladies, turning to the left; the left-hand lady moves through the middle, turning to the right of the right-hand lady, and the other lady follows suit, turning to the left of the gentleman. Note that you do not touch hands, as was done before, because that is not correct. [Do the chain] in such a way that when the eight *broken sequences* are completed everyone has returned to place. Then the gentleman *stamps* four times, beginning with the left foot; each lady does the same, one after the other. After this all do two *flourishes,* two *falling jumps,* one *reprise,* and one *flourish* to the left; and another *reprise* and *flourish* to the right. Finally do two *stopped steps,* and two *Sapphic steps* flankingly, beginning each movement with the left foot, and then the right.

In the fourth (and last) playing, do two *flourishes,* two *falling jumps,* and one *minim double* to the left; repeat to the other side. Then the gentleman does two *stamped sequences of the canary;* the ladies do the same, one at a time, as stated above. At the end the gentleman moves between the ladies with two *stopped steps,* taking the place of the right-hand lady; the right-hand lady does the same, going to the gentleman's place. The other goes to the other lady's place, all ending in a triangle, and making a *breve Reverence* as before, gracefully conclude this beautiful cascarda in time to the music. Note that when this cascarda is over, the gentleman must give the flower to the lady he chose first, and then take the other back to her place, taking his leave in the usual courtly manner.

[18] *Allegrezza d'Amore*

[19]
Amor Costante [*Constant Love*]
Balletto

Dedicated to the Most Illustrious and Excellent Lady
Costanza Sforza Buoncompagna, Duchess of Sora [*sic*]
(Fig. VIII)

Begin this dance in the position shown by the figure, with a *long Reverence* and two *breve continences*. Then do two *semibreve steps* and one *half-double sequence* to the left; repeat to the other side. After this do two *falling jumps* and one *Corinthian step* to the left; repeat to the other side. This done, do two *breve stopped steps* facing each other. Then the gentleman drops the lady's right hand, and both make a *Reverence* as before.

In the second playing, progress with four *breve sequences,* at the end of which drop hands in the usual courteous manner, and do two *semibreve steps* turning to the left, and one *breve sequence* facing towards each other; repeat to the other side. Then do two *Sapphic steps* flankingly, and one *half-double sequence* to the left; repeat to the other side. Finally do two *reprises,* two *falling jumps* to the left and one *half-double sequence* forward; repeat to the other side; begin all these movements, to be sure, first with the left foot, and then with the right.

In the third playing, take right hands in the usual courteous fashion, doing two *broken sequences* and two *Sapphic steps,* beginning with the left foot. Then dropping hands, do two *semibreve steps* turning to the left, one *Sapphic step* with the left hip in, while changing places, and two *falling jumps* (one with the right foot, the other with the left) facing towards each other, beginning all these movements with the left foot; repeat to the other side, taking left hands, and returning to place. After this do two *Sapphic steps* flankingly, and one *half-double sequence* to the left. At the end do two *reprises,* and two *falling jumps* to the left, and one *half-double sequence* forward; repeat to the other side.

The Sciolta of this Piece as a Saltarello

In this playing, take right arms and do two *broken sequences,* and then drop arms and do two more turning to the left, changing places and separating somewhat from each other. Then do two *steps* and one *broken sequence* forward (beginning all of these movements with the left foot), one *falling jump* to the right, and one *dexterous step* to the left; repeat to the other side with the right foot. Finally do two *broken sequences* flankingly, three *stamped sequences of the canary* (beginning with the left), and two *stamps* (one with the right, the other with the left); repeat to the other side. Also do two *flourishes,* two *falling jumps,* and two *Sapphic steps.* At the end, do two *semibreve stopped steps* forward, taking each other by the customary hand, and in the usual well-mannered fashion, with a *breve Reverence* in four triple beats, conclude this most beautiful of ballettos.

[19] *Amor Costante*

Forza d'Amore [*The Power of Love*]

Balletto

Dedicated to the Most Illustrious and Excellent Lady
Leonora Orsina Sforza, Duchess of Segne
(Fig. VII)

Begin this dance in the position shown by the figure, in the usual courtly manner, with a *long Reverence,* and two *breve continences,* as I have said for the other dances. Then take right hands, with one *stopped step* with the left foot, and a *half Reverence* with the right; repeat to the other side. After this take customary hands and do two *breve sequences,* and progress through the ballroom with two *breve stopped steps,* two *semibreve steps,* and one *breve ordinary sequence,* beginning everything with the left foot, and then with the right. This done, do one *dexterous step* to the left, and another to the right. Then do two *broken sequences* flankingly forward, and two *falling jumps.* Finally do two *breve ordinary sequences,* dropping hands at the end in the usual well-mannered fashion. Add two more *scurrying* [*sequences*] in the shape of an S.

The Galliard to this [*Balletto*]

In the second playing, the gentleman does one four-pattern galliard variation. Now if he wishes to do it gravely, he may do two *sequences* flankingly, two *grave falling jumps* (that is, *semi-minims*), and one *feigned sequence* (as described in the Bassa, et Alta), beginning with the left foot; the lady does the same. The gentleman then repeats the same variation, beginning it to the other side (that is, with the right foot); the lady does the same. This done, do four *dexterous steps* as a pedalogue: that is, the gentleman does one with his left hip in; the lady does another; the gentleman repeats this to the other side, with his right hip in; the lady does the same. Then do one *knot* and one *flourish* together; repeat to the other side. At the end do two *steps* forward, with two *Sapphic steps* flankingly in, beginning all the first movements with the left foot, and then with the right.

In the third playing, take right hands, doing two *semibreve steps* and one *breve sequence* to the left. Then do one *breve continence* with the right foot, and one *feigned sequence* with the left foot, dropping hands in the usual courteous fashion; repeat to the other side, taking left hands. Then dropping hands, do two *breve stopped steps,* and one *double sequence in French style,* progressing to the left; repeat to the other side. This done, repeat the pedalogue again, with all the other actions and movements I called for in the second playing.

The Sciolta of this Piece as a Saltarello

In this last playing make a *breve Reverence* in four triple beats, facing towards each other, with two *Sapphic steps* (one to the left, the other to the right). Then turn to the left with two *minim steps,* and one *broken sequence* forward. After this do a *knot,* two *flourishes,* and one *stopped broken sequence,* beginning with the left foot, and a *half Reverence* with the right; repeat to the other side. Finally, do two more *Sapphic steps* flankingly, with two *flourishes,* and two *falling jumps.* Then, while doing two *stopped semibreve steps* forward, gently take customary hands in the aforementioned courtly manner, and making a *Reverence* in time to the music, conclude this lovely and graceful balletto.

[20] *Forza d'Amore*

Bassa Honorata [Bassa, the Honoured One]

Balletto

Dedicated to the Most Illustrious and Excellent Lady
Costanza Savella Orsina, Duchess of Saint Gemine
(Fig. III)

Stand as shown in the figure, the gentleman taking the lady by the customary hand in the usual well-mannered fashion, with a *long Reverence* together, and two *breve continences.* Then take right hands and do two *ordinary sequences,* two *falling jumps,* and one *dexterous step;* repeat to the other side, taking left hands. Finally, the gentleman takes the lady once more by the customary hand, and both do the *continences* and *Reverences* as above, beginning all movements first with the left foot, and then with the right.

In the second playing, progress with two *breve stopped steps,* four *semibreve steps,* two *breve sequences,* and two *semibreve falling jumps,* ending with one *dexterous step* to the left, beginning all these movements with the left foot; repeat the same *sequences, falling jumps,* and *dexterous step* to the side. Now these two playings are called Symmetrical Sections.

In the third playing, the gentleman leaves the lady, and progresses some distance away to the left with two *semibreve steps* and one *breve sequence,* concluding this *sequence* by turning to face towards the lady (these movements begin on the left foot). Now progressing to the right, repeat to the other side. Then together do two *breve sequences* flankingly, two *falling jumps,* and one *dexterous step;* repeat to the other side. At the end, do two *continences* and a *Reverence* as above.

In the fourth playing, the lady alone does just what the gentleman did. Then do all the abovementioned movements together as before.

In the fifth playing, both do one *double in Italian style* to the left, and another to the right. After this, opposite each other, do the abovementioned *sequences* flankingly, the *falling jumps,* and the *dexterous step,* both to the left and the right, with the two *continences* and *Reverence.*

The Sciolta of this Piece is Done as a Saltarello

In this single playing, take right hands, and do two *broken sequences*, two *minim steps*, and one *Sapphic step* to the left; repeat to the other side, taking left hands. After this drop hands, doing two *Sapphic steps* flankingly backward, two *falling jumps*, two *minim steps*, and one *Sapphic step* with your left hip in; repeat to the other side. Finally do two *continences*, and in the usual courtly manner take customary hands, making a *Reverence* as before, and concluding this lovely balletto in time to the music.

[21] *Bassa Honorata*

[22]
Cesarina

Balletto

Dedicated to the Most Excellent and Illustrious Lady,
D[onna] Livia Orsina Cesarina, Duchess of Cività Nuova
(Fig. III)

Begin this most graceful balletto by standing as shown in the figure, making a *grave Reverence* in six beats of music, and two *semigrave continences* in three beats each. Then progress through the ballroom with four *breve sequences*. After this do two *semibreve steps,* and one *half-double sequence*, beginning with the left foot; repeat the same *steps* and *sequence* to the other side. This done, do one *dexterous step* to the left, and another to the right, with one *broken sequence*, two *minim steps* forward, and two *falling jumps*. Note that the *steps* and the *falling jumps* begin with the right foot. Finally, repeat the abovementioned *broken sequence* once more, with three *falling jumps*, and one *dexterous step*, with all the aforementioned movements to the other side.

In the second playing, progress with two *pulled stopped steps* and two *breve sequences*. Then do two *semibreve steps* and one *half-double sequence*, beginning with the left foot; repeat the same *steps* and *sequence* to the other side. After this do two *stopped steps*, two *broken sequences*, and two *falling jumps*, beginning with the left foot, do another *broken sequence* with the same foot, and three *falling jumps*, beginning these *falling jumps* with the right foot. This done, do the two *dexterous steps* again, and all the other movements described above in the first section; repeat to the other side, beginning with the *broken sequence* and the three *falling jumps*. Now this is called a Symmetrical Passage. Note that you drop hands with the last *falling jump*.

In the third playing, do two *sequences* flankingly, separating from each other. Then do one *knot*, two *flourishes* forward, one *half Reverence*, one *foot under*, and conclude with a *cadence*, beginning everything with the left foot. After this repeat the same variation again, beginning and ending it with the right foot. Then do two *stopped steps*, and two *sequences* flankingly. This done, do one *broken sequence* with the left foot, and three *falling jumps*, beginning with the right. Now turning your left hip in, do one *dexterous step*; repeat to the other side, turning your right hip in. Then turn to the left with one *broken sequence*, two *minim steps,* and two *falling jumps*, turning your left hip in on the last one. Note that the *broken sequence* is done with the left foot, and the *steps* and *falling jumps* begin with the right. After this, repeat the *broken sequence*, again with the three *falling jumps*, *dexterous step*, and all the subsequent movements mentioned in the first [playing], to the other side.

In the fourth (and last) playing, take right hands, doing two *steps* and one *half-double sequence*, beginning with the left foot, with one *continence* with the right, and one *feigned sequence* with the left, bending your knees a little in the manner of a *half Reverence*, and dropping hands at that moment in the usual courteous manner; repeat to the other side, therefore taking left hands. After this do two *stopped steps*, with two *dexterous steps* flankingly (first with the left hip in, and then with the right), and two *sequences* flankingly, separating from each other somewhat. Then do two *reprises with foot under* to the left, and one *flourish*, beginning with the left foot; repeat to the other side (to the right) with two *broken sequences* flankingly forward, and two *falling jumps*. This done, do two *sequences* flankingly, with two *stopped steps*. Finally, take customary hands in the usual well-mannered fashion, and make a *Reverence* as at the beginning, gently concluding this lovely and beautiful balletto. Now this is correct in theory.

[22]   *Cesarina*

23

Bellezze d'Olimpia [The Beauties of Olimpia]

Balletto

Dedicated to the Most Illustrious and Excellent Lady
Olimpia Orsina Cesi, Duchess of AquaSparta
(Fig. V)

In my first book I began this balletto with the gentleman standing to the right of the lady and then returning to her left, which was [both] bad style and ill-mannered, because in dancing the gentleman should always give precedence to the lady. Furthermore, I have noticed that another error occurred if one began this way, for, after completing the *Reverence* and *continences*, two *ordinary sequences* were done, and when one dropped hands, turning to the left with two more *sequences*, it was quite wrong not to turn right [afterwards]. Now to do it correctly I would like you to begin this way: stand opposite each other, as shown in the figure for Alta Regina,[1] with a *long Reverence* in the usual courteous manner, and two *breve continences*. Then do two *grave steps* turning to the left, and an *ordinary sequence* facing each other, beginning with the left foot; repeat to the other side. After this, opposite each other, do together two *broken sequences* flankingly, and three *falling jumps*; repeat to the other side. Then do two *stopped steps* forward, taking customary hands, and, in the usual courteous manner make a *Reverence* in time to the music.

In the second playing, progress with two *semibreve steps* and one *ordinary breve sequence*, beginning with the left foot; repeat to the other side. Then do two *stopped steps*, with two *ordinary sequences*, at the end of which drop hands in the usual courteous manner and do two more [*sequences*] *scurryingly*,[2] one to the left, and the other to the right (now if you do not wish to do them *scurryingly*, you may do them flankingly backward). Then, opposite each other, do two *broken sequences*, two *Sapphic steps* flankingly, two *continences*, and a *Reverence*, as above.

In the third playing, do a pedalogue. That is, the gentleman alone does one

---

[1] Fig. II; nevertheless, the figure given here by Caroso is Fig. V, which is slightly different.

[2] I.e., scurrying sequences? The reversed order of the words is kept here, since the context suggests that Caroso is considering all *sequences* in the same category at this point.

stopped step flankingly forward, and the lady does the same, beginning with the left [foot]; he repeats another one with the right, and she does the same. Then the gentleman does two *ordinary breve sequences* flankingly, and the lady does the same by herself. After this do two *broken sequences* flankingly together, and three *falling jumps*, beginning and ending with the left foot; repeat once more to the other side. Then do two *stopped steps* forward, taking both hands. Having done these *stopped steps*, the gentleman drops the lady's right hand in the usual courteous manner, and both make a *Reverence* at the end of this playing.

In the fourth playing, take right hands and do two *ordinary sequences,* dropping hands afterwards in the usual well-mannered fashion; then both turn to the left and do two more [*ordinary sequences*], changing places. After this do one *knot,* two *flourishes* forward, one *stopped step,* beginning these actions and movements with the left foot, and a *half Reverence* with the right. Note that in doing this *stopped step* and *half Reverence,* you should turn a little to the left; repeat to the other side. Then opposite each other do the *broken sequences* flankingly, and *falling jumps* twice, as stated above. Finally do two *stopped steps* and a *Reverence* in time to the music.

In the fifth playing, take left hands, and do the same as you did in the fourth playing to the other side.

In the sixth (and last) playing, take customary hands in the usual courteous and well-mannered fashion, just as you did when taking hands in the first playing, and do two *stopped steps*, two *semibreve steps,* and a *breve sequence;* repeat to the other side. Then do the two *broken sequences* and three *falling jumps*, as given above. At the end do two *stopped steps*, and taking customary hands, make a *long Reverence* as at the beginning, to conclude this balletto.

[23] *Bellezze d'Olimpia*

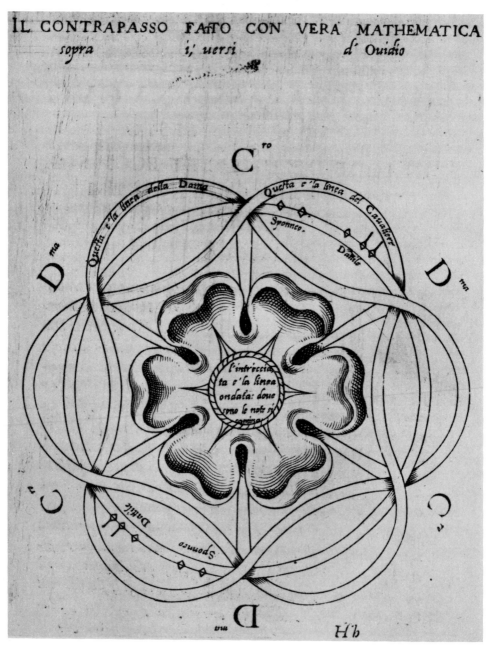

(*Title*) Contrapasso, created according to correct mathematical principles based on Ovid's verse [meters]. (*Top left*) This is the lady's path. (*Top right*) This is the gentleman's path. (*Top right* and *bottom left*) Spondeo, Dactyl. (*Center*) The chain is shown by the wavy line; one walks [along the line] where the notes appear.

24

Contrapasso Nuovo [New Counterpace]

To Be Performed by Six [Dancers]

Dedicated to the Most Illustrious and Excellent Lady
Cornelia Orsina Cesi, Duchess of Ceri

To do this Contrapasso requires the participation of three gentlemen and three ladies, who form a circle in the following order: that is, one gentleman and one lady. Now in time to the music all make a *long Reverence* without holding hands, and two *breve continences.* Then progressing in a circle to the left, do two *semi-breve steps* and one *breve sequence,* beginning with the left foot; repeat to the other side, progressing to the right. Note that this passage must be done once more, both to the left and to the right. After this, when the music changes, each gentleman takes the right hand of the lady standing to his right, and he does two *steps* and one *sequence,* as above, beginning with the left foot. Then everyone drops hands, and with his left hand the [gentleman] takes the left hand of the other lady whom he is opposite, with the same two *steps* and one *sequence,* beginning with the right foot, and continuing to change places. Now he should not be displeased upon finding himself without his lady the second time, since at the end of the third change (having continued on the above-mentioned terms in a circle) each one will once again discover himself to be with his own lady. This done, drop hands, and do two *steps* turning to the left, beginning with the left foot, and one *sequence* forward, bending your knees a little as in a *half Reverence;* repeat to the other side.

Chain Passage Around the Ring

Each gentleman takes his lady's right hand, and together they do one *breve sequence* with the left foot; then take the left hand of the other lady and do another *sequence* with the right foot, and continue thus, making a chain around the ring, until you have done six *sequences,* at the end of which everyone will have returned to place with his own lady. Now this chain takes three repetitions of the music.

After this do two *breve continences* together, and a *long Reverence,* with two *double sequences in French style* (one to the left, and the other to the right).

Everyone does two *breve sequences* forward, beginning with the left foot, and taking hands in a circle. Then do two *continences,* and dropping hands, do the same two *double sequences* as above.

Finally, do two *breve continences,* and two *breve sequences* flankingly, concluding in the manner of a *half Reverence,* and everyone taking his lady by the customary hand, in the usual courtly manner. At the end, do two *breve stopped steps* (one forward and the other back), and with a *long Reverence,* conclude this dance executed according to the correct rules, and following perfect theoretical and mathematical principles.

[24]   *Contrapasso Nuovo*

[25]
Specchio d'Amore [*The Mirror of Love*]
Cascarda

Dedicated to the Most Illustrious and Excellent Lady,
The Duchess of Atri
(Fig. VII)

Stand as shown in the figure, and do a *breve Reverence* and two *Sapphic steps*. Then do two *half-double sequences*, two *broken sequences*, two *flourishes*, and two *falling jumps*, beginning with the left foot. Note that all of these movements are done in three repetitions of the music. Then, to one playing of the reprise[1] of this piece, do one *stopped broken sequence* with the left foot to the left, and a *half Reverence* with the right. After this, to another playing of the reprise of this piece, repeat to the other side.

In the second playing, progress with one *half-double sequence* with the left [foot], two *flourishes*, and two *falling jumps*, beginning with the right foot; repeat to the other side. Then do two *broken sequences*, two *flourishes*, and two *minim steps*. After this, to the reprises of this piece, do the same *broken sequences* and *half Reverence* that I called for in the first playing. Now these two Passages are Symmetrical.

In the third playing, take right hands, doing two *broken sequences*, and two *Sapphic steps*. Then drop hands, with two more *broken sequences* turning to the left, and two more *Sapphic steps* (the first with the left hip turned in, and [the second] repeating with the right). Face towards each other and do one *reprise* and one *flourish*, beginning with the left; repeat to the other side. Do two *flourishes* forward and two *falling jumps*. Finally, to the two musical reprises do two *semibreve stopped steps*, two *falling jumps*, and one *Sapphic step*, beginning with the left foot.

In the fourth playing, take left hands and do everything you did in the third playing to the other side. Now the third and fourth sections are termed Well-Ordered.

---

[1] See music. This cadential pattern fits the musical definition of a reprise (see Hudson, 'Ripresa etc.').

In the fifth (and last) playing, progress to the left with one *half-double sequence* with the left foot, one *falling jump* with the right, and one *dexterous step* to the left; then progress to the right, repeating to the other side. Finally, do one *reprise* and one *flourish* to the left; repeat to the other side, with two *flourishes* forward, and two *falling jumps*. Then, to the reprises in the music, do two *minim stopped steps* flankingly forward, and having done this, take customary hands in the usual courteous manner. Now with a *Reverence* at the end of the music as at the beginning, conclude this lovely cascarda.

[25]   *Specchio d'Amore*

[26]

Contentezza d'Amore [*The Happiness of Love*]

Balletto

Dedicated to the Most Illustrious and Excellent Lady
Giulia Orsina Conti, Duchess of Poli
(Fig. VIII)

Stand opposite each other holding both hands, as shown in the figure, and make a *long Reverence* in time to the music, with two *breve continences*. Then do two *reprises,* two *falling jumps,* and one *breve sequence* to the left; repeat to the other side. At the end, the gentleman drops the lady's right hand, in the usual courteous manner, and both make a *Reverence* as before, beginning everything with the left foot, and then with the right foot.

In the second playing, progress together holding hands (not as before, when the lady progressed first, and the gentleman afterwards, for I say that to dance it thus was quite wrong). You must, then, do two *breve stopped steps* together, with two *semibreve steps* and one *breve sequence,* beginning with the left foot; repeat to the other side, both the *stopped steps* as well as the other movements, beginning with the right foot. After this, turn to face towards each other at the other end of the ballroom, without dropping hands, and do two *grave falling jumps,* each in one beat, and three quick [*falling jumps*], in the time of two beats,[1] beginning with the left foot. At the end do two *breve continences,* one with the left foot and the other with the right.

In the third playing, progress by doing the same passage to the other side, beginning with the right foot, and returning to the place where you began the dance.

In the fourth playing, take right hands and do two *breve sequences*, at the end of which drop hands in the usual courteous manner. Then turn to the left, with two more *sequences,* one going to one end of the ballroom, the other to the other end. This done, opposite each other, do two *stopped steps,* two more *sequences* flankingly, two *grave falling jumps,* and one *dexterous step,*

---

[1] *Sic.*

beginning these movements with the left foot. Finally, do two *stopped steps*, as above.

In the fifth playing, take left hands, repeating all these movements to the other side, beginning with the right foot.

The Sciolta of this Piece as a Saltarello

In the sixth (and last) playing, take hands as at the beginning, and do two *broken sequences* to the left. Then drop hands, with two *steps* turning to the left, and another *broken sequence* forward, changing places. After this take hands again, and repeat to the other side, returning to your own places. Do two *reprises*, two *falling jumps*, two *minim steps*, and one *Sapphic step* to the left; repeat to the other side. Finally, do two *minim stopped steps* forward, and in the usual courtly manner conclude this lovely balletto by doing a *breve Reverence* in time to the music. Note that you must join the left foot to the right at the end of the music, or else the dance will be quite wrong.

[26] *Contentezza d'Amore*

27

Bassa Savella [*?*]

Balletto

*Dedicated to the Most Illustrious and Excellent Lady
Livia Orsina Savella, Duchess of Castel Candolfo*[1]
(Fig. I)

In this balletto stand opposite each other as shown in the figure, taking customary hands in the usual courteous manner, and make a *long Reverence* together in four beats of music, with two *continences* (one with the left foot, the other with the right). Now take right hands, and do two *half-double sequences* to the left, and one *Corinthian step* (that is, three *reprises* and one *falling jump*), beginning with the left foot; repeat, taking left hands and beginning with the right foot.

In the second playing, take customary hands once more, progressing with four *half-double sequences.* Then take right arms, doing two *broken sequences* and two *pulled sequences,* and dropping arms, turn to the left with one *double [sequence]*, beginning everything with the left foot; repeat to the other side, taking left hands[2] and beginning with the right [foot].

In the third playing, turn to the left with two *half-double sequences,* two *Corinthian steps* flankingly forward (first with the left hip turned in, and then with the right hip), with two *pulled steps,* two *broken sequences,* two *minim steps,* and one *Sapphic step,* doing all these movements to the left; repeat from the beginning to the other side, turning right.

The Sciolta of this Piece

In the fourth (and last) playing, take right hands again, and do two *broken sequences.* Then drop hands, turning to the left with two *steps* and one *Sapphic step* with the left hip in, changing places; repeat to the other side, taking left hands. Do one *Sapphic step* to the left, and another to the right, with two *broken sequences* flankingly forward, two *flourishes,* and two *falling jumps.*

---

[1] *Sic.*
[2] *Sic.*

Finally, do two more *broken sequences,* and two *semibreve stopped steps,* and in the usual courteous manner take customary hands, making a *Reverence* in four triple beats, and gently concluding this dance in the German style.

[27]   *Bassa Savella*

28

Conto dell'Orco Nuovo [New (Version of the) Tale of the Ogre]

Balletto

*Dedicated to the Most Illustrious and Excellent Lady
Camilla Caetana Caetana, Duchess of Traetta*
(Fig. V)

To begin this dance stand as shown in the figure, doing a *breve Reverence*, two *Sapphic steps*, two *minim steps*, two *flourishes*, and two more *Sapphic steps*, standing still for half a beat. Then progress holding hands, doing four *pulled sequences* (or *ordinary* [*sequences*]). This done do one *Corinthian step* to the left, and another to the right. At the end, do two *broken sequences*, two *flourishes*, and two *falling jumps*, beginning these movements with the left foot.

In the second figure,[1] do two *semibreve steps* and one *breve sequence*, beginning with the left foot; repeat to the other side. After that repeat the abovementioned two *Corinthian steps*, and all the other movements done in the first playing. Now these two Passages are termed Symmetrical.

In the third figure, take right hands and do two *steps* and one *sequence* as before, progressing to the left, beginning with the left foot. Then do two *falling jumps*, each in one beat of music (the first with the right foot, the second with the left), with one *dexterous step* to the right. Dropping hands, do two *breve sequences* turning to the left, two *semibreve falling jumps* facing towards each other, and one *dexterous step* to the left at the end.

In the fourth figure, take left hands, repeating everything to the other side, and beginning with the right foot.

In the fifth figure, take customary hands once more, and do four *breve sequences*, two *Corinthian steps*, two *semibreve stopped steps*, and at the end, in the usual courtly manner, conclude this lovely balletto with a *breve Reverence*.

---

[1] See ch. 2 for a discussion of this term.

[28] *Conto dell'Orco Nuovo*

Furioso all'Italiana [*Furioso in Italian Style*]¹

Balletto

*Dedicated to the Most Illustrious and Excellent Lady
Camilla Piccolomini Conti, Duchess of Carpeneto*
(Fig. IX)

To begin with, three gentlemen stand in a line at one end of the hall, with an equal number of ladies at the other end; or two ladies and one gentleman [stand] at one end, and two gentlemen and one lady at the other end (as may be seen in the figure). Then all make a *long Reverence* together opposite each other, with two *breve continences*. After this the gentleman and lady who are in the middle lead the dance, doing two *half-double sequences* forward, at the end of which you bend your knees a little in the manner of a *half Reverence,* without touching right hands. Then change places, the lady doing two more *scurrying sequences;* now before she takes her place in the middle she acknowledges the person on her right, and while taking her place in the middle she acknowledges the other person on her left. The gentleman does one *half-double sequence* forward, and two *minim steps,* and acknowledging the ladies, places himself in the middle, doing two *falling jumps* (he does the *sequence* with his left foot, and he begins the *steps* and *falling jumps* with his right); the others follow with the same [movements] together. Then, having arrived [again] in line, do a hay (or chain) this way: the gentlemen do four *sequences* as above, [either] slowly, or *scurryingly,* beginning by turning to the right, and the ladies [turning] to the left, and so on. Then at the end of this section, the lady who was at the left will have arrived in the middle, while on the other hand the gentleman who was at the right will have arrived in the middle. Now by moving this way at each repetition of the music, everyone arrives at his own place [again], which would not happen if everyone began this hay (or chain) by turning to the left, as was formerly done in this dance.

¹ Florio, p. 200, defines 'Furiosa' as 'a kind of vine that bears grapes twice a year'. Since the prevalent figures in dances of this title are hays, or chains, a play of words may be implied in the title. *Furioso* also means 'furious', however, and the title may refer to a texted version of the music, now unknown, with an angry protagonist.

It is also to be noted that each of the people in the middle must take his own turn, as the first ones did, changing places. Thus, at the end of all three repetitions [of the music], each one will have returned to his own place.

The Sciolta of this Piece

When everyone has had a turn, and the leaders of the dance are in the middle again, all make a *long Reverence* together, and do two *sequences* forward, bending your knees a little at the end in the manner of a *half Reverence*. Note that if this dance is done by two ladies, with one gentleman in the middle, and two gentlemen and a lady, they should do it thus, and then do the chain, as I stated in the dance called Contrapasso Nuovo. Now the gentlemen touch hands with the ladies each time (now the right, and then the left), always changing ladies; the ladies do the same to the other side. And if you do the dance this way it is better, and more perfect in theory than if done by three (or six) gentlemen at one end of the hall, and as many ladies, who do the *long Reverence* and two *breve continences* in these playings, and after that begin the hay (or chain) in line, without following any rule, so that at the end, the leading man, when turning to make the chain, gives his right hand (which he had just dropped with the third lady) to the lady following him—and this is terribly wrong. And even if they would try to do it in the shape of a half-moon it would still be improper. Furthermore, it is not right for gentlemen to touch hands with gentlemen, or similarly ladies [with ladies]. Therefore let me say that it would be good if any gentleman who would like to do this balletto would do it as I have described above, for [then] it would be quite proper, and according to the Rules. Now if someone would like to do this chain with three (or six) gentlemen, and as many ladies, in two playings of the music, he should begin it along the length of the hall, with those who are in the middle approaching each other with one *sequence,* and taking right hands. Then change partners, taking left hands. After this give your right [hand] to the lady on your right. Now this should be done by both the gentlemen and the ladies. Then, when you are at the end of the hall, turn to the left, once again taking the right hands you have just dropped. This done, give your left [hand] to the next person, and so on, both gentlemen and ladies returning to place. But I repeat, that everyone should eschew doing this dance this way, for it is wrong.

When the Piece Changes

All make a *long Reverence* together (both gentlemen and ladies), and do two *breve sequences* forward, bending your knees a little in the manner of a *half Reverence.*

The Sciolta of this Piece

At the end of the two *sequences*, take hands in a circle in the usual courteous manner, and moving to the left, do two *reprises*, two *falling jumps*, and a *half-double sequence*, beginning with the left foot; repeat to the right to the other side. After this drop hands, doing two *half-double sequences* flankingly, two *Sapphic steps*, and another *half-double sequence* forward, beginning with the left. This done, take hands again in a circle, and do everything to the other side. Now similarly dropping hands, do the two *sequences, Sapphic steps*, and another *sequence* as above.

Another Change of the Piece

In this playing, let me say that it is not good to do what was done before, when the gentlemen made a *Reverence*, and after that the ladies, for then they found that they [already] had the left foot in back, with which they could not [then] make a *Reverence* in back, as I have said in my Rules; thus the dance was wrong. Therefore, in place of the two *Reverences*, let me say that with the left foot, which you have in back, do one *stopped broken sequence* to the left, and a *half Reverence* with the right; repeat to the other side. Now if done this way the dance will be absolutely correct.

Repeat the Sciolta Anew

In the last playing, everyone does two *broken sequences* together, with two *Sapphic steps* flankingly forward. Finally, do two *semibreve stopped steps*. Then, in the same courteous manner as at the beginning, each gentleman takes his lady gently by the customary hand, and in this way, and by making a *breve Reverence* in four triple beats, bring this graceful dance to an end.

[29] *Furioso all'Italiana*

Play ten times gravely

Sciolta [saltarello]

Play the Sciolta three times

In this [part of the] piece do a
Reverence and two *sequences* forward.

Having done this, play
the Sciolta once more.

Ghirlanda d'Amore [*The Garland of Love*]

Cascarda

Dedicated to the Most Illustrious and Excellent Lady,
D[onna] Marfisa d'Este Cibbo, Marquise of Carrara
(Fig. VII)

Begin this cascarda by standing as shown in the figure, in the usual courtly manner. [Then] do one *broken sequence* to the left, and when you make a *half Reverence* with the right, touch right hands; repeat to the other side. Then take customary hands, progressing with four *broken sequences*, two *half-double sequences*, two *flourishes*, two *minim steps*, and two more *broken sequences*. Finally, do two *reprises* to the left, two *falling jumps*, two *minim steps*, and one *Sapphic step;* repeat the same *reprises* and other movements to the other side, beginning the abovementioned movements with the left foot, except for the *half Reverence*. Now this is a Symmetrical Section.

In the second playing, take right hands and do two *broken sequences* and one *falling jump*, beginning with the left, and one *dexterous step* to the right. Then drop hands, turning to the left with two *half-double sequences*. Now opposite each other, do one *knot*, two *flourishes*, two *minim steps*, and one *Sapphic step*, beginning with the left foot; repeat to the other side. Finally, do two *reprises* to the left, two *falling jumps*, two *minim steps*, and one *Sapphic step*. Now do two *reprises* to the right, and three *falling jumps*, beginning with the right; and conclude with one *dexterous step* to the left. This is called a Well-Ordered Section.

In the third playing, take left hands, doing all the movements you did in the second playing to the other side.

In the fourth (and last) playing, turn to the left with one *half-double sequence*, using the left foot, one *falling jump* with the right, and one *dexterous step* with the left hip turned in; repeat to the other side. After that do two *flourishes* (or two *reprises*) to the left, two *falling jumps*, and one *Corinthian step* with the left hip turned in; repeat to the other side. At the end, do two *broken sequences* flankingly, two *minim steps*, two *falling jumps*, with two *semibreve stopped steps* forward; and in the same courteous manner, and making a *breve Reverence* in four triple beats, conclude this lovely and graceful cascarda.

[30] *Ghirlanda d'Amore*

7th course = F

[31]
Furioso alla Spagnuola [*Furioso in Spanish Style*]

Balletto

Dedicated to the Most Illustrious and Excellent Lady
Margarita Somaia Peretti, the Marquise [*of*] *Peretta*
(Fig. IX)

Begin this Furioso alla Spagnuola with three gentlemen and three ladies; that is, each gentleman takes his lady by the customary hand, all standing at the top of the hall in a straight line, and in the usual courtly manner, all making a *long Reverence* and two *breve continences*.

In the second playing, the middle gentleman and lady progress with two *half-double sequences*, taking each other by both hands after that (not [just] the right hand, as before, for that would be wrong). This done, take customary hands and do two *scurrying doubles*, going to the other end of the hall.

In the third playing, the other two gentlemen and their ladies do the same.

In the fourth playing, the gentleman who leads the dance (who is in the middle) does a hay in such a way that none [of the gentlemen] ever drops his lady['s hand]. Now everyone simultaneously does one *sequence* with his left foot. Note that the gentleman in the middle begins to make the chain (or hay) by turning to the left with one *sequence* and passing through the middle, while the couple on his left pass in front with another *sequence*, turning to the right, and the other couple on his right pass in front, turning to the left of the leader, and so on, until the couple which was on the right is in the middle. Now this couple will begin the fifth playing in the same manner as the head couple just did.

In the fifth playing, all three couples together make the same *Reverence* and two *continences* as at the beginning.

In the sixth playing, the couple standing in the middle repeats what the first couple did in the third playing.

In the seventh playing, the other two couples also repeat the same.

In the eighth playing, all do the hay as above, and the couple which has not been in the middle will arrive there.

In the ninth playing, all three couples once again do the abovementioned *Reverence* and *continences*.

In the tenth [playing], the couple in the middle does as those did who led off the dance.

In the eleventh [playing], the other two couples do together what they did the other times.

In the twelfth [playing], do the same chain (or hay), and the couple who began the dance should end in the middle, with the others in their places. Note, however, that at the end of the music you should form a triangle (that is, a circle).

The Sciolta of this Piece as a Saltarello

In the first playing, all do the *Reverence* and *continences* together, as above.

In the next two playings of this sciolta, do a chain as I described it in the dance called Barriera, and in the Contrapasso for six, in the time of six *half-double sequences,* so that each couple returns to its place.

When the Piece Changes

In this playing of the music all do two *continences* and a *Reverence* together, as above.

Repeat the Sciolta of this Piece as a Saltarello Four Times

In the first playing of this sciolta, all join hands in a circle in the usual courteous manner, and do two *reprises* to the left, two *falling jumps*, and a *half-double sequence,* beginning with the left foot; repeat to the other side, and conclude that *sequence* in the manner of a *half Reverence*.

In the second playing, all couples break the circle, but each gentleman continues to hold his lady by the customary hand, and do together two *half-double sequences* flankingly (one to the left, the other to the right), two *falling jumps,* two *minim steps,* and one *dexterous step,* beginning all these movements with the left foot.

In the third playing, take hands again in a circle, repeating the movements you did in the first playing to the other side.

In the fourth playing, do what you did in the second playing to the other side.

Here the Change of the Piece is Repeated

In this variation of the music, each gentleman takes his lady by the right hand, making a *long Reverence* together. This done, each turns to the lady on his left, and taking her by the left hand, both make a *Reverence* with the same foot.

The Saltarello is Repeated Again

In this last playing, each gentleman takes his lady by the customary hand in the usual courtly manner, with two *broken sequences* forward, and two *scurrying* [*sequences*], each returning to place in the same order with which you began this dance. At the end, do two *semibreve stopped steps,* each in one triple beat, and a *Reverence* in four beats, and beautifully conclude this graceful dance.

Use the Same Music as for Furioso all'Italiana on p. 258.

Contrapasso [Counterpace]

To Be Danced in a Circle

Dedicated to the Most Illustrious and Excellent Lady
Francesca Sforza della Cornia, Marquise of Castiglione
(Fig. V)

In order to do this Contrapasso, the gentleman who remains [on the dance floor] after the dance called Il Piantone, or after the Ballo del Fiore, calls up three, four, or six ladies [to dance] (more or less, as he pleases), inviting just one at a time and placing her at the top of the hall (or any other dancing place). Then, whether there are four or six of them, he will invite one gentleman less [than the ladies] (since with himself this will come to the right number). After this he will command the Master of the Ball to order this Contrapasso to be played. Now everyone forms a circle (that is, one gentleman and one lady, and so on) when the music begins, and all do a *long Reverence* and two *continences* (note that each gentleman faces his lady when he does the *Reverence* and *continences*). After this progress in a circle with two *semibreve steps* and one *breve sequence* to the left; repeat to the other side. Now do these movements once more as above, both to the left and to the right.

Here the Piece Changes, and is Played Three Times

When the music changes, take right hands and do two *steps* and one *sequence,* just as above, beginning with the left foot; repeat to the other side, taking left hands. Then drop hands, taking two *semibreve steps* turning to the left, and one *breve sequence,* bending your knees a little at the end in the manner of a *half Reverence;* repeat to the other side. Note that you must not do this as before, when two *sequences* turning to the left, and two more to the right were done, for this was very wrong.

In the second playing, take right arms, repeating what was done in the first section; repeat to the other side, taking left arms. Then do four *sequences* flankingly (two backward, separating a little, and two forward, approaching each other).

In the third playing, take both hands, and progress to the left with the abovementioned two *steps* and *sequence*, beginning with the left foot; repeat to the other side, also doing the aforementioned four *sequences* flankingly.

The [Original] Piece Starts Anew From the Beginning

In the first playing, progress to the left with two *breve sequences*; in the second [playing] do two *semibreve steps* and one *Sapphic step;* in the third and fourth playings, repeat to the other side, progressing to the right. Note that you must not do this as before, when you progressed in a circle with eight *sequences,* all to the left, for at the end you remained with your left foot in back, with which you made a *Reverence.* Let me say that because of this the dance was wrong, for if the first passages are to the left, and then to the right, and the turns as well, then why should you do one passage only with eight *sequences* in a circle? Let me say, then, that if you wish to do this dance perfectly, you must do it as I have said above.

Play the Changed Piece Three More Times

In the first playing, make a *Reverence* together, and two *continences.* Then do the abovementioned turns.

In the second playing, do two *steps* and one *minim double* (that is, the gentlemen forward and the ladies backward), beginning with the left foot; repeat to the other side (the ladies forward and the gentlemen backward). Now take note not to do it as before, when you did two *steps* forward and a *sequence,* and then with the same left foot which was in back, the gentlemen had to walk backward, for this was terribly wrong. If done the way I have just said, however, you will move most correctly and in an orderly way. This done, do the four *sequences* flankingly, as I stated for the second section of this changed music.

In the third (and last) playing, in place of what was done before—a *Reverence* by the gentlemen and a *half* [*Reverence*] by the ladies, and a repetition with the ladies making a *long Reverence,* and the gentlemen another, and then again another at the end of this playing—let me say that was most improper, for in one playing there is no time for three *Reverences.* And then (what would be even worse), after having done the four *sequences,* one should not make a *Reverence* with the same left foot, as I said before. Let me say, then, that in this playing you must do two *breve continences,* two *sequences* flankingly, and two *breve stopped steps* forward. Finally, in the usual courtly manner, every gentleman takes the hand of the lady on his right, and by making a *Reverence,* gently conclude this graceful balletto.

Play the Same Music as for Contrapasso Nuovo on p. 244.

[33]
Nido d'Amore [*The Love Nest*]

Balletto

Dedicated to the Most Illustrious Lady
Caterina Orsina Melchiori, Marquise of Torreto
(Fig. III)

In this lovely and graceful balletto, stand as shown in the figure, taking customary hands in the usual well-mannered fashion, and gently do a *long Reverence* and two *breve continences.* Then progress with two *half-double sequences,* two *flourishes,* two *minim steps,* and two *Sapphic steps.* When the music begins to run [sequentially][1] do two *broken sequences,* two *falling jumps,* and one *Corinthian step,* beginning all these movements with the left foot; after this repeat the *broken sequences, falling jumps,* and *Corinthian step* to the other side.

In the second playing, do one *pulled step* with the left foot, one *knot* with the right, two *flourishes,* and a *falling jump* beginning with the right foot, and one *Sapphic step* with the left; repeat to the other side. Then progress with two *minim steps,* one *knot,* two *flourishes,* and one *broken sequence,* beginning with the left foot; repeat to the other side. This done, repeat the sequential section once more; that is, two *Sapphic steps,* one to the left, the other to the right, two *minim steps,* and two *broken sequences,* at the end of which you drop hands, and repeat all the aforementioned movements scurryingly in the time of another sequential section, turning first to the left and then to the right, in the manner of an S. Face towards each other at the end.

In the third playing, the gentleman does one galliard variation of four patterns. The lady does a tordion pattern, but if she does not know how to do this, she should do two *sequences* flankingly, two *semibreve falling jumps,* and a *feigned sequence.* Both the gentleman and the lady begin this variation with the left foot, and conclude with it, so that this foot remains forward.

After the lady has finished her part (or variation), the gentleman does the aforementioned part again, beginning and ending it with the right foot. Take

---

[1] *'Alla Fuga della Sonata'.* This may refer to the second half of the duple-meter section, which runs sequentially downward.

care not to do it any other way, for that would make the dance quite wrong. The lady should do the same variation [as before], beginning and ending it with the right. At the [sequential] playing of the galliard do two *minim steps,* two *broken sequences* flankingly, two *falling jumps,* and one *Corinthian step,* beginning with the left foot; repeat to the other side.

The Piece is Played as a Saltarello

Take right hands and do two *broken sequences,* two *minim steps,* and one *dexterous step* to the left; then take left hands, repeating to the other side. This done, turn to the left with one *half-double sequence* with the left foot, one *falling jump* with the right, and one *dexterous step* with the left hip in; repeat to the other side. In the two sequential playings do the same movements that you did in the first playing: that is, two *broken sequences,* two *falling jumps,* and one *Corinthian step* flankingly in, beginning with the left foot, repeat to the other side.

Canary Music

Both turn to the left simultaneously with two *broken sequences,* two *minim steps,* and one *Sapphic step* with the left hip in, beginning with the left; repeat to the other side.

Here Do a Pedalogue

In half of this playing of the music for the canary, the gentleman does two *stamps,* and one *stamped sequence,* beginning with the left; the lady replies with the same footwork. After this the gentleman repeats this with the right; and the lady responds similarly. The gentleman does one *double canary sequence* with the left foot, the *tiny minced jumps* with the right (that is, three rapid *stamps*), ending with the a *stamped sequence* with the left; the lady repeats the same movements reciprocally. Now each does this one more time. To conclude, do one *stopped broken sequence* together with the left, and a *half Reverence* with the right; repeat to the other side.

Repeat the Pedalogue [Music] Anew

The gentleman does a slide forward on his heel, and one backward on his toe with his left foot, which is in back, and with the same [foot] one *dexterous step* with the left hip out; the lady does the same. He repeats the same variation to the other side; and so does she. This done, turn to the left and the right, as at the beginning of this canary. Finally, with two *semibreve stopped steps* forward, gently take customary hands in the usual courteous manner, and, with a *breve Reverence,* bring to an end this beautiful dance which is theoretically perfect.

[33] *Nido d'Amore*

Rotta [Saltarello]

Canary

Alta Vittoria [Great Victory]

Balletto

Dedicated to the Most Illustrious Lady
Laura Carrafa Theodola, Marquise of Calice
(Fig. I)

To begin this balletto, the gentleman takes the lady by the customary hand in the usual courtly manner, and both make a *long Reverence* in four beats of music, with two *breve continences,* each in two beats. Then progress with two *breve stopped steps,* four *semibreve steps* (one beat per step), and two *continences.* After this do two *breve sequences,* at the end of which drop hands in the usual courteous fashion in the manner of a *half Reverence,* and the gentleman moves to one end of the hall and the lady to the other end with two *scurrying sequences,* turning first to the left and then to the right in the shape of an S. Now face towards each other at the end, having begun all these movements with the left foot. Now do not dance it as before, when you turned only to the left, for this was wrong.

The Sciolta of this Piece as a Galliard

For his first four-pattern galliard variation the gentleman does whichever one seems best to him, provided it begins and ends with his left foot forward; he may also do some *capers* if he knows how. If he does not wish to do an altered variation,[1] however, he may do two *sequences* flankingly, two *semibreve falling jumps* (that is, *grave*), each to one beat, with a *breve feigned sequence,* at the end of which he bends his knee a little in the manner of a *half Reverence,* doffing his bonnet (or hat) from his head. After this the lady does one *knot,* two *flourishes,* two *quick steps* backward, two more *flourishes,* two more *minim steps,* two more *flourishes,* a *half Reverence* with the left, one *foot under,* and a *cadence* at the end, beginning all these movements with her left foot. Now she too should conclude with her left foot forward, for anything else would be wrong. And if she does not know how to do this variation, she may do what the

---

[1] '*Mutanze alterata'.* Another meaning of this term could be 'disturbed' variation, in the sense that it would be broken up and off the ground, hence 'high' ('*alta*').

gentleman did, with two *sequences* flankingly, two *grave falling jumps*, and one *feigned sequence*.

The gentleman repeats the same variation to the other side. The lady also does hers to the other side.

Note

[Formerly], when those two variations were over, it was customary to make two *Reverences* in this dance. That is, the gentleman made one with his left foot, which was already in back at the end of the galliard variation, and the lady made a *half* [*Reverence*]; then the lady made a *long Reverence,* and the gentleman another. Now this was improper, and made the dance wrong, for when the left foot was already in back, one could not have made a *Reverence* with that foot, for it is unnatural, and against the rule. Therefore I say that to do this dance so as to be correct in theory, do two *stopped steps* forward in place of the two *Reverences,* which is proper.

In these [next] four galliard patterns do this Symmetrical Variation together: first do two *reprises with foot under* to the left, and one *flourish;* repeat to the other side. Finally, do two *dexterous steps* flankingly in, beginning all these movements with the left foot. Now this is a Symmetrical Variation. If the lady does not know how to do this variation, however, she may do two *breve sequences* flankingly, and two *dexterous steps*, or two *continences.* After this *scurry* in the shape of an S with two more *sequences,* as I said above. Then approach each other, taking customary hands in the usual courteous fashion. Note that the gentleman should not cover his head in the short time in which he does four *broken sequences,* and then, when dropping hands, doff his bonnet once more, for this is unsightly. Furthermore, by remaining uncovered he appears the more dignified, honouring his lady even more, so that this is the well-mannered fashion for the gentleman [to follow].

The Sciolta of this Piece as a Saltarello

In this sciolta progress with four *broken sequences.* Then drop hands, turning to the left with two *minim steps,* and one *broken sequence* forward; repeat to the other side, turning to the right. Take note that this should not be done as before, when you turned only to the left with four *broken sequences,* and never to the right, for this was wrong. This done, do two *Sapphic steps* flankingly backward, and one *Corinthian step* with the left hip in; repeat to the other side. You may also do one *broken sequence* backward with the left, one *feigned* [*broken sequence*] with the right, and a *minim double* forward. Both patterns are correct.

Take note that you should not do as before, when you did two *broken sequences* backward, and then, with the left foot, which remained forward, you continued by walking forward; worse still, once you had completed those *broken sequences,* you did two *minim steps* forward, joining it to the right with the third one; then you repeated the above-mentioned *broken sequences* with the right foot, joining the right to the left on the third step. Now let me say that this involved two errors: the first, with [regard to] the *broken sequences,* was that the foot which remained forward should not have continued forward, for, as I said above, this is unnatural and against the rule; the second, was that it was wrong because the foot which joined the other one should have been the one to move next. For these two reasons the dance was wrong as it was done before. Let me say, then, that if you would like to do it properly, you will do what I have said above. After this, do two *reprises* to the left, two *falling jumps,* and one *minim feigned double.* If you would like to do it with even nicer movements, however, do one *knot,* two *flourishes,* two *minim steps* forward, and one *Sapphic step* with the left hip in; repeat to the other side. Now this section is done as a Saltarello, and is perfect in theory.

Canary

For this canary do four *broken sequences* forward, taking right hands, dropping hands at the end, and doing four more [*broken sequences*] *scurryingly* in the shape of an S, changing places; at the end of the *scurrying* [*broken sequences*] bend your knees a little in the manner of a *half Reverence.* Now take note that while the gentleman is doing his variation, the lady must make some graceful motions, so that she will not resemble a statue.

Gentleman's First Variation

The gentleman does the most beautiful variation he knows, and concludes by doing four *retreats,* with two *minim stopped steps* forward, without turning as above; [then] make a *Reverence.*

Lady's First Variation

The lady does another [variation] totalling eight patterns. Then she does the four *retreats* flankingly (that is, two *falling jumps,* and one *Sapphic step*). Conclude with the two *stopped steps* and the *Reverence,* as the gentleman did. This done, repeat the four *broken sequences,* taking left hands; then dropping hands, *scurry* with four more [*broken sequences*], as above. Repeat the same variations to the other side (first the gentleman and then the lady). Finally, after the lady has done the four *retreats,* both together turn to the left with two *broken sequences,* two *minim steps* forward, and one *Sapphic step* with the left hip in, beginning with the left foot; repeat to the other side. Then, with two *minim stopped steps* forward, take customary hands in the usual courtly manner, and making a *breve Reverence* in time to the music, and having joined the left foot to the right, bring this noble balletto to an end.

[34] *Alta Vittoria*

Sciolta [Saltarello]

Canary

Furioso Nuovo [The New Furioso]

To Be Done by Eight [Dancers]

Dedicated to the Most Illustrious Lady
Clelia Rebibba de Massimi, Marquise of Pressedi
(Fig. I)

Begin this balletto in this fashion: any gentlemen who would like to do it takes four ladies [to dance], placing two of them at one end of the hall, and the other two at the other end. Then he calls on three gentlemen (so that with himself there are four), two of whom go and, in the usual courteous manner, take the customary hands of the two ladies at one end of the hall, and the other two do the same. Take note that the gentleman who begins (or, to say it better, invites the others) should choose the first lady he asked [as his partner], for she must take precedence. Now she who was called up first should logically be the one who remains [on the ballroom floor] at the end of this dance, so that she may dance the ballo called Il Piantone, while the other [gentlemen] should take the ladies to their chairs when this dance is over.

Now when you begin this dance, you need to know that all eight always dance simultaneously. First, make a *long Reverence* (that is, *grave*) in four simple beats of music, followed by two *breve continences* (one with the left foot, the other with the right). Then all do a passage of four *half-double sequences*. Note that at the end of the [first] two *sequences*, each gentleman should take the right hand of the lady belonging to the gentleman who is passing through, in the usual courteous and well-mannered fashion. Then pass [each other] with two more *half-double sequences*, concluding by turning to the left, bending your knees a little in the manner of a *half Reverence*, having changed places; that is, the group of four who have been at one end of the hall will have moved to the other end, and the other [group] will have done the same, facing towards each other at the end of this playing of the music.

In the second playing, every gentleman takes his lady by the right hand (without doing the *Reverence* and *continences*), and do two *semibreve steps* and a *half-double sequence* (that is, one moves into the other's place); again, both groups of four will face each other. This done, do two *breve continences*. Take note that you begin the *steps* and *half-double sequence* with the left foot, while the *continences* begin with the right.

In the third playing, do the same passage as given for the first playing, but without doing the *Reverence* and two *continences,* and beginning all the movements with the right foot. Now in passing touch left hands, bending your knees a little in the usual courteous manner. At the end of four *half-double sequences* turn to the right, with each group of four in its original place facing each other at the end of the music.

In the fourth playing, each gentleman takes his lady's left hand once again, and beginning with the right foot do two *semibreve* steps and a *half-double sequence* (beginning with the right), each returning to your usual place. After this, do two *continences,* as above, beginning with the left foot, with each group of four facing towards the other, and ending in time to the music.

In the fifth playing, do two *breve stopped steps* forward. Finally, make a *long Reverence,* joining the left foot to the right at the end of the music. Now begin these movements with the left foot.

The Sciolta of this Piece in Proportion (That is, as a Saltarello), Played Twice

In these two playings of the piece in proportion, do a chain in a circle in the same manner as given for Il Furioso alla Spagnuola; do eight *half-double sequences,* however, so that at the end of the two playings [of music] each person has the left foot in back.

Here the Piece Changes as You See in the Tablature

In this playing of the music, do one *stopped step* forward with the left foot, which was in back, another with the right, and a *Reverence* with the left foot, as was said above.

Here the Piece is Played Again in Proportion, Four Times

In the first playing of this music, all join hands in a circle (that is, one gentleman and one lady, so that each gentleman is between two ladies, and each lady between two gentlemen), and do two *reprises* together to the left, two *falling jumps,* and a *half-double sequence* with the left foot. Now these movements are done to half of this music. Without dropping hands, do the same movements to the right, beginning on the other side, ending the first playing of the music this way.

In the second playing, drop hands and do two *broken sequences* turning left, one *half-double sequence* forward, and two more *half-double sequences* turning right, facing towards each other at the end.

In the third playing, take hands again in a circle, and repeat what you did in the first playing to the other side.

In the fourth playing, drop hands and do what you did in the second playing, but to the other side.

The Change of the Piece [is Played] Once

In this playing everyone does two *stopped steps* forward, and a *Reverence,* as given above.

Here the Piece is Played in Proportion Once More

In this playing, do two *Sapphic steps* flankingly backward, with two *broken sequences* flankingly forward. Then do two *semibreve stopped steps* (one forward, the other backward). At the end everyone takes customary hands, making a *breve Reverence* together, and each group of four is back in the position from which it began the dance.

Play the Same Music as for Il Furioso all'Italiana on p. 258.

36

Spagnoletta Regolata [*Well-Ordered Spagnoletta*]

Balletto

Dedicated to the Most Illustrious Lady
Gieronima Palavicina Montora, Marquise of Montoro
(Fig. IV)

Begin this Spagnoletta by standing as shown in the figure for Alta Regina and making a *breve Reverence*. Then do four *broken sequences* in a circle, and four *minim steps* facing towards each other. Take note that you should not do two *minim steps* forward, joining your left foot to the right afterwards, for this is not right, since one *minim step* is lacking. Let me say, then, that you should do as stated here. Having done these four *steps,* do two *reprises* to the left, two *falling jumps,* and one *minim double* turning left. Now if you do not wish to turn, do this *double* forward, beginning all these movements with the left foot; repeat the *reprises, falling jumps,* and *double* to the other side. Then do two *broken sequences* flankingly backward, one *ordinary* [*sequence*] with the left foot, another *feigned* [*sequence*] with the right, and one *minim double* forward with the left. Now in place of those two *broken sequences,* you may also do two *Sapphic steps;* and [you may do] one *Corinthian step* with the left hip in place of the *double,* for this way the dance is even lovelier; repeat to the other side. Note also that you should not do the *broken sequences* backward as before, since when you had done these two *broken sequences* backward, the left foot remained forward, and you then had to walk forward with it, which was an incorrect movement. Besides, in taking two *minim steps* forward, and joining the left to the right, you then used the right to repeat the abovementioned two *broken sequences* flankingly backward. Now this was also very wrong, because that foot which is joined [by the other] should always continue the movement. Now this is called a Symmetrical Passage.

In the second playing, do six *broken sequences,* progressing in a circle to the left, with all the actions and movements as above.

In the third playing, the gentleman turns left with two *broken sequences.* Then do two *minim steps* forward, and one *Sapphic step* flankingly (or one *minim double*); repeat to the other side. Then do two *reprises with foot under* to the left, two *falling jumps,* and a *Corinthian step* (or a *minim double* forward); repeat to the other side. After this do together the *broken sequences* flankingly backward, and the *double* forward, twice, as was given in the first playing.

In the fourth playing, the lady alone does what the gentleman just did. After this, do the *broken sequences* backward together, with all the other movements as above.

In the fifth (and last) playing, progress in a circle to the left, with two *minim steps,* two *falling jumps,* and one *Sapphic step,* beginning with the left foot; repeat to the other side. Then do the abovementioned *reprises* and *falling jumps,* with all the subsequent movements as above. Take note that when doing the two *broken sequences,* you do two *Sapphic steps* flankingly backward, with two *broken sequences* flankingly forward. At the end, do two *stopped minim steps* forward, and finish this Spagnoletta with a *minim Reverence.*

Play the Same Music as for Spagnoletta Nuova in the Style of Madrid on p. 194.

37

Ballo del Fiore [*Dance of the Flower*]

Balletto

*Dedicated to the Most Illustrious Lady Caterina Savella Savella,
Baroness of Rome*

The gentleman who would like to begin this dance will call upon the Master of the Ball, and ask him to have the Ballo del Fiore played. When the music begins, he does a *long Reverence* and two *breve continences.*[1] Then he progresses with four *half-double sequences,* approaching the lady he intends to invite to dance; and in the usual courteous manner he does two *breve stopped steps* forward and a *long Reverence.* He waits through one more repetition of the music for the lady to rise from her seat, and once she has risen, both do a *Reverence* and *continences* together as above, gently taking customary hands. Then in the next repetition [of the music] they progress with four *half-double sequences,* at the end of which the gentleman describes a half-moon with his hand, placing the lady opposite him, and with two *continences* and a *Reverence,* as courteously as above, leaves the lady at the end of the hall (or any other dancing place). Then he progresses again as at first, and following the same procedure invites another [lady], similarly progressing with her with the same movements he did with the first lady. Now when making a *Reverence,* all three should do it together. In the event that the gentleman wishes to take three [ladies], he must follow the same rule, setting her [the third lady] with all the others in a line. Then he progresses as above, and when he has reached the other end of the hall, he invites one gentleman [to dance]. As soon as that [gentleman] has approached him, he must be sure to place him on his right. After that all together do a *Reverence* and the *continences* as above. This done, progress with four *half-double sequences,* the ladies separating a little so that the gentlemen may pass between those who are at either end. Now the lady in the middle passes between the gentlemen and, in passing, everyone bends their knees a little simultaneously in the manner of a *half Reverence,* the gentlemen gently doffing their bonnets (or hats). Then do the other two *sequences,* everyone turning left and changing places. Facing towards each other, and with the left

---

[1] No figure is shown or cited for this dance.

foot, which remained in back, do two *breve stopped steps* and a *long Reverence*. Formerly, it was customary to do only one passage, but it is much better to do two, for in this way the gentleman who leads this dance will end up with his own lady, and will be able to take her right hand in a more orderly fashion than was possible before. Once again, [then], do the same passage with all its movements. At the end, both the gentlemen and the ladies are back in place.

In this playing of the music, the gentleman who leads repeats the first passage, approaching the lady who stands to the right of the others. In the second playing of the music he does two *stopped steps,* and [they make] a *Reverence* together. In the third playing take right hands in the usual courteous fashion, and do two *semibreve steps* and one *half-double sequence,* progressing to the left, and beginning all movements in this dance with the left foot; taking left hands, repeat to the other side. Take note that the other gentleman, at the same time that the first is taking hands, approaches [the lady], performing the same passage and other movements. Then that first [gentleman] takes the other lady, and this [gentleman] takes the first [lady], who has been left [by the first gentleman], and they continue thus. Take note that the first lady, once she has finished dancing with the second gentleman, goes and stands at the end of the hall where the gentlemen were, while the gentlemen, similarly, go to their [the ladies'] place. The other ladies, after each has finished her movements, place themselves in line next to the first. At the end, do two *continences* and a *Reverence,* progressing toward each other flankingly with four *half-double sequences,* two *stopped steps,* and a *Reverence.* The gentleman gives the flower to the lady of his choice (though in my opinion he should properly give it to the first lady he invited, for she should take precedence). After this, each gentleman takes one lady apiece, and repeats the first passage with the two *stopped steps* and *Reverence,* taking leave of her after having led her back to her place.

After this the lady who was given the flower follows the same procedure as the gentleman, inviting three gentlemen [to dance] one at a time, and only one lady, with two passages, as described above. At the end she gives the flower to the gentleman of her choice (though it would be best, as I said above, if she gave it to the one she invited first). Now the other two gentlemen take the ladies to their places with the abovementioned movements. Thus this dance will continue quite properly in this order.

[37]   *Ballo del Fiore*

Tordiglione [*Tordion*]

Balletto

*Dedicated to the Most Illustrious Lady
Costanza Offreda Giacovacci, Gentlewoman of Cremona and Rome*

To begin this balletto, the gentleman takes the lady by the customary hand, in the usual courtly manner,[1] and both do a *grave Reverence* in six beats of the music, and three *semigrave continences* in three beats each. Then progress with four *grave broken sequences.* This done, do one *reprise with foot under* to the left, two *falling jumps,* and three *semibreve steps,* each in one beat, beginning all these movements with the left foot. Do the same *reprises, falling jumps,* and three *semibreve steps* to the other side, dropping hands at the end.

In this next playing, take right hands and do two *grave broken sequences.* Then drop hands in the aforementioned polite manner, doing two more [*broken*] *scurrying* [*sequences*] (first to the left and then to the right), in the shape of an S, changing places, and ending these *broken scurrying sequences* facing towards each other, bending your knees a little in the manner of a *half Reverence.*

Gentleman's First Variation

In the first variation (or part), the gentleman does two *reprises with foot under,* two *flourishes* forward, two *minim steps* backward, two quick *Reverences* in the manner of three beats of the *little bell,* and one *foot under* to the right, beginning all these movements with the left foot. After this do two *flourishes* forward, two *minim steps* backward, and a *cadence,* ending with the left foot forward, as you began this variation. Now by doing it this way it will be quite correct. Otherwise, if you end the *cadence* with your right foot forward (as some do), let me say that this variation will be quite wrong. Take note that you must not conclude the variation at the end of the music with a *reprise with foot under,* slowly dropping the left foot down in front after that, for that is not proper. It is necessary that you do what I have said above, since galliard

---

[1] No figure is shown or cited for this dance.

variations must finish with a *cadence*. Repeat the same variation to the other side.

Lady's First Passage

In these eight patterns in which the gentleman does the aforementioned two variations (one of four patterns beginning with the left foot, and the same to the other side), the lady progresses with two *grave broken sequences,* two *ordinary* [*sequences*], and one *Sapphic step* to the left. Now these movements take one repetition of the music; repeat to the other side.

Lady's First Variation

The lady does the same variation with one foot and the other as the gentleman just did. If she does not know how to do it, however, she should begin with two *semibreve steps* (that is, slow), and two *Sapphic steps* flankingly in. After this turn to the left with two *broken sequences,* and end with another flanking *Sapphic step* with the left hip in, beginning these movements with the left foot; repeat to the other side.

Gentleman's First Passage

While the lady does the variation, both to the left and the right, he should do the same passage and the same movements that she did.

Gentleman's Second Variation

The gentleman does two *limping hops* with his left foot forward, two quick *half Reverences*, and a *knot,* beginning these movements with the left foot. Then do a *step in the air* with the right, two *flourishes* forward, two *minim steps* backward, two quick *half Reverences,* and a *foot under* with the right. At the end do a *half Reverence* with the left foot, a *foot under*, and a *cadence*, remaining with the left foot forward; repeat to the other side.

Lady's Second Passage

The lady repeats anew the same passage as at first, both to the left and to the right.

Lady's Second Variation

The lady begins this variation with one *knot,* two *flourishes* forward, two *minim steps* backward, two quick *half Reverences,* and two *falling jumps,* beginning these movements with the left foot. Then do two *flourishes* forward, and two *minim steps* backward, beginning with the right, and end with a *cadence* in time to the music, remaining with the left foot forward; repeat the same variation to the other side. Should it be the case, however, that she does not know how to do what has been described above, she may do it in this other, slower manner: that is, begin with two *dexterous steps* flankingly in to the left, stopping a little with each *dexterous step*. Then do one *knot*, two *flourishes* forward, a *half Reverence*, a *foot under*, and a *cadence*, beginning each movement with the left foot; repeat the same variation to the other side.

Gentleman's Second Passage

The gentleman does the same passage as before, both to the left and to the right. Having done this, both take left hands, repeating what they did when they held right hands, but each now returning to place.

Gentleman's Third Variation

In this third variation the gentleman does one *reprise with foot under*, and a *flourish* to the left; repeat to the other side. Then do one *knot* facing towards [your lady], two *minim steps* turning to the left, two *flourishes* forward, two more quick *minim steps* backward, a *half Reverence*, a *foot under*, and a *cadence*, beginning all these movements with the left foot; repeat to the other side.

Lady's Third Passage

The lady repeats the same passage as above.

Lady's Third Variation

The lady does the same variation that the gentleman did, first with one foot, and then with the other foot.

Gentleman's Third Passage

The gentleman progresses to the left with two *semibreve steps,* and two *broken sequences.* Then do a *knot*, two *flourishes,* and a *Sapphic step* with the left hip in, beginning these movements with the left foot; repeat to the other side.

Gentleman's Fourth Variation

In this fourth (and last) variation, the gentleman does one *reprise with foot under* to the left, and one *flourish;* repeat to the other side. Then do one *limping hop* with the left foot raised forward, one *step in the air* with the right, and a *cadence.* Then do a *little bound* to the left, a *foot under* with the right, and with the same foot do a *step in the air,* another with the left foot, two *flourishes* forward, a *half Reverence*, a *foot under*, and a *cadence*, landing with the left foot forward; repeat to the other side.

Lady's Fourth Passage

The lady does the same passage as above.

Lady's Fourth Variation

She does a *knot,* two *flourishes* forward, two *minim steps* backward, two more
flourishes, turning to the left, two more *minim steps,* two *flourishes* forward, a
half Reverence, a *foot under,* and a *cadence,* beginning everything with the left
foot; repeat to the other side.

Gentleman's Fourth Passage

He repeats what he did in the third passage, approaching the lady, without
doing this half of the variation together, which would be superfluous. Now
then, when they are both finished (the lady her variations and the gentleman his
two passages), he takes the lady by the customary hand in the usual courtly
manner. Together do two *reprises,* two *falling jumps,* and a *broken sequence* to
the left; repeat to the other side (to the right), beginning first with the left foot
and then with the right. Finally, do two *grave broken sequences* forward, two
flourishes, and two *Sapphic steps* (one to the left, the other to the right),
beginning the first movements with the left foot. This done, do two *semigrave
stopped steps,* and in the usual courteous manner conclude this most graceful
dance with a *grave Reverence.* Take note that you should not do it as before, for
that was wrong. The reason is that the passages did not fit properly, when you
did three *grave broken sequences* to the left, then three more to the right, and
two flankingly. The passages were incorrect, because the passage to the left did
not conclude in time to the music; instead the music came to an end with the
fourth *broken sequence,* which began to the right. Now it was also wrong for
another reason, in that when you did the *reprise* and two *falling jumps* they
were done four times, and were always to the left and never to the right. Then at
the end of this dance you did one *scurrying sequence* and a *Reverence,*
following no rule at all. Let me say, however, that if you would like to do this
dance, do it as I have said, because it follows the proper rules and is perfect in
theory, and quite correct.

[38] *Tordiglione*

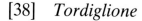

[39]
Vero Amore [True Love]
Balletto

Dedicated to the Most Illustrious Lady Arminia Mattei Santacroce,
Baroness of Rome
(Fig. VIII)

Take both hands, as shown in the figure for Contentezza d'Amore, and together, in the usual well-mannered fashion, do a *grave Reverence* in triple beats and two *semigrave continences,* each in three beats. Then drop hands without stopping at all, and do two *sequences* flankingly, two *falling jumps,* two *Sapphic steps* flankingly, with two *continences* as above. This done, take customary hands in the aforesaid polite manner, making a *Reverence* as above, beginning and ending all movements with the left foot.

In the second playing, progress together with four *breve sequences,* and two *falling jumps.* Then do two *half-double sequences,* two *falling jumps,* two *continences,* a *Reverence* as above, and two *falling jumps.*

Gentleman's Solo Variation

In the third playing, the gentleman alone does two *minim steps* forward, a *reprise with foot under* as in the galliard, and a *flourish* to the left; repeat the same *reprise* and *flourish* to the right, one *knot* with the left, and two quick *half Reverences* with the left foot in the manner of three beats of the *little bell.* Then immediately do one *falling jump* with the left, another with the right, a *step under of the foot,* and a *cadence* with the right in back. After this begin the same variation with that same right foot, which was in back. Now together do two *continences,* a *Reverence,* and two *falling jumps,* as above.

Lady's Solo Variation

The lady alone does the same variation that the gentleman did, and then together [they do] two *continences,* a *Reverence,* and the two *falling jumps.* Now in case she does not know how to do the *flourishes,* or does not know how to do this variation, she may do another which is easier, in the following way: after she has done the abovementioned *falling jumps* together with the gentleman at the end of the music, she should do two *ordinary sequences* flankingly, and one *broken sequence,* beginning these movements with the left foot, one *step* (also forward) with the right, and a *dexterous step* to the left; repeat the same movements to the other side, beginning with the right foot. Then together do the *continences, Reverence,* and two *falling jumps* as above.

In the fourth playing, take right hands and do two *ordinary sequences* to the left, two *falling jumps,* two *minim steps,* and one *Sapphic step.* Then drop hands and repeat the same movements and actions, taking left hands and beginning with the right foot. Now drop hands and do two *continences,* a *Reverence,* and the two *falling jumps* as above.

The Sciolta of this Piece as a Saltarello Played Only Once

In this playing of the music as a Saltarello, do two *pulled broken sequences,* two *flourishes,* and a *Sapphic step* to the left, beginning each thing with the left foot; repeat the same movements to the other side. Then, opposite each other, do two *stopped steps* forward, and taking customary hands in the usual well-mannered fashion, make a *breve Reverence* in four minim beats, thus gracefully concluding this balletto.

[39]   *Vero Amore*

Always play the Ritornello twice.

Ninfa Leggiadra [Lovely Nymph]

Cascarda

Dedicated to the Most Illustrious Lady
Laura Caetana Della Riccia, Baroness of Rome

To begin this beautiful cascarda, the gentleman and lady take customary hands
in the usual courtly manner,[1] and begin by making a *breve Reverence* in the
time of four triple beats. Then progress with two *breve half-double sequences*,
two *semibreve steps*, two *broken sequences*, and one *dexterous step*, beginning
each movement with the left foot. After this do two more *semibreve steps*, two
broken sequences, two *flourishes*, two *falling jumps*, and end with one
dexterous step, beginning with the right. Now this is called a Symmetrical
Section.

In the second playing, take right hands and do two *half-double sequences*,
and two *Sapphic steps*. Dropping hands, do two *steps* as above, turning left,
two *broken sequences*, and one *dexterous step* with the left hip in. After this do
two *steps*, two *broken sequences*, two *flourishes*, and one *Sapphic step*,
beginning with the right. At the end do one *dexterous step* to the left.

In the third playing, take left hands and do all those movements to the other
side. Now I term these two sections Well-Ordered.

In the fourth (and last) playing, do two *half-double sequences* flankingly,
two *Sapphic steps*, two *broken sequences*, two *flourishes*, two *falling jumps*,
two *semibreve steps*, and two *Corinthian steps* flankingly in, taking customary
hands. Finally, do two more *steps* backward and gracefully making a *breve
Reverence* as before, conclude this lovely cascarda.

---

[1] No figure is shown or cited for this dance.

[40] *Ninfa Leggiadra*

Ballo detto Il Piantone [*Dance Called the Sentinel*][1]

Dedicated to the Most Illustrious Lady
Bartolomea Senesia Baroness of N.

The gentleman begins this dance by doffing his bonnet (or hat), with a *long Reverence,* and two *continences.*[2] Then progress toward the ladies with two *semibreve steps* (that is, slow), and one *breve half-double sequence,* beginning with the left; repeat to the other side. Then with the left [foot] (which remained in back), do two *breve stopped steps* forward, looking at the lady you intend to invite, and making a *long Reverence* to her. After this wait while the lady rises from her seat, and when she has risen, both make a *Reverence* in the usual courtly manner, most gracefully taking customary hands. Having concluded the *Reverence,* progress with two *semibreve steps* and one *breve sequence,* beginning with the left foot; repeat to the other side, and at the end of the *sequence* with the right [foot] bend your knees a little in the manner of a *half Reverence,* and with this movement drop hands in the aforesaid polite manner. Then the gentleman covers his head, and with the same passage, goes to one end of the hall, while the lady does the same [passage], going to the other end of the hall. Now it will be up to the gentleman to decide how many times he wishes to do this passage. Finally, approaching his original place, with his left foot (which will be in back), he does two *stopped steps* and a *Reverence* as above. The lady turns to face towards the gentleman, making a *Reverence* to him at the same time. Now if the gentleman wishes to do this passage as a galliard [instead], with variations and *capers,* that is up to him.

The lady follows the same procedure given above, and she may also do the following passage leading [out]:[3] that is, four *semibreve steps* and one *breve sequence,* which must be done with more dignity. Take note that she should

---

[1] The meaning of 'Il Piantone' is obscure in the context of this dance. Florio: 'Any plant or tree to be set. Also a stock of a tree to graffe [*sic*] upon. Also any great stake or pile driven in the ground. Also a suddaine slip given to one, a cunning cheating trick'. The standard modern sense is given here.

[2] No figure is shown or cited for this dance.

[3] '*Passeggio ducale*'. In the context of the choreography, the term clearly refers to withdrawing or leaving, hence perhaps 'leading out'. The term is not used elsewhere.

never take her leave in the middle of the hall, but withdrawing towards the chair on which she had been sitting, and turning to face the gentleman, both make a *Reverence* in time to the music. She [should] make a swaying movement, turning her body a little toward the side on which she perceives her train, so that with this graceful movement (as I said in my note on how a lady should seat herself), her train will move into the space between the legs of her chair. Now before she is seated, she should acknowledge the other lady who is on her left.

To conclude, [let me say] that you should continue [the dance] this way, without failing to follow my advice in my Rules on how to do this dance, for by following these regulations, no one will ever be in the wrong.

[41] *Ballo detto il Piantone*

La Gagliarda detta la mezza notte

Cortesia [Courtesy]

Balletto

Dedicated to the Most Illustrious Lady
Eugenia Spinola Giustiniana, Gentlewoman of Genoa

To begin this lovely and graceful balletto, take customary hands in the usual courteous manner (as I have said for the other balletti),[1] making a *long Reverence* together, with two *Corinthian steps* (one to the left, the other to the right). Then progress with one *knot*, two *flourishes*, two *minim steps* forward, and a *Sapphic step;* repeat to the other side. This done, do two *breve half-double sequences*, at the end of which drop hands, bending your knees a little in the manner of a *half Reverence*. Then do another two *scurrying* [*sequences*], turning first to the left and then to the right in the shape of an S, and facing towards each other at the end of the music. Take note that all the first movements must begin with the left foot, and then with the right. Now this first section is called Symmetrical.

La Rotta as a Galliard

The gentleman alone does the first variation of four galliard patterns, [choosing] one that suits him best. If he does not know how to do one, however, he should do two *sequences* flankingly, two *semibreve falling jumps*, and one *feigned sequence*, concluding in the manner of a *half Reverence*, and beginning and ending with the left foot.

The lady does a tordion variation. Now if she does not know how to do one, she should do the abovementioned *sequences, falling jumps*, and *feigned sequence* that the gentleman did.

The gentleman does a second solo variation, but it must be the same [as the first], beginning and ending with the right foot, for if he does a different one with different movements, even if it is in time to the music, it will be wrong because it is necessary that the same movements be done as were done by the left foot. Now if you do it this way it will be correct and Well-Ordered. The lady does the same solo to the other side.

---

[1] No figure is shown or cited for this dance.

After this the gentleman alone does a Symmetrical Variation in four galliard patterns. That is, he does two *reprises with foot under* and one *flourish* to the left; and he repeats to the other side. Then he does two *broken sequences* flankingly, and two *semibreve steps* forward, at the end of which he should bend his knees a little in the manner of a *half Reverence*, beginning with the left foot. The lady then repeats the gentleman's solo.

The Sciolta of this Piece as a Saltarello

In this single playing of the sciolta, both together do one *knot*, two *flourishes*, two *minim steps* turning to the left, and one *Sapphic step* with the left hip in; repeat to the other side. Then do one *broken sequence* to the left with the left foot, and a *Reverence* with the right, and immediately a *reprise with foot under* to the right, a *flourish* with the left, and a *dexterous step* to the left; repeat to the other side. Finally, do two *broken sequences* flankingly forward, and two *Sapphic steps*. Now, in the usual courtly manner, take customary hands, doing two *minim stopped steps* forward, and make a *breve Reverence* to conclude this utterly beautiful balletto, [which is] correct in theory.

[42] *Cortesia*

Saltarello

Pungente Dardo [Stinging Dart]

Balletto

Dedicated to the Most Illustrious Lady
Clelia Cuppis Conti, Baroness of Rome
(Fig. II)

Begin this balletto by standing opposite each other, as shown in the figure for Alta Regina, and in the usual courtly manner, make a *long Reverence,* with two *breve continences,* strutting a little. Then take right hands and do two *semibreve steps,* and one *breve sequence* to the left, beginning with the left foot; repeat to the other side. After this drop hands, turning to the left with two *broken sequences,* and one *dexterous step* with the left hip in, beginning with the left foot, and with a *breve continence* to the right and a *breve feigned sequence* facing each other. Repeat to the other side, taking left hands. Now this is the first Symmetrical Section.

In the second playing, take customary hands in the same courteous manner and progress with four *breve sequences,* two *stopped steps* (also *breve*), and two more *sequences* as above. Then do the two *broken sequences, dexterous step, continence,* and *feigned sequence,* beginning first with the left foot and then with the right, in the same order I stated in the first playing above.

In the third playing, take both hands and do two *breve sequences* to the left, after which you drop hands, bending your knees a little in the manner of a *half Reverence,* and another two [*sequences*] turning left, separating somewhat and changing places, facing each other after you have finished them, and doing two *breve stopped steps,* and two more *sequences* flankingly. To conclude, repeat anew the *broken sequences, dexterous step, continence,* and *breve feigned sequence* (as much with one foot as the other), in the manner stated above.

In the fourth playing, take hands again and repeat to the other side.

The Sciolta of this Piece as a Saltarello

In this Saltarello playing, do two *breve sequences* turning to the left, with two *minim steps,* and a *Sapphic step* with the left hip in, beginning with the left foot and changing places; repeat to the other side, each returning to place. Then do one *stopped broken sequence* to the left with the left foot, and a *half Reverence* with the right; repeat to the other side. This done, do two *Sapphic steps* (one to the left, and the other to the right), two *flourishes* forward, and two *falling jumps*. After this do a *knot*, two *flourishes*, two *minim steps* and a *Sapphic step* flankingly in, beginning with the left foot; repeat to the other side. At the end do two *broken sequences* forward, and two *Sapphic steps;* at that moment take hands in the usual courteous manner, and do two *steps* backward, and with your left foot, which is forward, gently make a *breve Reverence,* bringing the left foot to the right in time to the end of the music, and gracefully putting an end to this balletto, which is perfect in theory.

[43]   *Pungente Dardo*

The Sciolta [saltarello]
is played twice

Rara Beltà [Rare Beauty]

Cascarda

*Dedicated to the Most Illustrious Lady
Giulia Mattei Cievoli, Gentlewoman of Rome*

To do this graceful cascarda, the gentleman takes the lady gently by the customary hand in the usual courtly manner, and you make a *breve Reverence* together, with two *Sapphic steps.*[1] Then do one *stopped broken sequence* with the left foot, and a *half Reverence* with the right; repeat the same *broken sequence* and *half Reverence* to the other side. After this progress with two *altered broken sequences,* three *stamped sequences in the canary,* beginning with the left foot, and two *stamps* (one with the right, the other with the left); repeat to the other side. At the end, do one *knot,* two *flourishes,* two *minim steps,* and one *Sapphic step,* beginning with the left foot; repeat to the other side. Now this is called a Symmetrical Section.

In the second playing, take right hands, and do one *stopped broken sequence* and a *half Reverence,* beginning first to the left, and then do two *Sapphic steps* (one to the right, the other to the left). After that take left hands and repeat to the other side. This done, turn to the left with two *broken sequences,* and one *Corinthian step* with the left hip in; repeat to the other side. Finally, face towards each other and repeat the above-mentioned movements: that is, the *knot, flourishes, steps,* and *Sapphic step,* as described in the first playing. Now this is called a Well-Ordered Section. Begin all the first movements with the left foot, except the *half Reverence.*

In the third playing, repeat anew all that you did in the second playing, but to the other side.

In the fourth (and last) playing, progress to the left with two *minim steps,* two *broken sequences,* and one *Sapphic step* with the left hip in; repeat to the other side. After this do a *stopped broken sequence* to the left with the left foot, taking right hands, and then quickly make a *half Reverence* with the right; dropping hands, repeat to the other side, taking left hands. This done, do a *reprise with foot under* to the left, and one *flourish* forward; repeat to the other

---

[1] No figure is shown or cited for this dance.

side, adding two *Sapphic steps* flankingly. Finally, do two *flourishes,* two *falling jumps,* and two *broken sequences.* Then take customary hands in the usual courteous manner, and do two *minim stopped steps* forward, concluding this lovely and graceful cascarda with a *breve Reverence.* Now this last section is termed Symmetrical. Begin all these movements with the left foot.

[44]   *Rara Beltà*

Amor Prudente [Prudent Love]

Cascarda

Dedicated to the Most Illustrious Lady Lucretia Cesi Malvasia,
Gentlewoman of Rome and Bologna
(Fig. II)

To begin this cascarda, stand opposite each other as shown in the figure for Alta Regina, and in the usual courtly manner do a *minim Reverence,* two *flourishes* forward, and two *falling jumps.* Then do two *minim steps* forward, and one *Sapphic step* to the left; repeat to the other side. Progressing to the left, do two *broken sequences* and one *half-double sequence,* beginning with the left; repeat to the other side. After this do one *stopped broken sequence* to the left with the left foot, and a *half Reverence* with the right; repeat to the other side. Opposite each other, do two *flourishes* (or two *reprises*), two *falling jumps* (beginning with the left to the left), two *minim steps,* and one *Sapphic step* with the left hip in; repeat to the other side, except that in place of the two *minim steps,* you do one *Sapphic step* to the right, and the other to the left, as I said above.

In the second playing do one *reprise* and one *flourish* to the right with the right foot in place of the *minim Reverence;* repeat to the other side. Then repeat the same movements and all the actions you did in the first playing, beginning with the right foot.

In the third playing, take right hands, and do one *half-double sequence* with the left foot, two *minim steps,* and one *Sapphic step* to the right. Begin the *steps* and the *Sapphic step,* however, with the right foot. Now drop hands, repeating [the same movements] and turning to the left. Then opposite each other, do two *reprises,* two *falling jumps,* two *flourishes,* and one *Sapphic step,* beginning with the left foot; repeat to the other side. After that do one *stopped broken sequence* to the left with the left foot, and a *half Reverence* with the right; repeat to the other side. This done, do two *flourishes,* two *falling jumps,* two *minim steps,* and one *Sapphic step,* beginning with the left foot; repeat to the other side. Finally, do two *Sapphic steps* (one to the right, and the other to the left).

In the fourth playing, repeat all the abovementioned movements and actions you did in the third playing, but begin them with the right foot. To do anything else would render this cascarda wrong.

In the fifth (and last) playing, do two *minim steps* to the left, two *falling jumps,* two *flourishes,* and one *Sapphic step,* beginning with the left foot; repeat to the other side. Then do one *knot,* two *flourishes,* two *minim steps* turning to the left, and a *broken sequence* forward; repeat to the other side. After that do one *reprise with foot under* and one *flourish* with the left; repeat to the other side, with two *flourishes* forward, and two *falling jumps.* Finally, do two *broken sequences* flankingly forward, two *Sapphic steps,* and two *stopped steps* (one forward, the other backward). Now gently conclude this cascarda with a *minim Reverence.*

[*Play the same music as for Alta Vittoria, the Sciolta (Salterello) and (Canary) on p. 273.*]

[46]
Donna Leggiadra [Gracious Lady]
Cascarda

Dedicated to the Most Illustrious Lady
Isabella Castella Malvasia,
Gentlewoman of Bologna

To begin this cascarda, stand opposite each other, and make a *breve Reverence* in the usual courtly manner.[1] Then progress in a circle to the left with four *broken sequences,* two *Sapphic steps,* and two *minim stopped steps* (one forward, the other back). Finally, do two *reprises* and two *falling jumps* to the left, and one *minim double* turning to the left, beginning all these movements with the left foot. Now, in time to the end of the music, do two *minim steps* forward (the first with the right foot, the second with the left).

In the second playing, progress to the right with six *broken sequences,* repeating all the abovementioned movements to the other side, as I described them in the first playing.

In the third playing, the gentleman alone does two *flourishes,* two *falling jumps,* and a *stopped broken sequence* to the left, beginning with the left foot, and then a *half Reverence* with the right; repeat the same movements to the other side. Then together do two *minim stopped steps* (one with the left foot forward, the other with the right backward), and two *half-double sequences* (one to the left, the other to the right).

In the fourth playing, the lady does what the gentleman did in the third playing.

In the fifth (and last) playing, do two *semibreve steps* together, taking right hands. Then do one *half-double sequence,* beginning with the left foot; taking left hands, repeat to the other side. At the end, do two *minim stopped steps,* and with a *breve Reverence,* gently conclude this lovely and graceful cascarda.

---

[1] No figure is shown or cited for this dance.

[46]   *Donna Leggiadra*

Selva Amorosa [*The Forest of Love*]

Balletto

Dedicated to the Most Illustrious Lady
Francesca Silvestra Ciecolini,
Gentlewoman of Mont'Alto and Macerata

To begin this balletto stand opposite each other without holding hands,[1] and when the music begins, make a *long Reverence* with two *continences* in the usual courtly manner. Then take right hands and do two *breve half-double sequences,* at the end of which drop hands, bending your knees a little in the manner of a *half Reverence,* and turn to the left with two *minim steps,* two *flourishes* forward, two more *minim steps,* and one *Sapphic step* with the left hip in, changing places, and beginning all these movements with the left foot; repeat to the other side, taking left hands, and returning to your own places. Finally, take both hands and do two *continences.* Then the gentleman drops the lady's right hand, gently doffing his bonnet (or hat), and both make a *long Reverence.* Now this is a Symmetrical Section.

In the second playing, progress with two *half-double sequences.* Then do a *reprise with foot under* to the left, and a *flourish* forward; repeat to the other side. Do two *minim steps* forward, and one *Sapphic step,* beginning all these movements with the left foot; repeat from the beginning to the other side. After this do two *half-double sequences,* concluding in the manner of a *half Reverence.* Now drop hands in the usual courteous manner, and do two more [*sequences*] *scurryingly,* turning first to the left and then to the right in the shape of an S. Now this is a Well-Ordered Section. Take note that the gentleman should go to one end of the room and the lady to the other.

The Sciolta of this Piece as a Galliard

In this variation of the piece the gentleman does a four-pattern galliard variation (whatever suits him best), beginning and ending it with his left foot.

The lady alone does one *knot,* two *flourishes,* two *semibreve steps* forward (that is, slowly), turning to the left, with two *flourishes,* two more *steps* as

---

[1] No figure is shown or cited for this dance.

above, a *half Reverence,* a *foot under,* and a *cadence,* beginning and ending with the left foot. Now should she not know how to do this variation, she may do two *sequences* flankingly, two *semibreve falling jumps* (that is, *grave*), and conclude with a *feigned sequence.*

The gentleman repeats his solo variation, beginning to the other side.

The lady also repeats her first solo to the other side. Now this is called a Well-Ordered Variation.

In the fourth playing of the music, the gentleman alone does the following Symmetrical Variation this way: begin with two *reprises with foot under* to the left, and one *flourish;* repeat to the other side. Then do the *five steps of the galliard* (as they are usually termed) twice, beginning all these movements with the left foot.

The lady does the same variation, but should she not know how, she may do two *sequences* flankingly, two *broken sequences,* and two *minim steps* forward, bending her knees a little in the manner of a *half Reverence.* Finally, do four *scurrying sequences,* as described above, taking customary hands at the end in the usual well-mannered fashion.

The Sciolta of this Piece as a Saltarello

In this sciolta, progress with one *knot,* two *flourishes,* two *minim steps,* and one *Sapphic step.* Repeat to the other side. Then drop hands and do two *minim steps* turning left (beginning all these movements with the left foot), one *falling jump* to the right with the right foot, and one *dexterous step* with the left hip in with the left foot; repeat to the other side. After this do two *reprises* to the left, two *flourishes,* two *falling jumps,* and one *broken sequence;* repeat to the other side. At the end do two *Corinthian steps* flankingly in, two *minim stopped steps* forward, after which you take customary hands in the usual well-mannered fashion, and gently conclude this lovely and graceful balletto with a *breve Reverence.*

[47] *Selva Amorosa*

[Galliard]

[Saltarello]

48

Fulgente Rai [Brilliant Rays]

Cascarda

Dedicated to the Most Illustrious Lady Flaminia Fondra Sardini,
and to the Most Illustrious Gentleman Allessandro Fondra,
Her Brother, of Lucca
(Fig. II)

To begin this lovely and graceful cascarda, stand opposite each other as in the figure for Alta Regina, and in the usual courtly manner make a *breve Reverence* with two *Sapphic steps*. Then take customary hands and progress with four *broken sequences*. After that do two *minim stopped steps* forward[1] (one forward, the other backward), and two more *Sapphic steps,* beginning all these movements with the left foot. After that do one *stopped broken sequence* with the same foot, and a *half Reverence* with the right; repeat to the other side. Finally, do two *reprises,* two *flourishes,* two *minim steps* forward, and one more *Sapphic step* to the left; repeat to the other side. Now this is a Symmetrical Section.

In the second playing, take right hands and do two *broken sequences,* and one *flourish,* beginning with the left foot, and one *dexterous step* to the right with the right foot; then drop hands and repeat the same movements turning to the left. Facing towards each other, do two *minim stopped steps* (one forward, the other backward), and two *Sapphic steps* flankingly, a *broken sequence,* a *half Reverence* together, a *reprise* to the left, two *flourishes,* two *minim steps,* and a *Sapphic step,* as I described in the first playing.

In the third playing, take left hands and do every movement to the other side, as you did in the third playing,[2] and these two sections are termed Well-Ordered Sections.

In the fourth (and last) playing, do one *knot,* two *flourishes,* two *minim steps* to the left, and one *broken sequence,* beginning with the left foot; repeat to the other side. Then do one *reprise with foot under* to the left, and one *flourish;* repeat to the other side, adding one *stopped broken sequence* with the left foot,

---

[1] *Sic.*

[2] *Sic.* Caroso apparently means the second playing.

and a *half Reverence* with the right; repeat the same *reprises, flourish, broken sequence,* and *half Reverence* to the other side. This done, do two *Corinthian steps* flankingly with your hips in. Finally, do two *stopped steps* forward, after which take customary hands gently, and with the abovementioned courtesies conclude this most graceful cascarda with a *breve Reverence.*

[48] *Fulgente Rai*

49

Alta Cardana [Great Lady Cardana]

Cascarda

Dedicated to the Very Illustrious Lady
Gieronima Cardana Arca, Gentlewoman of Rome

Begin this cascarda in the usual courtly manner,[1] and take customary hands, with a *breve Reverence* and two *Sapphic steps.* Then progress with four *broken sequences,* one *reprise with foot under* to the left, and one *flourish;* repeat to the right, continuing with two *broken sequences,* two *flourishes,* two *minim steps,* and finally a *Corinthian step* to the left; repeat to the other side. Finally do two *reprises,* two *falling jumps,* and a *minim double* to the left, beginning with the left; repeat to the other side.

In the second playing, take right hands and do two *broken sequences,* one *falling jump* to the left, and one *dexterous step* to the right, dropping hands at this point; repeat to the other side, turning to the left. After this, repeat the *reprise* and *flourish* (both to the left and to the right), the two *broken sequences,* two *flourishes,* two *minim steps,* and one *Corinthian step,* beginning these movements with the left foot; repeat to the other side. At the end do those two *reprises,* two *falling jumps,* two *flourishes,* and one *Sapphic step* to the left. Now do two *reprises* to the right, two *falling jumps,* and one *broken sequence,* beginning with the right, and one *Sapphic step* to the left. Now this I call a Well-Ordered Section.

In the third playing, repeat to the other side, taking left hands.

In the fourth (and last) playing, do one *pulled step* with the left foot, and a *limping hop* with the same foot, raising the right, after which you do one *step in the air* with the left, and a *cadence;* repeat the same *limping hop, step in the air,* and *cadence* to the other side. Then do one *minim step* with the right, and a *Sapphic step* to the left; repeat the same movements from the beginning, beginning them to the other side. This done, do the abovementioned *reprise* and *flourish* (both to the left and to the right), with all the other movements described in the second playing, up to the *Corinthian step.* At the end do two

---

[1] No figure is shown or cited for this dance.

broken sequences flankingly, and two *Sapphic steps*. Then take customary hands in the usual courtly manner, and do two *minim stopped steps* forward, and a *Reverence* with the left foot.

[49]   *Alta Cardana*

Commentary: Notes on the Musical Transcriptions

General Principles

The commentary (1) cites any changes in mensuration and/or barring made in the transcription;(2) cites concordances with *Il Ballarino* and with other pieces in *Nobiltà di dame* (because Caroso titles his rules for steps *Trattato Primo* and his dances *Trattato Secondo*, references to *Il Ballarino* are, e.g. II, f. 169ᵛ); (3) uses the Helmholtz system for pitch names:

C   B   c   b   c'   b'   c"   b"

(4) notes all corrections or editorial additions; (5) discusses special problems germane to the individual dance; (6) uses modern noteheads in showing original time values; and (7) uses tr. = transcribed; t=tactus; tabl. = tablature.

[1] *Celeste Giglio*

(1) Soprano *g'* emended from *f'*; (2) soprano *eᵇ"* emended from *e"*; (3) bass *d* emended from *c*; (4) soprano *bᵇ'* emended from *a'*; (5) soprano *g'* emended from *a'*; (6) tabl. *e'* emended from *e♯'* (course 2, cipher ○ for 1); (7) (bars 37, 38) each bass *d* emended from *c*; (8) soprano *f♯'* = ♩ emended from ♩.; (9) mensural modulations between successive dances in 'Celeste Giglio' are notated in the original with more care than usual — they occur in the final bars of the first movement (bar 39, where the last two bars of the duple movement shift to triple in preparation for the galliard); and at the end of the galliard (bars 72, 73, where the bars in 3 ♩ shift to 3 ♩ in preparation for the saltarello); (10) tabl., last *bᵇ'* emended from *a'* (course 1, cipher 1 for ○);(11) tabl., ♩. emended from ♩; soprano *eᵇ"* emended from *e"*; (12) bass *d* emended from *c*; (13) (bars 64a & b; 1st and 2nd endings) the 2nd ending in bar 64b is adjusted to:

64a   64b   65

from original:

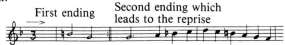

First ending

Second ending which
leads to the reprise

64b: *b′* lute part emended to correspond to 64a; **(14)** bass *b*♮′ emended from *b*♭′; **(15)** bass *d – B*♮ emended from *c – B*♭; **(16)** (tabl. bar 73, upbeat) ♩ emended from ♩.; **(17)** tabl., missing notes *f′ – g′* supplied by analogy to bar 76, and confirmed in the British Museum copy of *Nobiltà di dame*; **(18)** soprano *e*♭″ emended from *e*″; **(19)** interpolation of notes missing in the recurring cadence formula | ♩ ♩ | ♩. |; **(20)** tabl., final chord emended from ♪.

[2] *Nuova Regina*

(1) Bass *c* emended from *B*♭; **(2)** soprano *d′ – e′* emended from *e′ –f′*; **(3)** soprano *e′ –f′* emended from *d′ – e′*; **(4)** bass *c* emended from *B*♭.

[3] *Alta Regina*

Closely similar to, though not exactly identical with *Il Ballarino*, II, f. 9ʳ; 'Leggiadre Ninfe', f. 146ᵛ, and 'Cesarina', f. 151ᵛ, both tablatures notated 3♩. ♪♩|; 'Squilina', f. 44ᵛ, tablature notated 3 ♩. ♪ ♩|, and mensural soprano ₵3♩. ♩ ♩ | like the notation here.

(1) Bass, ♭ symbol printed as ♮; **(2)** (bars 4, 5, & 6) bass durations, ♩. emended from ♩; **(3)** tabl. *c′*, ♪ emended from ♪; **(4)** chord ♩ emended from ♩; **(5)** bass *d* emended from *c*; **(6)** tabl., final chord, double dots after ciphers transcribed: (see ch. 7).

[4] *Amorosina Grimana*

The first sentence of the text hints that the music is to be played in fast triple beats, each equal to the dotted minim (as in the cascarda 'Alta Regina', originally notated 3 𝅜 ♭ | ♭ 𝅜 | but transcribed at half value). A suggested adjustment of the duple notation into triple is appended here. Concordance: 'Pavaniglia', *Il Ballarino*, II, f. 39ᵛ, notated ₵ ♩ ♩ ♩ ♩ |.

(1) Soprano *f*♯′ emended from *f*♮′; **(2)** final soprano *a′* emended from *g′*; **(3)** bass *e*♭ emended from *e*♮′; **(4)** (bars 6 & 7) each *f*♯′ in soprano emended from *f*♮′ ; **(5)** bass *c* emended from *B*♭ ; **(6)** cadence adjustment of two G-chords, ♩ ♩ | emended from tr.♩ ♩ |.

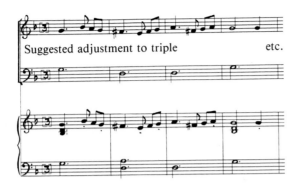

Suggested adjustment to triple   etc.

[5] *Laura Suave*

In this set of variations on the famous melody and bass of the 'Aria di Fiorenza', Caroso provides one of his most 'fleshed-out' scores. It is marred, however, by an abundance of printing errors, most of them rhythmic. The opening rhythmic motive ♩ ♫ ♩ ♩ emerges as a basic figuration, but is not stated clearly until bar 8, so unclear is the notation at the beginning. Accompanying this motive in many sections are fast chordal repetitions within a slow harmonic rhythm, suggesting the influence of contemporary Italian and Spanish guitar strumming techniques. With so many notes and rhythmic changes per bar, the chance of a printing error is further increased whenever a 7th-course cipher ○ has its own rhythmic symbol, which is typically printed in front of the cipher above the staff. The symbol may seem to align rather with the preceding cipher formation, and, indeed, may throw off the placement of subsequent symbols in the bar.

This is the only time in *Nobiltà di dame* that a galliard is barred by the perfect breve under 3 (bar 21). Reading at half value is suggested, with bar 21 united with bar 20 and treated as a 2nd ending by adjusting bar 20 to triple:

Cavalieri, the original composer of the 'Aria di Fiorenza', assigns ○3 to his version in the ballo of the Intermedio VI of 1589 (see D. P. Walker, ed., transcription of the ballo music in *Les Fêtes de Florence: Musique des intermèdes de 'La Pellegrina'*, pp. 140–54).

The use in the galliard of double dots in the tablature between repeated chords (see pp. 168) may have caused further displacement of the rhythmic signs in some of the problematic measures. The rhythmic interpretation adopted here (♩ ♩. ♪ ♩ ♩ ♩ ♩) is based on the clear notation in the original of bars 33 & 34; consecutive double dots, as in bars 29 & 30, are interpreted as ♩ ♩. ♪ ♩. ♪ ♩ ♩ ♩; it is possible, however, that ♩ ♩. ♪ ♪ ♩ ♩ ♩ was intended. For examples and discussions of these types of strumming rhythms in early seventeenth-century guitar tablatures, see Johannes Wolf, *Handbuch der Notationskunde* (Leipzig, 1913–19), II, ch. 3; Joseph Weidlich, 'Battuto Performance Practice in Early Italian Guitar Music (1606–1637)', *Journal of the Lute Society of America* XI (1978), pp. 76–7.

(1) (Bars 1–3 & 6, tabl.) [C] ♩ ♫ ♩ ♩ ♩ | ⫽ | ⫽ | & | ⫽ |

emended from: [C] ♩ ♩ ♩ ♩ ♩ ♩ | ♩ ♩ ♩ ♩ ♩ ♩ | ♩ ♫ ♩ ♩ | & | ♩ ♫ ♩ ♩ |;

(2) (bars 4a & 4b, tabl.) final chord in 1st ending adjusted to ♩ for repetition of strain; same chord in 2nd ending = ♩; $d'–eb'$, ♫-anacrusis to second strain, is printed after the repeat sign in original tablature, as shown above the transcription; (3) tabl., first chord = ♩ emended from ♩; (4) tabl., rhythm ♩ ♩ ♩ of bass courses on $F–f–Bb$ emended from ♩ ♩ ♩ for harmonic reasons; (5) tabl., ♩ g' emended from a' (course 1, cipher ○ for 2); (6) tabl., ♩ ♫ ♩ ♩ ♩ emended from ♩ ♪ ♩ ♩ ♩ (𝄾 misplaced to left); (7) tabl., by analogy to bar 40, 1st e' = ♩ emended from ♩ (𝄽 misplaced to left), and bass d realigned to the right under chord $f' – a'$; (8) 6th minim is placed after the repeat sign, functioning as an upbeat to bar 26 in the tablature, and understood to be a minim rest in the staff notation; (9) tabl., ♩ ♩ ♩ ♩ emended as follows: (a) 1st minim: Bb chord is compressed from the broken chord of the tablature: [music] for [music] ; (b) 2nd and 3rd minims: ♩ ♩ ♩ emended from ♩ ♩ ♩ (𝄽 misplaced to left); (10) bass eb emended from $e♮$; (11) tabl., by shifting original rhythmic symbol 𝄽 two places right: ♩ ♩. ♪ ♩. ♩ ♩ ♩ emended from 7-beat bar ♩ ♩. ♪ ♩ ♩ ♩ ♩ ♩; (12) tabl., original places rhythmic symbols before two nearly consecutive 7th-course ○-ciphers (F here); shifting original symbols 𝄽 and 𝄾 produces ♩ ♩. ♪ ♩. ♩ ♩ ♩ ♩ emended from 6½-beat bar ♩ ♩. ♪ ♩. ♩ ♩ ♩ ♩ (13) tabl., ♩ ♩. ♪ ♩ ♩ ♩. ♩ emended from 7-beat

bar | 𝅗𝅥 ♩ ♩ 𝅗𝅥 𝅗𝅥 𝅗𝅥 ♩ 𝅗𝅥 |: **(14)** bass *c–d* & soprano *c"–a'* = 𝅗𝅥 𝅝 emended from

𝅝 𝅗𝅥; **(15)** final soprano *a'* emended from *b♭'*; and final bass *A* emended from
B♭'; tabl., minims 3–6 = ♩ ♩ ♩ ♩ ♩ ♩ emended from ♩ ♩ ♩ ♩ ♩ ♩.;
(16) bass *B♭* emended from *c;* tabl., 1st minim: *B♭* chord emended from broken
chord arrangement (as in bar 26; see n. 9); **(17)** tabl., *f♯–a–f♯* emended from
c♯–f–c♯ (ciphers 1–○–1 misplaced one course too low); **(18)** tabl., 2nd minim, *f'–*
f = ♩ ♩ emended from ♩ ♩ (ʅ misplaced to left); final chord on 6th minim is
added to complete the bar (entrance into the saltarello is on the downbeat,
without an upbeat); **(19)** bass *G* emended from *F;* **(20)** soprano *g'* emended from
a'; **(21)** soprano *a'–b♭'* emended from *g'–a';* **(22)** bass *e–d–c* emended from
d–c–B♭; **(23)** tabl., *f'* = ♩ emended from ♩.; **(24)** extra bar added (last ♩ of bar 80
& ♩ of bar 81) to parallel the previous strain and to fit the choreography; repeat
signs added for the repetitions of the canary; **(25)** tabl., chord *f–a,* emended from
a–d' (○ ciphers misplaced one course too high on courses 2 & 3 rather than 3 &
4).

[6] *Alta Gonzaga*

Strain endings are not adjusted for repetition because they do not seem to be
needed except for the last strain.

   (1) Soprano *b♭'* emended from *b♮';* **(2)** soprano *g'* emended from *f';* **(3)** bass *B♭*
emended from *B♮;* **(4)** soprano *b♭'* emended from *b♮'*. This is the only passage in
coloration in the book; the bass coloration on *d – G – A* is split between the end
of one staff and the beginning of another and is notated ⌐♦·♦·♦⌐; probably
|♦ ♦|♦ ♦ | is intended; **(5)**·(bars 20a, 20b, cadence adjustments): 1st ending,

cued by the inclusion of an upbeat chord on F after the cadence on D (| 𝅝 :||: ꜰ |);
2nd ending, adjusted for repetition from the beginning.

[7] *Passo e mezzo*

Concordance: *Il Ballarino*, II, f. 49ʳ, ₵ | 𝅗𝅥 ♩ | ♩ ♩ ♩ ♩ |; 'Ardente Sole', f. 18ʳ.
   (1) Bass *c* emended from *d;* **(2)** tabl., chord *a'–d'* = ♩ emended from ♪ (ꜰ
misplaced to left); **(3)** soprano *c♯'* emended from *c';* **(4)** bass *d* emended from *c;*
(5) soprano *d'* & bass *B♭* emended from *c♯'* & *B,* respectively; **(6)** soprano *d'* &
bass *d* emended from *c'* & *e,* respectively; **(7)** soprano *d'* emended from *f'*.

[8] *Barriera*

It is suggested that the duple sections be read with note values halved.
Concordance: *Il Ballarino*, II, f. 78ᵛ; for 6-course lute, no staff notation, no
signature. The version in *Nobiltà di dame* is heavily revised.
   (1) Tabl., ♩ ♩ ♩ ♩ emended from ♩ ♩ ♩ ♩ (ꜰ for ꜰ); **(2)** tabl., ♩ ♩ ♩ ♩

emended from ♩♩♩♩ (𝄽 for 𝄾); (**3**) bass *G* emended from *F;* (**4**) tabl., 1st ♩
emended from ♩ (𝄾 misplaced to left); (**5**) tabl., *e'* emended from *e*♭*′* (course 2,
cipher 2 for 1); unique use of sign C in tabl. in *Nobiltà di dame;* (**6**) tabl., *c* added,
as in bars 22 & 69; (**7**) the conflicting signatures C/₵ in the original are
transcribed as C, since the strain they introduce is identical to bars 17–24 and
41–8 in C; (**8**) tabl., *c* emended from *a* (course 5, cipher ○ for course 4, cipher 4);
(**9**) bass *A* emended from *G;* (**10**) tabl., ♩. emended from ♩ (𝄾 for 𝄾); (**11**) tabl., ♩
understood (symbol not clear); (**12**) tabl., ♩ ♩ ♩ emended from ♩ ♩ ♩ (𝄾
misplaced to left); (**13**) bass = 𝅜. emended from 𝅜.

[9]   *Spagnoletta Nuova*

Concordance: *Il Ballarino,* II, 'Spagnoletta', f. 163ᵛ.

(**1**) An extra bar is needed after bar 30 to complete the 8-bar phrase
paralleling bars 17–24 if the third strain, a 'canary' variant in minor mode, is
interpreted as beginning with the upbeat to bar 33; (**2**) final C-major chord on
the third beat of this bar is omitted in the transcription to conform to modern
practise.

[10]   *Gagliarda di Spagna*

Concordance: *Il Ballarino,* II, f. 24ʳ; mensural soprano, ₵♩ ♩ ♩ ♩.

(**1**) *b*♭*′* emended from *b'* (course 1, cipher 1 for 2); (**2**) first *a* emended from *b*♭
(course 4, cipher 2 for 3); (**3**) bass *d* emended from *f* (course 5, cipher ○ for 3);
(**4**) ♩ emended from ♩..

[11]   *Bassa, et Alta*

This piece has been rebarred to show its rhythmic organization, which may hark
back to earlier times: (○= 𝅜 𝅜) (see Daniel Heartz, 'The Basse Dance, its
Evolution circa 1450 to 1550', *Annales Musicologiques* VI [1958–63], p. 321).
For a short discussion of a concordance with a 'Baxa et Alta' in the Mudarra
MS, see John Ward, *The Vihuela da Mano and its Music (1536–1576),*
unpublished Ph.D. dissertation (New York University, 1953), pp. 147–9. The
'Alta' and 'Gioioso' sections in the text are unmarked in the original music; the
'Gioioso' may refer to a descendant of the fifteenth-century French basse danse
and Italian ballo, 'Rôti bouilli joyeaux'/'El gioioso' (see Heartz, 'A 15th-century
Ballo: *Rôti Bouilli Joyeaux*', *Aspects of Medieval and Renaissance Music: A
Birthday Offering to Gustave Reese,* ed. Jan La Rue [New York: W. W. Norton,
1966], pp. 359–75). Note the typical alternation in this triple dance of the
division of the breve bars into 3 x 𝅝 and 2 x𝅝.. Concordance: *Il Ballarino,* II, f.
155ᵛ.

(**1**) Treble, 6th ♩ chord *d'–a* emended from *g'–d'* (courses 2 & 3 for 1 & 2,
ciphers ○ & ○; see also bars 5 & 11); (**2**) 1st ♩ emended from ♩; (**3**) 4th ♩ = *g*

emended from *b* (course 4 for 3, cipher 2); 5th ♩ = *d′–a* (see fn. 1); **(4)** ♩ = *b♭* emended from *b♮* (course 3, cipher 1 for 2); **(5)** ♩ ♩ ♩ ♩ ♩ emended from ♩. ♩. ♩. ♩. ♩.; **(6)** *c′–b♭* emended from *f′–e♭′* (course 3 for 2, ciphers 3 & 1); **(7)** (bars 36, 37): ♩ emended from ♩. on chord before repeat sign, and continuing up to ♩ ♩; bass *G* of first chord after repeat sign emended from *c* (course 6 for 5,cipher ○); **(8)** bass *c* added; **(9)** ♩ emended from ♩. on minims 3, 4, & 5; **(10)** *f′* emended from *e′* (course 2, cipher 3 for 2); ♩ ♩ ♩ ♩ emended from ♩ ♩ ♩ ♩; **(11)** cadence adjustment: final chord reduced to minim from semibreve.

[12]   *Altezza d'Amore*

(1) ♩ ♩ ♩ ♩ ♩ emended from ♩ ♩ ♩ ♩ ♩ (omission of 𝆏 over 2nd note); **(2)** *g′–a′* = ♩ ♩ emended from ♩ ♩ (𝆏 misplaced to left); **(3)** ♩ ♩ ♩ ♩ emended from ♩ ♩ ♩ ♩ (omission of 𝆏 over 3rd note); **(4)** (bar 52, 1st ending) the rubric designating a 1st ending includes bar 51; **(5)** (bars 52a & b) the rubric makes clear that these two bars comprise a 2nd ending though they are notated after the double bar as ‖♩ ♩|♩ ‖; the final chord in bar 52b is emended to ♩. from ♩. The sign 3, usually employed to mark off the change into the following rotta (saltarello), is missing here; **(6)** (bars 54 & 55) *f′–e♭′–d′–d′* = ♩ ♩|♩ ♩ |emended from ♩ ♩. |♩. ♩|; **(7)** *f′* = ♩. emended from ♩; **(8)** *b♭′* = ♩ emended from ♩.; **(9)** *c′* = ♩ emended from ♪; **(10)** *a–g–f* emended from *d′–b–a* (ciphers ○–2–○ misplaced 1 course too high); **(11)** *g* = ♩ emended from ♩; **(12)** cadence adjustment ♩ from ♩..

[13]   *Coppia Colonna*

Note values of first movement halved. Galliard originally barred in duple under the sign 3 is regrouped into triple bars as 3♩=[1t]. Many of the rhythmic ambiguities and errors in 'Coppia Colonna' have been carried over from the piece in *Il Ballarino* and present problems in interpreting the author's intent. Concordance: *Il Ballarino*, II, 'Copia Felice' [*sic*], f. 58ᵛ, ₵.

   (1) ♩ ♩ ♩ ♩ emended from ♩ ♩ ♩ ♩ (𝆏 for 𝆏), transcribed as ♩ ♩ ♩ ♩ at half value; **(2)** bass *B* emended from *e* (course 5 for 6, cipher 4); **(3)** (bars 20a & 20b, 40; 1st and 2nd endings) unusual notation at transition from duple to triple; structural repeat sign lacking (requiring cadence adjustment of an added ♩); the galliard is barred in duple (by the ○) and has been corrected to agree with the 3 (the 3 is lacking in 'Copia Felice' at this juncture); **(4)** (bar 25) ♩ ♩ ♩ ♩ emended from ♩ ♩ ♩ ♩ (𝆏 for 𝆏); **(5)** *e♭′* added; supplied from 'Copia Felice'; **(6)** (bar 33, after double bars) ♩ ♩ ♩ ♩ ♩ emended from ♩ ♩ ♩ ♩ ♩ (𝆏 misplaced two notes to left); **(7)** cadence adjustment: ○ .

[14]   *Rosa Felice*

(1)♩ ♪♩ ♩ emended from ♪♩ ♩ ♩ (missing 𝄵 on 1st pulse, and 𝄒 𝄒 misplaced to left).

[16]   *Doria Colonna*

Concordance: *Il Ballarino*, II, sciolta of 'Pavana Matthei', f. 113ᵛ.
    (1) ♩ emended from tr.𝅗𝅥 .

[17]   *Alta Colonna*

Concordances: *Il Ballarino*, Balletto 'Bellezze d'Olimpia', II, f. 66ʳ (first strain) and Balletto 'Coppia Cappelli', II, f. 91ʳ (first strains); both notated ₵–|𝅗𝅥 𝅗𝅥|, whereas 'Alta Colonna' is notated 3𝅗𝅥 𝅗𝅥 𝅗𝅥|.
    (1) e^b emended from *e* (course 5, cipher 1 for 2).

[18]   *Allegrezza d'Amore*

Concordance: *Il Ballarino*, II, f. 109ʳ.
    (1) Bass *d* emended from e^b (course 5, cipher 2 for 3); (2) bass e^b emended from *d* (course 5, cipher 3 for 2); (3) ♩ emended from 𝅝 .

[19]   *Amor Costante*

Concordances: *Il Ballarino*, II, f. 27ᵀ; successively, ₵𝅗𝅥|𝅗𝅥 𝅗𝅥|and ₵ 3𝅗𝅥|𝅝 𝅗𝅥| in mensural soprano; also in *Il Ballarino*, cascarda 'Meraviglia d'Amore', II, f. 138ᵛ, identical tablature to the sciolta of 'Amor Costante'.
    (1) (Bars 17–24) final duple strain is faulty and incomplete. Through structural analogies of characteristic head motives and cadence formulae, interpolations provide the necessary 8-bar structure; the rubric in *Il Ballarino* which specifies that this strain, a 'ritornello', should be played twice is omitted in *Nobiltà di dame*, but apparently applies to 'Amor Costante' as well. In bar 17 the head motive is interpolated; (2) *f'–e'–d'* emended from *b♭'–a'–g'* (course 2 for 1, ciphers 3–2–○, as in bar 23); harmonic bass *c* added; last two chords added by analogy to bar 23; (3) head motive interpolated; (4) ♪♩ ♩ ♪ interpolated by analogy to parallel structure in bar 18; (5) bass *c* added as in bar 19; (6) (bars 24a, b) missing notes ♩ ♪ of cadence motive ♩ ♪ ♩ interpolated (see bar 8), then assimilated to 3𝅗𝅥 𝅗𝅥 𝅗𝅥 in 2nd ending; (7) ♩ emended from tr.♪.

[20]   *Forza d'Amore*

(1) (Bars 1–16) the sign 3 with barring every three minims is more typical of an internal galliard movement of a balletto suite than of an opening movement. Though the entire first movement can be performed in triple as

written, the first playing of this movement may in fact be intended to be performed in duple (the suggested opening appended here), since the texts for the second and third playings of the movement are specifically under the heading 'La sua Gagliarda'; (2) ♩ ♩ ♩ ♩ emended from ♩ ♩ ♩ ♩ (♪ misplaced to left); (3) the *bb′* is probably intended. For another example in the same context see Negri, 'Galleria d'Amore', galliard, bars 7–8; (4) *c′* (course 3, cipher 3), indistinct cipher supplied from British Museum copy of *Raccolta;* (5) ♩ ♫ ♩ ♩ emended from ♩ ♪ ♩ ♩ ♩ (♪ misplaced to left). The C and the barring in duple in the original suggest that the grouping here should be 3 ♩ = [1½t], a slower triple than before (see 'The Musical Edition', p. 58), with the possibility of regrouping into 2 ♩ for repetitions of the strain; (6) *f′* on downbeat (course 2, cipher 3 misplaced to right); (7) ♩ ♫ emended from ♩ ♩ ♩ (♪ for ♪); (8) ♩ emended from ♪ (♪ for ♪).

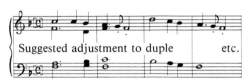

Suggested adjustment to duple   etc.

[21] *Bassa Honorata*

Concordance: *Il Ballarino*, II, f. 76[r].

(1) (Bar 16b, 2nd ending) 3 ♩. ♪ ♩ ♩ ‖ ♩ | =triple adjustment of the original ending leading into the saltarello: tr. ♩ ♫ | ♩ ‖: 3 ♪ ♪ ♩|; (2) *A* deleted (erroneous cipher 1 on course 6); (3) finger dot under 2nd chord emended from misplacement under 1st chord; (4) (bar 48) ♩ emended from tr. ♩..

[22] *Cesarina*

Concordance: *Il Ballarino*, II, 'La Gagliarda detta Cesarina' to 'Il Piantone', f. 183[v]; the two versions are obviously related musically; the later version in triple clarifies many of the rhythmic problems of the unbarred earlier setting, apparently including the notation of rests in the tablature.

[23] *Bellezze d'Olimpia*

Transcription rebarred in 3 ♩ =[1½t]. The music employs three levels of ternary rhythmic groupings: ○.(○ ♩=1½t) as in bars 1–4; hemiola (○ ○ ○=3t) as in bars 6 & 7; and ♩.(♩ ♩ =¾t) as in bar 9. Concordance: *Il Ballarino*, II, f. 66[r]; ₵ - ♩ | ♩ ♩| in mensural soprano.

[24] *Contrapasso Nuovo*

Transcription rebarred in 3♩ =[1½t]. Concordance: *Il Ballarino*, II, f. 148ᵛ.

(**1**) 3rd ♩, *g* emended from *a*♭ (course 4, cipher 2 for 3); (**2**) soprano *a′* emended from *e′* (course 1 for 2, cipher 2); (**3**) bass *c* added; and 3rd ♩ emended from ♩ (⌐ for ⌐); (**4**) bass *B*♭ added; (**5**) treble *e*♭′ added; (**6**) (bars 20a, & 20b) cadence adjustments for 1st and 2nd endings; chord of 2nd ending (○) appears in the original as a 13th bar to the strain but minus bass *f*.

[25] *Specchio d'Amore*

Concordance: *Il Ballarino*, cascarda 'Laccio d'Amore', II, f. 142ʳ.

(**1**) Bass *c* added.

[26] *Contentezza d'Amore*

Concordance: *Il Ballarino*, II, f. 61ᵛ; successively, ₵ ⌐ ♩ ♩ | ♩ ♩ and ₵3○ ♩ | in mensural soprano.

(**1**) Bass *d* emended from *A* (course 5 for 6, cipher 2); (**2**) ♩ ♫ ♩ ♫ emended (similar to bar 2) from ♩ ♩ ♩ ♫♫ (halved); (**3**) (bars 16, 17) conjectural interpolation ♫♫ : ♫♫ as in bars 13 & 20; (**4**) bass *c–d* emended from *G–A* (course 5 for 6,ciphers ○, 2); (**5**) (bars 24a, 24b) cadence adjustments; 1st ending, added ♩ for repeat of strain; 2nd ending, added ♩ ʔ in preparation for entrance into the sciolta on the downbeat; (**6**) suggested *F* for *A*.

[27] *Bassa Savella*

Concordance: *Il Ballarino*, balletto 'Bassa Ducale', II, f. 53ʳ; successively, ₵♩. ♩ | & ₵3♩. ♩ ♩ | in mensural soprano.

(**1**) 1st bass *a* emended from *b*♭ (course 4, cipher 2 for 3); (**2**) (bars 30a, 30b) original gives these two bars as consecutive 30 & 31; the transcription treats the final bar as a 2nd ending, 30b. Bar 30b, *d* added.

[28] *Conto dell'Orco Nuovo*

Concordance: *Il Ballarino*, II, f. 51ʳ; ₵ ⌐ ♩ | ♩ ♩ | in mensural soprano.

(**1**) ♩ adjusted from ○.

[29] *Furioso all'Italiana*

Transcription: note values halved for opening duple section and fast triple sciolta (saltarello), but not for the third section which, barred in the original by the ○ in ₵, is rebarred in 3♩ =[1½t]. The same music is specified for 'Furioso alla

Spagnuola' (No. 31) and 'Furioso Nuovo' (No. 35); the directions given in the rubrics here, however, do not necessarily apply to the other two dances. Concordance: *Il Ballarino*, II, f. 150ʳ.

(1) Final ♩ emended from tr.♪; (2) bass *d* emended from *g* (course 5 for 4, cipher 2); (3) (bars 8a, 8b) 1st ending, final chord= ♩ adjusted from tr. ♩ for the repetitions of this strain; 2nd ending, triple adjustment from duple 1st ending; (4) (bar 24b, 2nd ending) ♩. adjusted from tr.♩; (5) (bar 32, cadence adjustment) ⸴ added to lead back into sciolta, bar 9.

[30] *Ghirlanda d'Amore*

Concordance: this cascarda is a slightly simpler version of the rotta (saltarello) of 'Nido d'Amore' in *Nobiltà di dame*, p. 268.

(1) ♫ emended from ♩ ♩.

[33] *Nido d'Amore*

Concordance: the rotta (saltarello) of 'Nido d'Amore' is related to the cascarda 'Ghirlanda d'Amore', No. 30 in *Nobiltà di dame,* p. 260; the main difference is that the 3rd strain of 'Nido d'Amore' is two bars longer.

(1) *a'* emended from *b♭'* (course 1, cipher 2 for 3); (2) (bar 13a, 1st ending) ♩ adjusted from ♩ for repetition of strain; (3) cadence adjustment for second ending; (4)♩ ♩ reads ♩ ♩ in 'Ghirlanda d'Amore', No. 30; (5) *f'* = ♩ emended from ♪ (by analogy to bar 59); (6) (bar 61) last beat ♫ emended from ♩ ♩; (7) (bars 71a, 71b) ♩ supplied for missing rhythmic symbol.

[34] *Alta Vittoria*

Transcription: note values of first movement (duple) and third movement (saltarello) halved. Concordances: (1) *Il Ballarino:* (a) balletto 'Alta Vittoria', II, f. 104ᵛ; notational differences between the two versions occur primarily at transitions into the successive dance movements; (b) cascarda 'Florido Giglio', II, f. 32ᵛ, notated ₵3 ◦ ♩ (the almost identical saltarello of 'Alta Vittoria' is notated 3 ◦ ♩ ⎮); (c) 'Il Canario', II, f. 182ʳ, and the canary movement of 'Alta Ruissa', II, f. 176ʳ notated 3 ◦ ♩ (in 'Alta Vittoria' it is notated 3♩ ♩⎮). (2) *Nobiltà di dame*, p. 304, No. 45, the cascarda 'Amor Prudente' is identical to the sciolta (saltarello) and canary of 'Alta Vittoria'.

(1) 1st *f'* emended from *e'* (course 2, cipher 3 for 2); (2) ♩ ♫ (as in *Il Ballarino*) emended from ♫♩ (♮ misplaced to the left); (3) (bar 16a, 1st ending) ♩ emended from tr.♪ for repetition of strain; (4) (bar 16b, 2nd ending) the galliard, barred by the semibreve, is prefixed by the sign 3, which is missing

in *Il Ballarino;* cadence rhythms are obscure, with original alignment thus:

Pitches		a'	a'	‖	c" b'| a'	g'|

| *Il Ballarino* | ‖ | ♪ | ‖ | ♪ ♪ | ♪ | ♪ |

| *Nobiltà di dame* | ‖ | ♪ | ‖3 | ♪ | ♪ | ♪ | ♪ |

(5) ♩. ♩ ♩ (as in *Il Ballarino*) emended from ♩ ♩ ♩; (6) 3rd ♩, chord *g'–e* emended by deletion of an extraneous *d'* (course 2, cipher ○); (7) bass *d* emended from *A* (course 5 for 6, cipher 2); (8) obscure rhythms at split cadence-bar; as transcribed | ♩. ♩ ♩ | ♩ ╌ ‖ ♩ ♩ |, it is more in line with ♩. ♩ | ♩ ♩ | ‖ ╌ ♩ ♩ | from *Il Ballarino*, but with the rest moved before the double bar. Original notation is:

| *Il Ballarino* | 𝅝. | 𝅗𝅥 | 𝅗𝅥 | 𝅗𝅥 | 𝅗𝅥 | ‖ | ╌ 𝅗𝅥 𝅗𝅥 |

| *Nobiltà di dame* | 𝅝. | 𝅗𝅥 | 𝅗𝅥 | 𝅗𝅥 | 𝅗𝅥 | ‖ | 𝅗𝅥 𝅗𝅥 𝅗𝅥 |

Chords are spelled here as in bar 24; (9) final soprano *g'* emended from *a'* (course 1, cipher ○ for 2); (10) irregular barring in the tablature may designate a structural division between two phrases of four galliard patterns each; thus the original | 𝅝 | 𝅘𝅥 𝅘𝅥 𝅘𝅥 | 𝅘𝅥 𝅘𝅥 | is transcribed | 𝅝 𝅗𝅥 𝅗𝅥 𝅗𝅥 ‖ 𝅗𝅥 𝅗𝅥 |; (11) bass *B♭* (𝅗𝅥.) added, analogous to bars 19 & 23; (12) *e'* emended from *d'* (course 2, cipher 2 for ○); (13) 𝅗𝅥 ‖ 𝅗𝅥 𝅗𝅥 | emended from tr.𝅗𝅥. ‖ 𝅘𝅥𝅮𝅘𝅥𝅮 |; (14) the 12-bar canary of 'Alta Vittoria' is directly related to the music of 'Il Canario' in *Il Ballarino*, as shown in the examples below: Ex. A is the entire 'Il Canario' tune; Ex. B is the cadence (bars 79 & 80) of both the saltarello to 'Alta Vittoria' and 'Florido Giglio' plus the 12-bar canary of 'Alta Vittoria'; and Ex. C is the edited transcription of Ex. B. The first two bars of the canary tune in Ex. A, notated ₵3 𝅝 𝅗𝅥, coincide with the cadential bars of the saltarello and the two-minim upbeat to the canary of 'Alta Vittoria' in Ex. B. The remainder of the canary tune in Ex. B has been added in the original in a notation one level lower (| 𝅗𝅥 𝅗𝅥 |), the more usual notation in *Nobiltà di dame*. The strange 3 𝅗𝅥 𝅗𝅥 | 𝅗𝅥 | at the end of the strain may be a reminder that in repeating the canary the two minims of the upbeat previously notated in [C] 3 ‖ 𝅗𝅥 𝅗𝅥 | are to be read as ‖ 𝅗𝅥 𝅗𝅥 |; (15) *c'* emended from *b'* (course 3, cipher 3 for 2).

Ex. A: 'Il Canario' *(Il Ballarino)*

(13)

Ex. B: End of saltarello (or 'Florida Giglio') and Canary of 'Alta Vittoria'

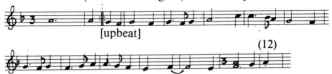

[upbeat]

(12)

Ex. C: Transcription of B

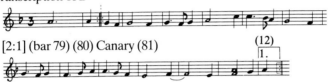

[2:1] (bar 79) (80) Canary (81)   (12)
                                                    1.

[37]   *Ballo del Fiore*

Concordance: *Il Ballarino*, II, f. 159^r.

(1) ♩. emended from tr. ♩ .

[38]   *Tordiglione*

Concordance: *Il Ballarino*, II, f. 169^v, identical tablature. In spite of its length of only twelve semibreves (with two nearly identical phrases of six semibreves each), the music can be reshaped into a variety of duple and triple groupings, depending upon the needs of the choreography, e.g.:

1st half

[39]   *Vero Amore*

Transcription: rebarred in 3♩ =[1½t]. Concordance: *Il Ballarino*, 'Balletto Amor mio', II, f. 107^r. The qualification of the opening *Reverence* of this dance as *Riverenza grave 'alla battuta tripla'* is unique, for elsewhere Caroso uses the term '*battuta tripla*' to mean a dotted minim, but here it may mean a dotted semibreve or breve (Rule XXI). According to Collins, however, the term '*tripla*' in the seventeenth century may simply mean any kind of triple measure (see bibliography in 'The Musical Edition').

Caroso provides no music for the sciolta; he may intend the given music to be read at two different levels of triple grouping, one to accommodate the first slow movement and another for the sciolta as a saltarello, with both versions to be read from the same score. The first bars of the sciolta, in halved note values, are projected:

[The Sciolta of this piece as a Saltarello] etc.

[40]   *Ninfa Leggiadra*

(1) *f′* emended from *c′* (course 2 for 3, cipher 3); (2) *f′–c′–f* emended from *c′–a♭′–c* (courses 2–3–4 for 3–4–5, ciphers 3–3–○); (3) & (4) bars 16 & 24 are added for completion of the musical structure of a 4-bar phrase.

[41]   *Ballo detto Il Piantone*

Transcription: first movement rebarred in 3 ♩ =[1½t]. For the second movement, 'La Gagliarda detta Mezza notte', an exact rhythmic interpretation has not been determined; therefore, rhythmic symbols from the unbarred tablature are placed above the appropriate transcribed pitches, and bass pitches are written as blackened note-heads without specific rhythmic duration. Concordance: *Il Ballarino,* II, f. 183^V & 184^r; and balletto 'Alta Ruissa', II, f. 176^r (first movement only).

(1) D-minor triad emended from 4-note chord with cipher 3 on course 1 (*b♭′*) — *Il Ballarino* shows the triad; (2) 5 pitch-rows between the asterisks: rhythmic symbol at the beginning of the series emended from ; (3) bass *g* emended from *d* (course 4 for 5, cipher 2); (4) last 4 pitch-rows: rhythmic symbols emended from (misplaced to right).

[42]   *Cortesia*

Concordance: *Il Ballarino,* II, f. 5^V, 'Alba Novella'; the two scores are related, but 'Cortesia' is more elaborate melodically and harmonically: it dispenses with the fourth strain of both the first movement and the concluding saltarello; it inserts a galliard/tordion; it halves the note values of the first movement of 'Alba Novella'; and it retains the same level of notation for the saltarello (3 𝅗𝅥 𝅗𝅥 𝄽), but bars it by the perfect semibreve 3 𝅗𝅥.　𝅗𝅥. | (the only time this barring occurs in *Nobiltà di dame*).

(1) *a′–g′–f♯′=* 𝅘𝅥 𝅘𝅥𝅘𝅥 emended from ♪ 𝅘𝅥 ♪ (𝄼 𝄼 misplaced to right); **(2)** *g′–b♭′–a′–g′=*𝅘𝅥𝅘𝅥𝅘𝅥𝅘𝅥 emended from 𝅘𝅥 𝅘𝅥 𝅘𝅥 𝅘𝅥 (𝄽 for 𝄼); **(3)** *G* added (given in 'Alba Novella'); **(4)** (bars 29–32) 𝅘𝅥 from * * emended from 𝅝 (𝄼 for |); **(5)** 𝅗𝅥 𝅘𝅥 𝅘𝅥 𝅗𝅥 emended from 𝅗𝅥 𝅝 𝅗𝅥 𝅗𝅥 (incorrect rhythmic symbols).

[43]　*Pungente Dardo*

Transcription: first movement rebarred in 3 𝅗𝅥 =[1½t]; bars 15–18 and the saltarello movement transcribed at half value. Concordance: *Il Ballarino*, II, f. 89ᵛ.

(1) *c′–b♮=* 𝅗𝅥 𝅗𝅥 emended from 𝅗𝅥　𝅗𝅥 (𝄽 for 𝄼); **(2)** *d′* emended from *g′* (course 2 for 1, cipher ○); **(3)** the 3 in this case may signify a triple grouping of undiminished semiminims (𝅘𝅥) equal to ¾ of the semibreve of the previous section (𝅘𝅥=𝅘𝅥), as signalled by the fact that the original barring by the 𝅝 in the first section carries over into the strain in 3 through 𝅘𝅥s, as shown above the score, creating some strange syncopations and disguising the true triple grouping. Once the temporal relationship is established, barlines begin to mark off the intended fast triple:
etc.

[44]　*Rara Beltà*

(1) Strain lacks one bar — conjectural bar interpolated.

[45]　*Amor Prudente*

Concordance: *Nobiltà di dame*, p. 274; the sciolta (saltarello) and canary of 'Alta Vittoria' are identical to 'Amor Prudente' (i.e., the identical plate was used in the printing). See the commentary to those movements (p. 327) for corrections and editorial additions.

[46]　*Donna Leggiadra*

Concordance: *Il Ballarino*, II, f. 123ʳ, cascarda 'Gloria d'Amore'.

(1) 𝅗𝅥 emended from 𝅗𝅥. (𝄼 for 𝄽); **(2)** 𝅗𝅥 𝄽 emended from 𝅝 (𝄾 for |); **(3)** 𝅗𝅥. emended from 𝅘𝅥 (𝄽 for 𝄼); **(4)** 𝅗𝅥. emended from 𝅝 (𝄾 for |).

[47] *Selva Amorosa*

The use of what appear to be triplets at the level of ♩ ♩ ♩ or ♪♪♪ within imperfect prolation (as in bars 8 & 10, 29 & 33), and the frequency of higher fret positions than normal in *Nobiltà di dame,* set this work apart from the other balletti. Possibly the triplets may be performed: ♩ ♩ ♩ = ♩ ♩♪, and ♪♪♪ = ♪ ♪♪ (see Collins's reference in 'The Musical Edition', p. 57).

(1) (Bars 12, upbeat, & 13; strain 3) ♪ (*. . . . . .*) emended from ♩ (♮ for ♭); (2) f♯ added to chord as in bars 23–4, 39–40, etc.; (3) (bars 16, upbeats, & 17 & 18) upbeat e′ emended from b (course 2 for 3, cipher 2); rhythm in the opening bars of the galliard ‖: ♩ ♩ | ♩ ♩ ♩ ♩ ♩ | ♩ ♩ ♩ | emended from the original rhythm as shown above the score; (4) ♩. emended from ♩ (♭ for ♮); (5) ♩. emended from ♩ (♭ for ♭); (6) (bars 43–6) c′ (course 3, cipher 3) moved left to 1st chord of the bar; all ♩ (*. . .*) emended from ♩ (♮ for ♭); (7) | ♩. ♩ ♩ |

or

emended (by analogy to bar 51) from | ♩ ♩ ♩ |; (8) Cadence adjustment for transition to fast 3; unusual barring in the repeat sign of the tablature may be an attempt to notate a rest: | ♩ |: |:3 ♩ | ♩ ♩ |.

[48] *Fulgente Rai*

Concordance: *Il Ballarino,* II, f. 120[r], sciolta of the balletto 'Rustica Palina'.

(1) ♩. ♪ ♩ emended from ♩ ♪ ♩ (tr. ♮ for tr. ♭); (2) (bars 24a & b) 1st ending = ♩; 2nd ending = ♩ for return to beginning.

[49] *Alta Cardana*

(1) A misprinted cipher 1 on course 6 ($A♭$) is deleted from the F-major chord; (2) cadence adjustment (♩ for tr. ♩.).

Glossary

The following glossary consists of those words relating to music or dance, or to both music and dance, that appear frequently in *Nobiltà di dame*, and whose Italian equivalents may either be of special importance for the reader to know, or have been translated in a special way because of their choreographic or musical context. Wherever there may be valid questions about the choice of an English term, an explanation is offered. All step types are not listed, however (for such a listing see the text itself), nor is this glossary intended to be a complete index of terms.

ENGLISH | ITALIAN

acknowledge, pay one's respects   *salutare*
The best translation for 'salutare' would seem to be 'salute', in the older sense in which it applies to non-military actions (for example, a lady 'saluting' a gentleman upon meeting him). The possible confusion 'salute' might produce in modern readers, however, coupled with the fact that the exact movement implied by 'salutare' is not made clear by Caroso, has prompted the choice used here.

alta   *alta*
This term is not translated, as it may have a specific meaning (see ch. 2).

approaching each other   *accostandosi*

back, backwards, behind, outward   *in dietro*

ball   *ballo, festa, festino*

balletto   *balletto*
This term is not translated, because it may have a specific meaning (see ch. 2).

ballo/dance   *ballo*
This term is translated as 'dance' when it is used generically, as in Rule XXV: '*a fare i Balli, i Balletti, & altre sorte di Balli*', 'to do balli, balletti, and other kinds of dances'.

bassa   *bassa*

This term is not translated, as it may have a specific meaning (see ch. 2).

beat   *battuta*

The term 'battuta' has numerous meanings. With regard to movement, it may mean a stamp or a clap (e.g., Rule XXIII. '*Seguito battuto del Canario*', '*stamped sequence in the canary*'). With regard to step durations, 'battuta' may mean 'tactus', 'beat', or 'pulse', that is, a recognizable, recurring, and finite unit of time, its precise meaning to be understood in context. When it is qualified further, as listed below, it takes on additional meanings.

ordinary beat	*battuta ordinaria*
perfect beat	*battuta perfetta*
simple beat	*battuta piane*
triple beat	*battuta tripla*
true beat	*vera battuta*

bend   *piegare*

While 'plié' would be the closest cognate in English, it suggests a ballet movement that is deeper and more turned out than the evidence of the sixteenth century warrants. See, for example, Negri's illustrations for the preparations for turns, or landings after jumps; and note Caroso's disapproving comments about a position of the feet '*che l'un piede mira à Sirocco, & l'altro à Tramontana*' (original, p. 13), 'in which one foot looks to the south and the other to the north'.

body   *vita*

Today the term '*vita*', when given an anatomical meaning, refers specifically to the waist. Caroso, however, clearly understands it as 'body', in the sense of the 'torso' or 'trunk'. Since in most cases the latter two terms do not work in the contexts in which they appear, I have used 'body', e.g., '*tenendo ben distesa al vita*' (Rule II), 'keeping your body quite straight'. This is in line with Florio's definition: 'Used also for the stature or proportion of man or woman' (p. 63). Further evidence for this meaning is found in Negri, in his description of '*salto tondo*', '*turning jump*': '. . . *avertendo che nel voltare attorno, si hà d'accompagnare la vita dritta è raccolta insieme, cioè la testa, le braccia, le gambe*', '. . . note that in turning around, you should keep your body upright and assembled, that is, the head, arms, and legs'.[1]

---

[1] Negri, p. 75.

bow	*chinare, inchinare*

This term is distinguished from '*Riverenza*' (*Reverence*), a larger movement.

breve (musical)	*breve*
broken	*spezzato*
cadence	*cadenza*
canary	*canario*
canary pattern	*tempo di canario*
caper	*capriola*

This is the English term of the period, used here instead of the modern '*cabriole*', because its execution is different. Florio: '*Caprióla*. . . . Also a Capriole or Caper in daunceing' (p. 83).

cross caper	*capriola intrecciata*

This is the English term of the period. The term '*entrechat*' of modern ballet is obviously a cognate, but stylistic differences in execution warrant the use of the old term.

cascarda	*cascarda*

Since this term for a dance type is used only by Caroso, and since it may have a specific meaning, it has been retained (see ch. 2).

changing places	*cambiando luogo*
changing step, exchanging step	*cambio, scambiata*
chasing step	*recacciata*
chopines	*pianelle*

This is the current translation. In sixteenth-century England this type of shoe was also known as 'pantofle'.

circle	*ruota*
clap hands	*battuta sù le mani, battuta di mano*
clap right hands	*dandosi una botta alla man destra*

coda, codetta — *chiusa*

Florio: 'a close or shutting up of anything' (p. 99). Caroso's use of the word is often similar to that of a musical codetta; that is, a small cadential section used as a refrain (see 'Pavaniglia' choreography). Choice of 'coda' or 'codetta' depended on this: when the *chiusa* of a dance was short and treated as a refrain, 'codetta' was used; when a *Chiusa* appeared only at the end of an entire dance and was of some length, 'coda' was the translation (see 'Passo e mezzo' choreography).

continence — *continenza*

The cognate was chosen because it most nearly approximates the definition by Caroso.

Corinthian step — *Corinto*

This is a play on words described by Caroso, who says that the title of the step derives from *cuore* (heart) (original, p. 64). It is unlikely that there is a further pun here with *corrente*, a dance which appears in two printed sources at this time (Negri and Arbeau). Caroso's *Corinto* is a step pattern only, not a choreography, and only one step within Negri's dance ('*sottopiede*', '*foot under*') is a component of Caroso's *Corinthian step*. This *foot under* is also common to many other dances. Arbeau's *courante* choreography seems even more distant.

customary hand(s) — *man' ordinaria*

dance — *ballo*

See ch. 2 for a discussion of this term. Also see ch. 5 for definitions of dance types.

dactylic step — *dattile*

dancing master, Master of the Ball — *Maestro di Ballo*
master of ceremonies

The usage in English depends upon the context. 'Master of the Ball' may be used when the context makes it clear that he is functioning as a modern master of ceremonies (that is, running the event of the ball), rather than acting as a teacher at a dancing lesson.

dancing place — *luogo dove si ballerà*

This is a common English term of the period.

dexterous step — *destice*

double — *doppio*

dropping hands — *lasciandosi*

end of the hall   *capo della sala*

The term 'top of the hall' is common in English country dancing, along with its counterpart, 'bottom of the hall'. In Caroso's case, however, *'capo della sala'* refers to either end of the hall.

facing towards each other   *in prospettiva*

The meaning of this term is not clear in *Nobiltà di dame*. In *Il Ballarino*, however, Caroso says, '. . . . *in prospettiva, cioè all'incontro à i circostanti'* (f.58ʳ). Thus it appears to mean that the partners face each other along a diagonal, as some of the figures seem to indicate, so that they appear to face some of the onlookers as well.

falling jump   *trabucchetto [sic]*

Florio, pp. 570–71: *'Trabochetti*, pitfalls, traps, or gins; *Traboccare*, to fall down, . . . to reele, to stagger, to stumble; *Trabócco*, a downe-fall. . . . a reeling, a staggering, or a stumbling'. Secondary meanings of *trabócco* of trebuchet, or trebucket, having to do with an engine for catapulting stones (military), or a small delicate balance, suggest the same movement described by Caroso (Rules XXIX and XXX).[2]

feet apart/disparate   *piedi dispari*

feet together, parallel   *piedi pari*

feigned   *finto*

fingerbreadth   *dita*

five steps   *cinque passi*

This is a standard synonym for the basic galliard step pattern (French: *cinq pas*; English: *sinkapace*). *'Sinkapace'* was not adopted here, as *five steps* was also a common term in sixteenth-century English, and *'sinkapace'* was not a translation, but a transliteration.

flanking, flankingly   *fiancheggiato, fiancheggiando*

The cognate term 'flanking' has been adopted here because it is as ambiguous as the original definition (original, p. 94). and the descriptions of the *Sapphic step, dactylic step*, and *Corinthian step* (Rules LXVI, LXVII, LXVIII). That is, a flanking movement is called for, but whether this is on a diagonal or straight toward the partner is not clear, since the degree of pivot on the standing foot at the beginning of the movement is not specified.

---

[2] *Garzanti Comprehensive Italian-English English-Italian Dictionary*, ed. Mario Mazon (New York: McGraw-Hill Book Company, 1961).

flourish   *fioretto*

Caroso's descriptions of the various kinds of *fioretti* make it clear that he considers them to be embellishments. Hence the old cognate seems the best translation (note that *fioretto* was a common musical term for embellishment).

foot stamping in the canary   *battuta di pié al canario*

foot under   *sottopiede*

forward, in front of   *innanzi*

fundamental law   *vera regola*

When Caroso refers to this (e.g., original, p. 63) he is speaking of perfect symmetry.

galliard   *gagliarda*

galliard pattern   *tempo di gagliarda*

gently   *gentilmente*

This is to be taken in the old sense: politely, genteelly, courteously.

grace   *gratia*

Caroso uses this term often in the sense of a specific ornament, just as it was employed in musical terminology.

grave (time value)   *grave*
     See ch. 2.

hall, ballroom   *sala*

hip, side (part of body)   *fianco*

inward, in   *per dentro*
     outward, out   *in dietro*

jump, hop, leap   *salto, saltino*

The exact meaning of these terms depends upon their context.

knot   *groppo*

limping hop   *zoppetto*

little bell	*campanella*
little bound with feet together	*balzetto à pié pari*
little mill	*molinello*

Florio: '*Molinello*, any kind of little mill. . . . Also as *Ventarello*' (p. 319). '*Ventarello*. . . . Also a paper windmill that children use to play with at a stick's end' (p. 593). Another meaning of the word is 'whirl'. My choice is influenced by the fact that a number of folk dances and folk-dance figures which involve similar movement use the terms 'windmill' or 'mill'.

little side stamping step	*costatetto*
long (time value)	*longa, lunga*
Master of the Ball, dancing master (see 'dancing master', above.)	*Mastro/Maestro di Ballo*
measure (as propriety, restraint)	*misura*
minim (time value)	*minima*
music, piece	*musica, sonata, suono*

See below under 'piece' and 'tempo'.

opposite (each other)	*all'incontro*
passage	*passeggio*

Symmetrical Passage	*Passeggio Terminato*

See Caroso's explanation of this term in 'Alta Regina'.

Well-Ordered Passage	*Passeggio Regolato*

See Caroso's explanation of this term in 'Amorosina Grimana'.

pattern	*tempo*

See the discussion of 'tempo' in ch.2.

pedalogue	*pedalogo*

See Caroso's explanation of this term in 'Laura Suave'.

perfect in theory, perfect theory	*perfetta theorica, vera theorica*

Caroso employs these terms to indicate that he has adhered to the law of perfect symmetry, and to other rules concerning the way one foot must follow the other.

piece, music *sonata*

The term 'sonata' has always referred to an instrumental piece; it was first used with this meaning in the sixteenth century, but its later meaning has varied through the centuries. Caroso employs it to mean 'sound' and 'sound-piece'; that is, the music for an entire dance (if it is in a few strains with no changes of meter), or all of the music in the *initial* segment of a balletto suite, or simply music which is highly distinctive. In the latter two cases it refers to recognizable music: the initial movement of a balletto which is then varied ('*Tutta la Sonata si scioglierà in Gagliarda*', 'The sciolta of this entire piece as a Galliard' ['Laura Suave']); or canary music ('*alla Sonata del Canario*', 'When the Canary Music [is Played]' ['Celeste Giglio']). 'Tune' is not a suitable translation, as in some cases the music is not dominated by a tune, but is essentially a chord progression. The term 'sonata' was discarded because in a balletto suite it may refer to the first movement only, and this may be confusing to modern readers who define 'sonata' as an entire multi-movement work.

progress/promenade (verb) *passeggiare*

progressing *passeggiando*

Modern English for '*passeggio*' is 'passage' or 'promenade'. Thus '*passeggiare*' is 'to make a passage' or 'to promenade', and '*passeggiando*' is 'promenading'. In fact, the Italian terms always signify that the couple travel across the floor side by side as in a promenade. In modern parlance, however, 'promenade' is specific to a walk (as in American square dancing's call, 'Promenade all'), while in Caroso's usage the movements called for may include elaborate footwork with kicks and leaps. What remains clear is that the basic meaning of '*passeggiare*' is 'to progress', to move across the floor instead of remaining on place. This is the translation used here, except in Rule VIII, where the term implies a walk only.

put under *sommessa*

Caroso's definition of this step is virtually indistinguishable from the *foot under*, or '*sottopiede*'. That it is given a separate definition suggests either that there is a distinction Caroso does not make clear, or that he has taken two separate terms of identical meaning, perhaps from two dance traditions of different geographical provenance. In Rule LVI, in fact, Caroso says, '. . . *Sommessa, cioè, un Sottopiede*', '*Put under*, that is, a *foot under*'.

pulled sequence *seguito trangato*

Florio: '*tranghiottito*, gulped, glutted, gorged, devoured, or swallowed down' (p. 573). See next entry for a discussion of *trango*.

pulled step	*trango*

The translation of '*trango*' is problematic. 'Pulled' corresponds most closely, perhaps, to Caroso's derivation of the term (Rule XIX), but the definition in Florio should be kept in mind when doing this step (see previous entry).

quick	*presto*

reprise	*ripresa*
mincing reprise	*ripresa trita*
reprise with foot under	*ripresa sotto piede*

retreat	*retirata*

Reverence	*Riverenza*

rotta	*rotta*

This term is rarely used in the dance text (see 'Cortesia', orig. p. 338). It seems to be equated with sciolta when it appears as a musical heading (e.g., 'Altezza d'Amore'). Garzanti gives as a second meaning for *rotto*, '*sciolto*, broken; broken off'; Apel defines *rotta* as a rhythmically varied afterdance in the fourteenth century.[3] In seventeenth-century guitar tablatures (e.g., Montesardo, 1606). Richard Hudson takes this term to mean 'rhythmic alterations of the sort found in dance pairs'.[4] Florio: '*rotto*, broken. . . . Also a fraction in Arithmetike' (p. 454). Both senses agree with Caroso's usage.

Sapphic step	*Saffice*

The translation is derived from Caroso's description of the term, with its play on words with Sappho (Rule LXVI).

sciolta	*sciolta*

In Caroso's usage the term always refers to a change from initial strains in duple to strains in triple, a vivid reflection of the word's basic meaning, 'loosening, broken'. The nature of the triple varies so widely, however, that no satisfactory solution has been found in English. All sciolte are after-dances (a term rejected as not suggesting specifically a dance in triple, and not as descriptive as 'sciolta'), and all, without exception, are variants on the original music in duple. That the sciolta is not, as Moe suggests[5], a specific type of dance, is evident in the headings cited on p. 9.

---

[3] *Harvard Dictionary of Music*, 2nd ed., p. 741.

[4] Richard Hudson, 'The *Folia* Dance and the *Folia* Formula', *Musica Disciplina* 25 (1971). 199–221.

[5] Lawrence Moe. *Dance Music in Printed Italian Lute Tablatures from 1507 to 1611*, p. 32.

Negri uses the term also, but for a strain in duple at the end of a dance, following a galliard and identical to the opening strain.[6] Thus his usage disagrees with Caroso's. See also ch. 5, '*Balletto*'.

scurrying   *scorso*

Caroso's description of the steps used in executing the *seguito scorso* suggests this cognate as the best translation.

section   *tempo*

See ch. 2 for a discussion of '*tempo*'. 'Section' is synonymous with 'playing', and is used when it specifically refers to the choreography that takes place during one playing of the music, as:

Symmetrical Section   *Tempo Terminato*
Well-Ordered Section   *Tempo Regolato*

semibreve (time value)   *semibreve*

semigrave (time value)   *semigrave*

sequence   *seguito*

Since the patterns of the *seguito (e.g., spezzato, seguito spezzato-scorso, seguito battuto)* consist of a sequence of steps, it has seemed best to use a parallel term.

shakes   *tremulanti*

The description of this term suggests it is intended as an ornament. Indeed, it is never called for in Caroso's choreographies, and this may imply that it is to be improvised. The term 'shake' was commonly used for one kind of musical ornament; the movement Caroso calls for is admirably suited to this word.

side (direction)   *fianco/lato/man*

All three Italian words seem to be used synonymously. If there are, in fact, any distinctions among them. Caroso's usage is not systematic enough to justify distinctions in English such as 'flank', 'side', or 'hand', except when '*man*' is used with reference to taking or clapping hands.

somewhat   *alquanto*

sliding   *schisciato*

---

[6] Negri, p. 162.

spondaic step	*spondeo*
stamps	*battute di piedi*
step	*passo*
stopped	*puntato*

strutting, swaggering   *pavoneggiare, pavoneggiandosi*
    Florio: *Pavoneggiare*, to gaze fondly, or like a Peacocke proudly to court and wantonize with himself'. (p. 362).

symmetrical   *terminato*
    See 'Amorosina Grimana' for Caroso's explanation of this term.

taking (hands, arms)   *pigliandosi*

thrust   *spingere*
    Among the varied meanings of '*spingere*' (to push, to shove, to drive, to thrust), 'thrust' has seemed the most appopriate when the movement is to be above the ground (as in the description of the opening movement of the *Reverence*). Since 'thrust' is equally valid whether the movement is high or low, it also seems to preserve this ambiguous aspect of the original. In the case of canary steps, however, '*spingere*' has been translated as 'push', because the movements are clearly sliding or shuffling along the floor.

time   *tempo*
    See ch. 2 for a full explanation of this term.

in the time of three galliard beats   *á tempo di tre battute della*
                                           Gagliarda

at the same time   *à stesso tempo*

tiny minced [jumps]   *trito minuto*
    The exact movement intended by Caroso in his description of this step pattern is unclear, but does not suggest a mincing, affected, or effeminate movement. Hence the more literal 'minced' is used, retaining some ambiguity.

turning jump   *salto tondo*
    The standard modern term for this is *tour en l'air*. The preparation and execution of this movement is quite different from that of ballet, however, so a more literal term has been adopted.

turn, twirl, whirl   *pirlotta, zurlo*
    Florio: '*Pirlare*, to swirl or turn round as a top' (p. 383). '*Zurlo*, any kind
    of top. . . . Also a round or turning trick in dancing' (p. 617).

variation   *mutanza*
    For a discussion of Caroso's use of the term, see ch. 2.

Figures to the Dances

Some two-thirds of the dances in *Nobiltà di dame* have full-page illustrations showing the correct opening position. A number of others refer back to figures shown previously. In fact, only nine different pictures are involved, which are simply duplicated as required. We reproduce them here as they appear in the Forni facsimile (the basis for the present work), noting the dances to which they refer. It is worth commenting that only Figure I is completely new. The others are either exact reproductions of plates which had appeared already in *Il Ballarino,* such as Figure IV, or are printed from modifications of the old plates (Figures II and V). The modifications are chiefly in details of dress (the size of the gentleman's trunk hose and hat, and the shape of the lady's false sleeves and hair ornaments), and we may assume they were added to update the older plates in style.

It is important to note that the various copies of *Nobiltà di dame* still extant show evidence of changes, errors, or omissions made during the process of printing. Figure I, for example, is missing from 'Nuova Regina' in the particular copy of 1600 used by Forni to prepare its facsimile reprint,[1] but a blank page at that spot leads to the conclusion that it was omitted by error in the original print. The Figure has been supplied here from the same page in the New York Public Library copy (the same illustration appears in the copy at Harvard University (dated 1605). Figure II, a modification of Figure IV, is not in either copy owned by the New York Public Library; Figure IV (the older plate) is used instead. However, the Forni facsimile gives Figure II to illustrate all the dances listed here (that is, only one dance, 'Laura Suave', has Figure IV); in the copy at Harvard University Figure IV appears with 'Alta Regina' besides 'Laura Suave'. While the situation is confusing, the result is identical, for no changes in dance position occur. Such variations in the several printings are typical of early printing practises.

---

[1] The editor assumes that the Forni copy was not tampered with before the facsmile was made.

I. Nuova Regina, Bassa, et Alta, Altezze d'Amore, Rosa Felice, Bassa Savella, Alta Vittoria,
Furioso Nuovo

II. Alta Regina, Alta Gonzaga, Coppia Colonna, Barriera Nuova, Conto dell'Orco Nuovo, Spagnoletta Regolata

III. Amorosina Grimana, Gagliarda di Spagna, Bassa Honorata, Nido d'Amore

IV. Laura Suave

V. Passo e mezzo, Barriera, Bellezze d'Olimpia, Contrapasso in Ruota

VI. Spagnoletta Nuova, Cesarina

VII. Doria Colonna, Forza d'Amore, Specchio d'Amore, Ghirlanda d'Amore

VIII. Alta Colonna, Amor Costante, Contentezza d'Amore, Vero Amore

Giac. Franco f.

IX. Allegrezza d'Amore, Furioso all'Italiana, Furioso alla Spagnuola

Table of the Rules for Dancing

[The table is modified to serve as an index as follows: words added to render the terminology consistent with the titles to the step definitions in the body of the text are bracketed; the Roman numerals designate the numbers of the rules in the text; the original step names are added and bracketed to facilitate identification.]

Table of the Notes on Deportment

[The Roman numerals have been added editorially to correlate with the text.]

Table of Dances, and Those To Whom They Are Dedicated

[The original Italian table does not include the type of each dance, which has been supplied from the dance texts or suggested editorially in brackets. The dances are numbered by the editor.]

[A]

C

D

F

G

L

N

P